Weaving Designs by Bertha Gray Hayes

Miniature Overshot Patterns

Norma Smayda, Gretchen White, Jody Brown, Katharine Schelleng

Schiffer Publishing Ltd
4880 Lower Valley Road • Atglen, PA 19310

Dedication

To the memory of Bertha Gray Hayes,
her spirit of creativity and celebration,
and her love of pattern and color.

Library of Congress Control Number: 2008941024

Designed by Stephanie Daugherty
Type set in GoudyOlSt BT/Dutch809 BT

ISBN: 978-0-7643-3246-3
Printed in China
10 9 8 7 6 5 4

Title page: Designs are selections from Bertha Gray Hayes' recently discovered patterns.

Other Schiffer Books on Related Subjects:
Color and Fiber, Patricia Lambert, ISBN:0-88740-065-5, $49.99
Weaving As An Art Form, Theo Moorman, ISBN: 0-88740-068-X, $12.99
The Art of Weaving, Else Regensteiner, ISBN:0-88740-079-5, $34.95
Geometric Design in Weaving, Else Regensteiner, ISBN:0-88740-078-7, $29.95
Weaver's Study Course: Sourcebook for Ideas and Techniques, Else Regensteiner, ISBN:0-88740-112-0, $19.95

Published by Schiffer Publishing, Ltd.
4880 Lower Valley Road
Atglen, PA 19310
Phone: (610) 593-1777; Fax: (610) 593-2002
E-mail: Info@schifferbooks.com

For our complete selection of fine books on this and related subjects, please visit our website at **www.schifferbooks.com**. You may also write for a free catalog.

This book may be purchased from the publisher. Please try your bookstore first.

We are always looking for people to write books on new and related subjects. If you have an idea for a book, please contact us at *proposals@schifferbooks.com*

Schiffer Publishing's titles are available at special discounts for bulk purchases for sales promotions or premiums. Special editions, including personalized covers, corporate imprints, and excerpts can be created in large quantities for special needs. For more information, contact the publisher.

Contents

Foreword 4

Acknowledgments 6

Weavers Speak Out on Bertha Gray Hayes 7

Preface 9

Introduction 12

1. Bertha Gray Hayes' Development as a Weaver 14

The Shuttle-Craft Course in Weaving 14

The National Conferences of American Handweavers 16

2. Bertha Gray Hayes' Weaving 23

Her Looms 23

Her Unique Patterns and How She Named Them 23

Selected Pages from the Workbook 25

Oddments of a Weaver at Work 30

Name Drafts: Bertha Gray Hayes' "Personalized Designs" 31

Publications 33

3. The Sample Cards 34

Miss Hayes' List of Sample Cards 36

Alphabetical List of Sample Cards 36

The 72 Sample Cards 37

Computer-generated Drawdowns of the First 72 Designs 110

4. Recently Discovered Patterns 164

Thirteen Handwritten Drafts from the Workbook, Designs 73 to 85 166

Woven Samples and Computer-generated Drawdowns, Designs 73 to 85 168

Additional Handwritten Drafts, Woven Samples, and Computer-generated Drawdowns, Designs 86 to 92 181

5. Other Weavings by Miss Hayes 194

6. The Story Continues 202

Glossary 203

Endnotes 206

Bibliography and Suggested Reading 207

Index 208

Foreword

A Historical Perspective

Handweaving has been part of the domestic scene in Rhode Island since European families first settled in the region. The stereotypical view of a colonial woman as she spins and weaves by the hearth of her home is just part of the picture. Settlers produced wool, hemp, and flax for spinning yarn and weaving cloth to meet their needs, but artisans also made fabric for sale or barter as early as the seventeenth century. New Anglican settlers who immigrated with the Massachusetts Bay Company had textile production skills and knowledge. Several groups of these people, disenchanted with their life in the Massachusetts Colony, moved to Rhode Island in the seventeenth century and set up spinning wheels and looms. Records show full and part-time weavers working in the state ever since.

Early farmers gradually increased their flocks of sheep, often with governmental encouragement. The increasing presence of fulling mills throughout the area is evidence of handwoven wool fabric production. Many Rhode Island farmers grew flax for seed and oil; the remaining stalks yielded bundles of fibers that were past their prime, but still made usable yarns and cloths. Some of those extant fabrics have brown streaks probably due to the late harvesting of the plants. Settlers imported cotton fibers from the Caribbean islands for blending with flax and weaving fabric, but not many extant early fabrics are 100 percent cotton.

According to civil and family records, professional weavers, family members, and servants produced utilitarian cloth for apparel and home furnishings during the eighteenth and early nineteenth centuries. Weaving in families such as the Carders, Brownings, and Hazards is well documented. Many lightweight wool blankets, small-figured linens, and geometrically patterned coverlets along with a few apparel fabrics survive from this era in Rhode Island.

In 1790, when Samuel Slater and his partners built a cotton yarn-spinning mill in Pawtucket and other entrepreneurs followed suit, the state had weavers who could make the yarn into fabric. Power-loom technology was decades behind the innovations in spinning, and until the 1840s, handweavers worked in workshops or took yarn home to weave. These weavers throughout southern New England produced both utilitarian cloth and fancy weaves. "Cash paid for weaving" painted on a wall in the Luther Store Museum in Swansea, Massachusetts testifies to the putting-out system in which weavers picked up yarn at the Luther Store and returned woven fabric for credit or cash. Hand weaving with commercially spun yarn continued for wool fabrics longer than for cotton, but as mills installed power looms, the employment of handweavers diminished and would never recover.

The dominance of power looms did not kill interest in handweaving. Again, family records show multi-generational involvement in weaving. Well-known late nineteenth-century weavers William Rose and his sister Elsie Rose learned how to warp looms and create patterns from their maternal grandparents. William, better known as Weaver Rose, became a well-known Rhode Island personage. He and Elsie are best known for their coverlets, and along with other area weavers kept the craft alive into the twentieth century.

The American response to the British Arts and Crafts Movement also played a role in promoting handweaving in the new century. Various groups across America promoted handweaving, and museums mounted exhibitions of handwoven textiles. Schools such as Berea College in Kentucky taught weaving and produced high quality products. Two additional Appalachian institutions—the Pi Beta Phi

Settlement School (1912) and Pine Mountain Settlement School (1913)—offered instruction in weaving taught by skilled instructors. A later Appalachian school, Black Mountain College (1933), also played a role in reinvigorating the craft.

Of great importance to Bertha Gray Hayes was the role that Mary Meigs Atwater, also born in 1878, and Osma Gallinger played in creating opportunities for weavers to learn and share their enthusiasm. Their work made the National Conferences of American Handweavers possible. As authors and teachers, these two women published much useful information for weavers. They recognized Miss Hayes' talent and encouraged her to continue with her unique contribution.

Bertha Gray Hayes continued the strong weaving tradition in Rhode Island that had begun in the seventeenth century. The members of the Weavers' Guild of Rhode Island and the Moonlight Weavers Guild as well as the students of the Saunderstown Weaving School further the tradition today.

Margaret T. Ordoñez, PhD
Professor of Textiles,
Fashion Merchandizing & Design
Director,
Historic Textile and Costume Collection
University of Rhode Island
Kingston, Rhode Island 02881

Acknowledgments

We gratefully acknowledge The Rhode Island Foundation and The Edward J. and Virginia M. Routhier Foundation, both of which generously supported this project.

We are also deeply indebted to Kenneth D'Ambrosio, Principal & Creative Director of Cote & D'Ambrosio. Ken has guided us through the professional aspects of this book, and without his cheerful volunteer input, our efforts at publishing would not have been as successful.

This project was a group effort of the Weavers' Guild of Rhode Island (WGRI) to disseminate information about Bertha Gray Hayes and her designs. Many people contributed to its completion. Each has brought her own area of expertise. Contributions were large and small, and all were essential. However, as in many group projects, some individuals stand out. In this case a number of weavers need to be spotlighted for their particular drive, energy, and hard work.

The spark for this project was Sara (Sally) DuBois' zeal for the preservation of Miss Hayes' work and the retelling of her life. Sally has worked long and tirelessly, combing through Miss Hayes' notebooks, deciphering name drafts, researching public records, and interviewing people who knew her. Without her passionate dedication to understanding and sharing Miss Hayes' life and work, there would be no book.

Antonia (Tony) Kormos brought her superb color sense and her considerable computer skills to the original scans of the sample cards. In addition, she wove eight of the samples missing from the seventy-two cards and eighteen of the "unwoven drafts" from Miss Hayes' workbooks. Tony also created the first versions of the computer-generated drawdowns for all the designs. Without her expertise, we would still be floundering.

Brenda Bolster, with extraordinary energy, expertise, and determination, secured necessary funding for this project. Her superb sense of style and insistence on giving Bertha Gray Hayes' miniature overshot patterns the best possible presentation have made this book infinitely better. Brenda reflects Miss Hayes' creativity and attention to detail in demanding the best that can be.

Norma Smayda, teacher and founder of the Saunderstown Weaving School, has provided a physical space and a warm, open, and inspiring atmosphere in which to learn. Her knowledge and experience are deep and wide, and her pleasure in our learning and growth is genuine.

Norma Smayda, Jody Brown, Gretchen White, and Katharine (Katie) Schelleng shared the writing of the text, and Jody and Gretchen did the computer work necessary to pull the parts together and get the manuscript to the publisher. Using Fiberworks PCW, Gretchen White meticulously prepared all drawdowns for Bertha Gray Hayes' threadings.

Katie and Norma have curated exhibits and given gallery talks.

Heartfelt thanks go to Marty Cavanagh and M. Virginia (Ginny) Walsh for their terrific support throughout this project, and to all those others who offered their experience and expertise.

We deeply appreciate Schiffer Publishing for recognizing the worth of this book, and are grateful to Nancy Schiffer and Stephanie Daugherty for seeing it to completion with grace and style.

Weavers Speak Out on Bertha Gray Hayes

I have long been charmed by Bertha, as I affectionately think of her, as a person and a weaver. Her attention to detail was truly remarkable as shown by the hours she must have spent, early mornings and while traveling, to create nearly 100 original designs. She worked out each threading, made drawdowns of each, then wove each fine sample. Her interests in visual design and current events (World War II, movies, popular songs) are displayed in her patterns, whether created as name drafts or because of their visual representation. I am inspired to share Bertha's fascination of weaving with others.

Norma Smayda

The first time I saw the seventy-two sample cards of Bertha Gray Hayes, I was intrigued both by the many weaving designs and colors they presented. Each new card intensified my interest, and I wanted increasingly to know about them and the person who had made them. Over the past few years as I studied and learned more about Miss Hayes and her work, I felt it extremely important that her work should be seen and appreciated by other weavers and therefore spent time arranging comprehensive exhibits and lectures to do just that.

Katie Schelleng

I find Bertha and her work unique, lively, and most interesting. She created these lovely patterns using names that included World War II themes, the period in which she worked, adding historical value and liveliness. What was happening in the world, in American handweaving, and in her social life are all in her choice of name drafting from which she created the patterns. It's a great opportunity to record a portion of the history of weaving that will fascinate weavers and non-weavers alike.

Marty Cavanagh

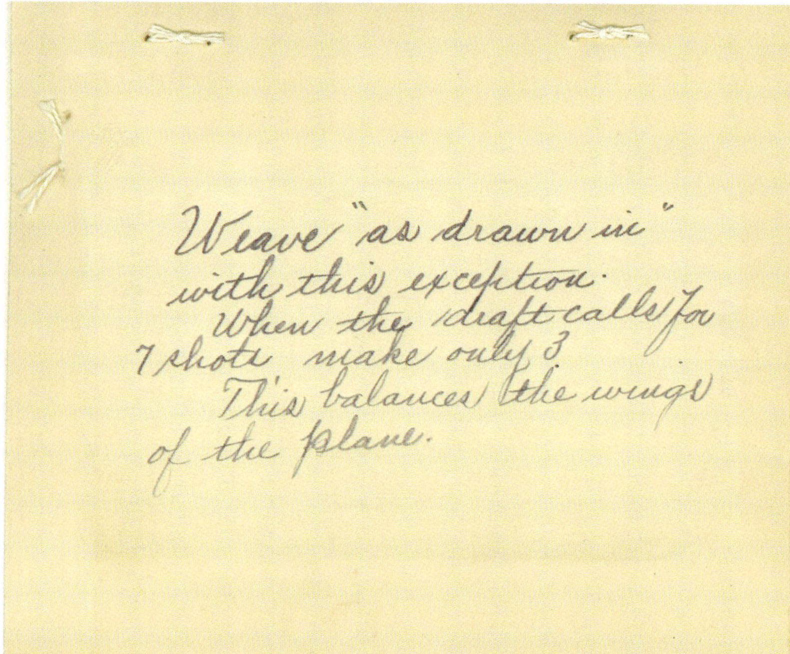
Weave "as drawn in" with this exception:
When the draft calls for 7 shots make only 3
This balances the wings of the plane.

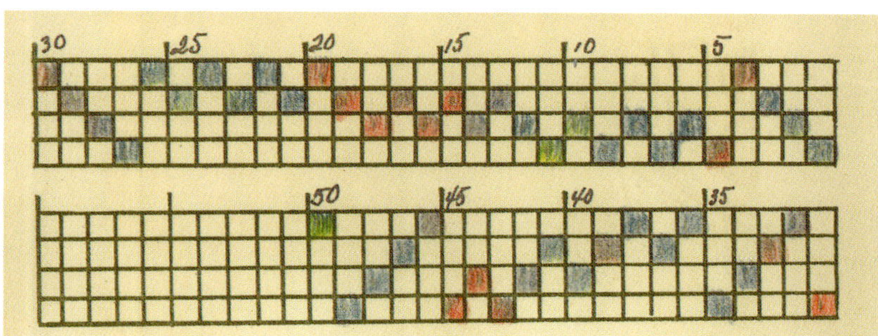

One morning arriving at the weaving school I heard Norma and others talking about Bertha. I asked, "Who is Bertha?" And Norma started the story of Bertha Gray Hayes. I found myself strolling into Bertha's romantic lifetime, the "Roosevelt Era"— the years 1933 through 1947— hence, her Designs called *Stars of Victory*, *Bomber Flight*, *Parachute*, and *Victory*, for instance. A flight of fancy, and I see Bertha coming home from work, putting on a Nelson Eddy record, and sitting with a glass of sherry, designing her patterns to the big band tunes — every new design a true treasure.

Brenda Bolster

When I first thumbed through Bertha's sample cards, they pulled at me on many levels—the asymmetry and whimsy; the evidence of passionate, careful, and detailed work; and the existence of another era in our own through these tangible remains of World War II, its themes and music. Bertha's overshot designs were "new" and different, even now. As we began to go through Bertha's notebooks, her personality and work habits emerged, and I realized how much I liked and respected her and appreciated her "Scotch thrift," endless creativity, and generosity of spirit.

Jody Brown

Sally, for a long time, talked about the Bertha Gray Hayes miniature samples. When they were at Norma's library I looked at them, found them charming, and something I would like to have in my weaving records. I asked Norma if I could borrow them and scan them into my computer. After scanning and making a few printouts and taking them to the Guild meeting, many members wanted to have a printout. (No thank you, not with my slow home equipment.) I guess that's when the idea to publish them in book form started.

Tony Kormos

Bertha's love of designing saw her through the tough times at the very end of her life. The names of those she met while in hospital, the name of that hospital, itself, the name of the very disease that killed her, all were transformed into weaving patterns. Working with the computer drawdowns, preparing them for publication, I have seen the beauty of her designs, the pattern elements that shift and change, regroup, and reappear. Working with others on this project, I have been struck by how our diverse skills and strengths complement one another, providing just what was needed for the tasks at hand. The sense of group purpose has been wonderful. The threads of our lives have been woven into a fabric both strong and fine.

Gretchen White

Preface

The year 2007 was the sixtieth anniversary of the founding of the Weavers' Guild of Rhode Island (WGRI) and the sixtieth anniversary of the death of Bertha Gray Hayes, a long-time resident of the state, weaver, and designer of many miniature overshot patterns. Miss Hayes was a self-taught weaver who was very active in the first and subsequent National Conferences of American Handweavers. Also, she was recognized by Mary Meigs Atwater, Osma Gallinger, Marguerite P. Davison, and Harriet Tidball for her contributions to American handweaving.

How Bertha Gray Hayes' sample cards and notebooks came to reside with the WGRI is a story of serendipity. In 1976, Norma Smayda, of the Saunderstown Weaving School in Rhode Island, first saw a shoebox containing Miss Hayes' seventy-two sample cards and the stamp used to create the threading grid on those cards, and some scrapbooks, at the home of Isabel Boan in Westport, Massachusetts. These items had been given to Mrs. Boan by Claire Chrostowski, her weaving teacher. After Miss Hayes' death, her estate sold three looms to Mrs. Chrostowski: an eight-inch Structo loom (model No. 240), a sixteen-inch table loom, and a thirty-six-inch eight-shaft loom. Mrs. Chrostowski may well have acquired Miss Hayes' sample cards, notebooks, and weaving samples at this time. After she moved to Florida, Mrs. Chrostowski sent the written and woven work of Miss Hayes back north to Isabel Boan, who wanted them in safekeeping in Rhode Island. Mrs. Boan gave them to the Weavers' Guild of Rhode Island, in the care of Norma Smayda who has stored them at the Saunderstown Weaving School ever since.

For the Summer 1986 New England Weavers' Seminar *NEWSLetter* sample, Elizabeth Fletcher of WGRI wove a Bertha Gray Hayes miniature overshot pattern (*Petite*) and Sally DuBois wrote an accompanying history of what was known of Miss Hayes at the time. This material went to all members of the New England Weavers' Seminar.

At the October 1986 meeting of the Weavers' Guild of Boston, Mary Yusko introduced Norma Smayda and Sally DuBois to Thelma Shilhan, another Boston Guild member. Mrs. Shilhan said she "had some things from a long-ago weaver, Bertha Hayes" and thought they should be returned to Rhode Island, but did not have them with her that day. At the November 1986 Boston Guild meeting, Mrs. Shilhan turned over the "box of things" to Sally DuBois. This box included Miss Hayes' handwritten "Workbook," which contained the seventy-two designs, with threadings and drawdowns, of her miniature overshot patterns, as well as an additional thirteen unnumbered threadings with drawdowns. Other items included a notebook of poetry about handweaving, copied in Miss Hayes' handwriting, a small handmade album with fifty-four skeleton drawdowns, and her scrapbook containing the Shuttle-Craft Course in Weaving (a correspondence course by Mary Meigs Atwater) and many articles on weaving. All these items are now kept at the Saunderstown Weaving School.

We refer to these materials as the Bertha Gray Hayes Archives. The Archives include:

> Box of seventy-two sample cards: with threadings and handwoven samples by Miss Hayes. Nine of the woven samples were missing, and eight replacements were woven by Tony Kormos and one by Sandra Reynolds.
>
> Workbook: with handwritten drafts for the seventy-two sample card designs, plus another thirteen drafts, assorted Shuttle Service Leaflets (Creative Crafts), and eight woven pieces.
>
> Pink Scrapbook: with a pink and gray cover woven in monk's belt. It contains the Shuttle-Craft Course in Weaving by Mary Meigs Atwater (a correspondence course, Seattle, Washington, 1922) and many articles on weaving from newspapers and magazines.
>
> Conference Journal: notebook of information about the first three National Conferences of American Handweavers (1938, 1939, 1940),

including the official logs of the conferences, as well as Miss Hayes' handwritten notes.

Butternut Workbook: binder with a blue and white cover woven in overshot, containing nineteen handwritten patterns. The cover fabric and the first pattern are called *Butternut*. Two of the patterns within are original to Miss Hayes: *Old Fashioned Garden* and *Summer and Winter Weave*.

Red and White Album: small handmade album with a handwoven cover in overshot, containing fifty-four skeleton drawdowns.

Gold Binder: binder with a cover woven in overshot, containing the "Guidance Book for Conference of American Handweavers, 1946, Washington, D.C."

Large brown envelopes: many with drafts glued to them, including two of the new drafts — *Rosette* and *Afterthought*.

Binder: with a blue and white cover woven in overshot, empty.

Small notebook of poems about weaving, in Miss Hayes' handwriting.

Metal stamp of threading grid, for use on sample cards.

Several dozen unused sample cards, with logo on front.

Framed group photograph of the attendees at the 1940 National Conference of American Handweavers.

Box of twelve samples of square braids and a lined double purse in overshot fabric.

Box of assorted weaving notes, some on discarded Providence Gas Company file cards, and twenty-one samples. Many of these samples were woven at the National Conferences.

A manila envelope containing 47 2" x 3" graphed designs for handwoven greeting cards.

In recent years, with advice from textile conservators at the University of Rhode Island, the Bertha Gray Hayes material has undergone conservation—i.e., removing staples, sewing the samples to the cards, putting acid-free tissue paper between the woven samples and their design cards, and keeping papers and other woven samples in acid-free boxes.

At the New England Weavers' Seminar in July 2007, held at Smith College in Northampton, Massachusetts, the WGRI curated the Special Exhibit of Bertha Gray Hayes' sample cards, notebooks, and weavings, bringing Miss Hayes' original items together for public viewing for the first time. The response to the exhibit was enthusiastic. Studying all these materials gives us a rare window into the creative mind of an original designer and handweaver at work.

Harriet Tidball, in 1956, printed seventy drafts "derived, by analysis, from a set of samples woven by members of a study group."[1] Miss Hayes' seventy-two miniature overshot sample patterns (plus three additional patterns) were published in 1957 in a black and white publication by Creative Crafts, under the direction of Osma Gallinger. Possibilities for faithful color reproduction of the actual sample cards have increased exponentially since 1957, and the WGRI wishes to share our delight over Bertha Gray Hayes' original sample cards with other weavers. More importantly, Sally DuBois found an additional thirteen threadings with drawdowns in the Workbook, and Norma Smayda found another seven patterns: two in the Workbook (*Jitterbug-enlarged* and *Meigs Mountain in Crackle Weave*), two in the Butternut Workbook (*Old Fashioned Garden* and *Summer and Winter Weave*), one in the Red and White Album (*Meigs Mountain-bookmark*), and two glued to large brown envelopes (*Rosette* and *Afterthought*). Tony Kormos has woven all of these except the crackle and summer and winter weaves. This book includes these patterns as well as color reproductions of some of Miss Hayes' other weavings and some pages from her design workbooks showing how she worked. We also have added computer-generated drawdowns including tie-ups and treadlings for all ninety-two patterns for those who might wish to weave these original and unusual designs.

Because the Gallinger and Tidball publications of Bertha Gray Hayes' patterns are not complete, as we now know, and often show only variations of Miss Hayes' threadings, we recognize the importance of publishing this work with Miss Hayes' sample cards and new patterns from her workbooks.

Miss Hayes was meticulous in her use of fine yarns, a correct and even beat, and a traditional treadling (as drawn in). The earlier publications have not been as consistent as Miss Hayes in these details, and much of the original charm of her samples was lost.

Figure 1. Binders with handwoven covers. Left to right: Blue and White Binder, Gold Binder, Red and White Album, Pink Scrapbook, Butternut Workbook. *Photograph by Robert Schelleng.*

Introduction

Overshot is a twill-based, supplementary-weft weave structure that was introduced into the United States by European weavers and then flourished in the Hudson River Valley, New England, and Appalachia during the nineteenth century. Traditionally, it was woven with a cotton yarn for warp and weft in a plain weave, with a heavier pattern weft yarn of cotton or wool. Many delightful and often dramatic patterns are possible on four shafts. The maximum width of the pattern blocks is determined by the practical length of the weft floats. Unlike other weft-patterned weaving, the overshot structure is identified by its three distinct areas: the balanced plain weave area, the pattern area of weft floats, and the half-tone area with pattern and ground weave showing equally.

Bertha Gray Hayes appears to have been charmed by overshot patterns early in her weaving career. She may have discovered these patterns through the Shuttle-Craft Course in Weaving, for affixed to the first page of her Pink Scrapbook is the overshot pattern *Wreath Rose* (Lesson III, Diagram 7). Miss Hayes then took this old, beloved weave structure, common in early American coverlets and the basis for many traditional designs, and gave it a twist. The patterns are unusual in her frequent use of asymmetry. Mary Meigs Atwater called Miss Hayes' work of the "modernistic" type and noted that very little of this type had been done in four-harness overshot.[2]

As such, it was new and valued. Additionally, in designing the patterns, her use of name drafts that reflect the music and events of her era (the years surrounding World War II) and her social circle gives the patterns historical interest. The resulting miniature overshot designs are unique, visually playful, and compelling—weavers love them. The sheer volume of Miss Hayes' original designs and her willingness to share them with other weavers brought her national recognition during the first decade of the National Conferences, beginning in 1938. Moreover, twenty additional patterns have been discovered in her workbooks that beg sharing.

Miss Hayes' complete passion for and absorption in weaving is inspiring to other weavers, and her care in presenting and recording her work is an instructive standard. The presentation of her designs on "sample cards" was most unusual, and the effort needed to create them was significant. Miss Hayes had stamps made to print her insignia on the front and the threading grid on the inside of the cards, opposite a small handwoven sample of the pattern. As Marguerite Davison said, they "were marvels of neatness and originality."[3] The sample cards were treasured by other weavers, who got them from Miss Hayes. In 1956, Mrs. Tidball thought that only two complete collections of the sample cards existed—belonging to Mrs. Bertha Tanner of Paradise, California, and Mrs. Genevieve Shields of San Gabriel, California. However, we know of at least two other sets, including Claire Chrostowski's collection, currently at the WGRI, and Osma Gallinger's, which was the basis of her publication of 1957. The awe and pleasure of today's weavers who have access to the box of sample cards at the Saunderstown Weaving School make us eager to share the work of this remarkable woman.

The story of Bertha Gray Hayes is that of a woman weaving and designing before and after working at a six-day-a-week job, during the first half of the twentieth century, when handweaving was making a reappearance on the national scene. This was a period of two world wars and a major economic depression. Scarcities and limited leisure time provided the backdrop for her self-instruction and the dedication to pursue her passion for weaving. Contact with other weavers took place primarily by mail and at national conferences. The Workbooks, the Pink Scrapbook, and the Conference Journal give us a window into the creative life of a woman immersed in weaving and design. Her original hand-drawn drafts and woven samples of seventy-two miniature overshot patterns are our fortunate inheritance of her intense focus and interest.

We know little of Miss Hayes beyond the legacy of the seventy-two original sample cards. She was born to Ansel Gray Hayes and Maria Elizabeth Dunlap Hayes, October 19, 1878, in Middleborough, Massachusetts. Miss Hayes had a younger brother Ansel (born 1880), who did not survive infancy, and no other known siblings.[4] She died in Providence, Rhode Island, December 10, 1947.[5] She is listed in the Providence City Directory beginning in 1914 and ending with her death. During her thirty-three years in Providence, she lived in seven different residences. From 1931 to 1947, she was employed by the Providence Gas Company, variously listed in the City Directory as "clerk" and "bookkeeper." In 1940, she was listed as "accountant" and "professional weaver."[6] At that point, Miss Hayes, a charter member of the National Conferences of American Handweavers, had attended the first three meetings and gained national recognition for her weaving.

Bertha Hayes was remembered by her co-workers at the Providence Gas Company as having a disciplined posture, neatly trimmed light hair, a youthful appearance, and beautifully tailored clothes. They said, "Weaving was her life." Much of her weaving was done in the early morning (one of her patterns is *Daybreak*), and she took her weaving, including pillow tops, handbags and sewing accessories, to work to be seen and shared with co-workers. Miss Hayes invited them to her home for tea, and to see her weavings. She gave Pearl Spencer, a young friend, a sewing basket and a thimble holder. She often designed patterns for friends based on their names, a technique known as "name drafting."[7]

We have talked recently with Jane and Mary McKivergan who knew Miss Hayes when she rented an upstairs apartment from their parents on Grove Avenue in East Providence in 1946-1947, until she died. Thomas McKivergan, their older brother, now deceased, was fourteen years old, Jane was ten, and Mary was six at the time they knew her. They remember Miss Hayes as a fine lady, always cheerful, proper, and refined, who often invited them upstairs to see her loom and watch her weave. In the eyes of a six year old, the loom was large, both high and wide, had treadles and was made of brown wood. They remember the rhythmic sound they could hear from downstairs. Jane and Mary still have dolls given them by Miss Hayes. She made the dolls adorned in crocheted dresses. Miss Hayes must have held these children in high esteem to have created and woven their name drafts.[8]

Miss Hayes shared weaving ideas with Mrs. MacAllister and Mrs. Batchelder, both charter members of the Weavers' Guild of Rhode Island, founded in 1947.[9, 10] Had Miss Hayes lived longer, she, too, would undoubtedly have become a charter member.

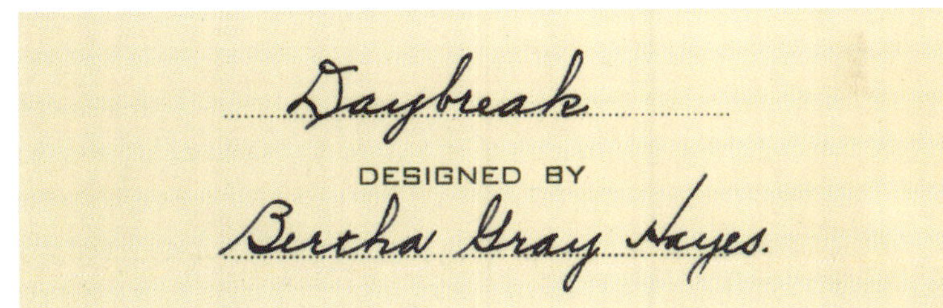

1. Bertha Gray Hayes' Development as a Weaver

The Shuttle-Craft Course in Weaving

In 1923, Miss Hayes became a charter subscriber to the Shuttle-Craft Course in Weaving, a correspondence course published by Mary Meigs Atwater. She kept a scrapbook of nearly seventy pages of the lessons for this course, as well as another 130 pages of articles, news clippings, and notes on weaving into the 1940s. The Pink Scrapbook is covered in handwoven fabric of pink, black, and dark red on a white warp, woven in monk's belt. She glued three small overshot samples and an advertisement from the Shuttle-Craft Company inside the front cover of her scrapbook (Figure 2) and more samples inside the back cover. Figure 3 is a sample page from Section III, Lesson 5 in the correspondence course. These lesson plans have been cut to fit on the pages where possible; others, measuring up to 13.5 inches by 20 inches, fold out. They cover topics such as parts of a loom, setting up a loom, knots, and diverse weave structures. The articles came from magazines, newspapers, and pamphlets. One article appears to have been sent to Miss Hayes as it had a handwritten note on it: "This article is pretty elementary for you but it just shows what simple stuff gets printed. Why don't you sell your fine ideas?"[11]

Some articles inspired Miss Hayes to write ideas for weaving projects in her scrapbook; for example, one of them was for a bag using three-harness weaving. In reference to one article, she commented in the margin that she met the people being written about at a recent national conference of handweavers. Another article inspired her to detail the cost of threads and other materials for a pillow and a runner and the hours taken to weave them, against the sale price of the articles, showing a good profit—without counting the labor.[12] (See Figure 4.)

Figure 2. Inside front cover of Pink Scrapbook.

Figure 3. Shuttle-Craft Course in Weaving, Section III, Lesson 5 from Pink Scrapbook.

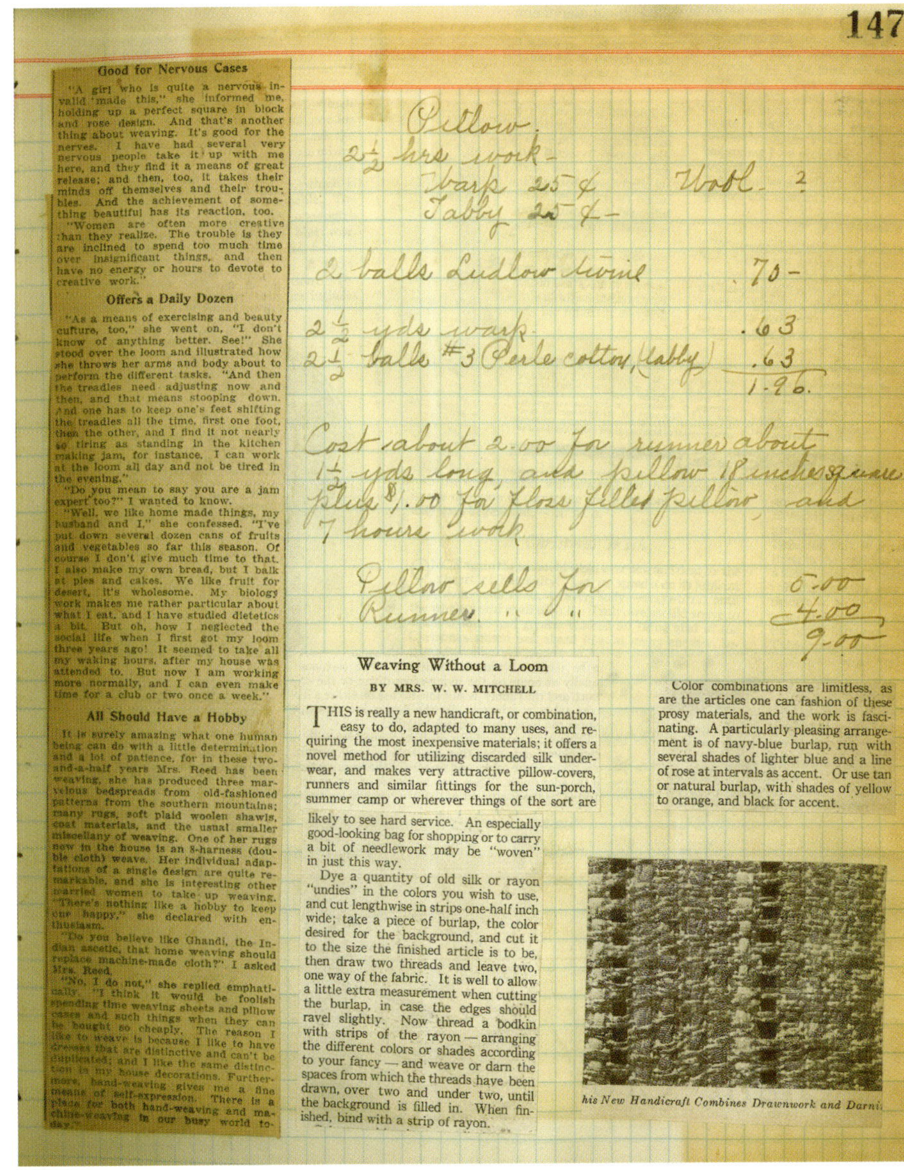

Figure 4. Record Keeping for Hours and Materials Cost, from Pink Scrapbook.

The National Conferences of American Handweavers

Miss Hayes seems to have emerged on the national handweaving scene with the First National Conference of American Handweavers in 1938, at Waldenwoods in Hartland, Michigan. From 1938 through 1947, Miss Hayes annually contributed an original pattern to the national conference, the first nine of which she attended. At the first ten conferences, a loom threaded to the Bertha Gray Hayes pattern for that conference allowed weavers to weave a sample. These drafts appeared in subsequent Shuttle Service (Creative Crafts) leaflets by Mrs. Gallinger, and Miss Hayes kept these leaflets in her workbooks

Personal communication from Josephine Del Deo (Jo), daughter of Osma Gallinger, supports what we already know about the relationship between Mrs. Gallinger and Miss Hayes. Jo, for whom Miss Hayes designed the pattern *Cheerio*, was active at the many conferences her mother organized.

> As to her patterns, which she provided my mother as complimentary in those years, I do recall them as lovely 4-harness designs . . . and in traditional style but original. My mother admired her as an accomplished weaver, and they had a great deal of correspondence, I believe, back and forth. . . . My mother's admiration of her abilities and contributions were always made manifest in the ways in which she featured these patterns of Bertha's quite often in her directional leaflets, which were part of a mail-order business as well as part of the conference patterns which she advertised as Creative Crafts leaflets subsequent to the conferences.[13]

Waldenwoods, site of the early National Conferences of American Handweavers, was part of John Robert Crouse's vision for the Hartland Area Project in which crafts, including weaving and loom making, would provide employment and income for area residents creating "things useful and beautiful" in a spirit of cooperation. John Robert Crouse and his uncle, H. A. Tremaine, of Hartland, Michigan, sold Crouse and Tremaine Carbon Works, which later became Union Carbide, to devote themselves to establishing the Hartland Area Project. Waldenwoods, part of the Crouse farm, was set aside for business conferences, and buildings were erected in 1924-1925. In 1933, J. R. Crouse brought Osma Couch to Hartland to instruct the area residents in the art of weaving. In 1934, Cromaine Crafts, named to honor Crouse and Tremaine and directed by Osma Couch, was opened, offering weaving products and other crafts. Soon after, woodworkers began constructing looms for sale.[14]

Osma Couch Gallinger (by now married to Milo Gallinger) organized the first National Conference of American Handweavers at Waldenwoods in 1938. Annual conferences, which continued for more than twenty years, originally met at Waldenwoods and convened in Pittsburgh in 1943, New York City in 1944, Indianapolis in 1945, Washington, D.C. in 1946, and Salem, Oregon in 1947. The first conferences, held in the summers, lasted two to three weeks. Although we have no knowledge of where conferences were held after 1947, we know that the *Stagger* pattern was chosen for the 1951 conference in honor of Miss Hayes. Additionally, Osma Gallinger indicated that the *Needlepoint* pattern was selected by the National Conference of American Handweavers "as one of the most practical of Bertha Hayes' creations."[15]

Miss Hayes placed two letters received after the 1938 conference at the beginning of her Conference Journal. These are described on page 165 and shown in Figures 5, 6, and 7. One was from Mary Meigs Atwater, the Director of the Conference and the acknowledged "dean" of American handweaving. The other was from Osma Gallinger, the Director of Cromaine Crafts and the organizer of the conference. Both women played a large part in Miss Hayes' weaving life: Mrs. Atwater as teacher and inspiration, and Mrs. Gallinger as friend and outlet for Miss Hayes' miniature overshot patterns. Many of these appeared in the newsletters of *Cromaine Crafts* and later *Creative Crafts*.

In the log of the first conference (1938), Mrs. Gallinger noted:

> Miss Bertha Hayes of Providence, R.I. presented her own original design, 'The Flower of Cromaine' [created while at the conference] to Cromaine Crafts. Fine work, and most thoughtful, Miss Hayes. Mrs. Atwater expressed her approval and it was decided to thread this pattern in a loom so that we could all see it.[16]

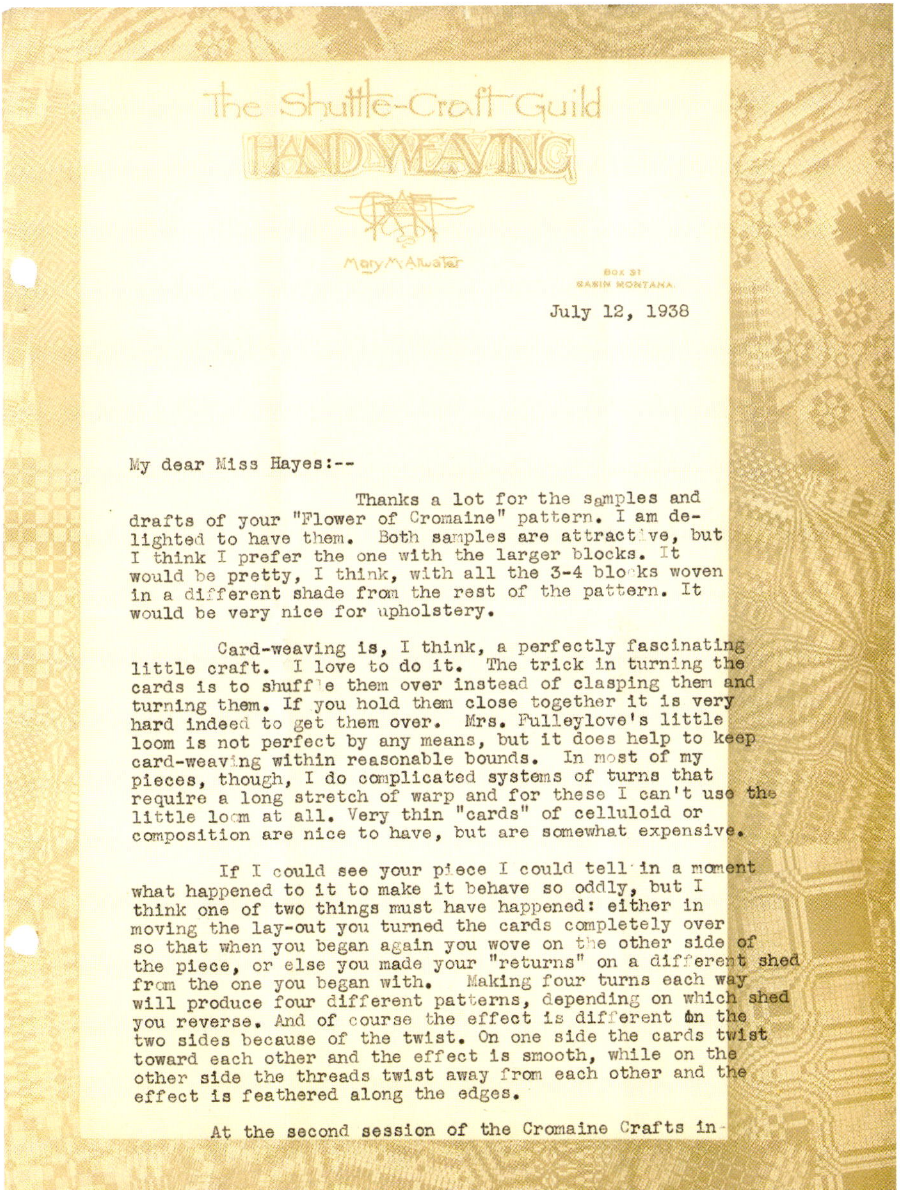

The Shuttle-Craft Guild
HAND WEAVING
Mary M. Atwater
BOX 31
BASIN MONTANA

July 12, 1938

My dear Miss Hayes:--

Thanks a lot for the samples and
drafts of your "Flower of Cromaine" pattern. I am de-
lighted to have them. Both samples are attractive, but
I think I prefer the one with the larger blocks. It
would be pretty, I think, with all the 3-4 blocks woven
in a different shade from the rest of the pattern. It
would be very nice for upholstery.

Card-weaving is, I think, a perfectly fascinating
little craft. I love to do it. The trick in turning the
cards is to shuffle them over instead of clasping them and
turning them. If you hold them close together it is very
hard indeed to get them over. Mrs. Fulleylove's little
loom is not perfect by any means, but it does help to keep
card-weaving within reasonable bounds. In most of my
pieces, though, I do complicated systems of turns that
require a long stretch of warp and for these I can't use the
little loom at all. Very thin "cards" of celluloid or
composition are nice to have, but are somewhat expensive.

If I could see your piece I could tell in a moment
what happened to it to make it behave so oddly, but I
think one of two things must have happened: either in
moving the lay-out you turned the cards completely over
so that when you began again you wove on the other side of
the piece, or else you made your "returns" on a different shed
from the one you began with. Making four turns each way
will produce four different patterns, depending on which shed
you reverse. And of course the effect is different on the
two sides because of the twist. On one side the cards twist
toward each other and the effect is smooth, while on the
other side the threads twist away from each other and the
effect is feathered along the edges.

At the second session of the Cromaine Crafts in-

Figure 5. Letter from Mary M. Atwater, page 1.

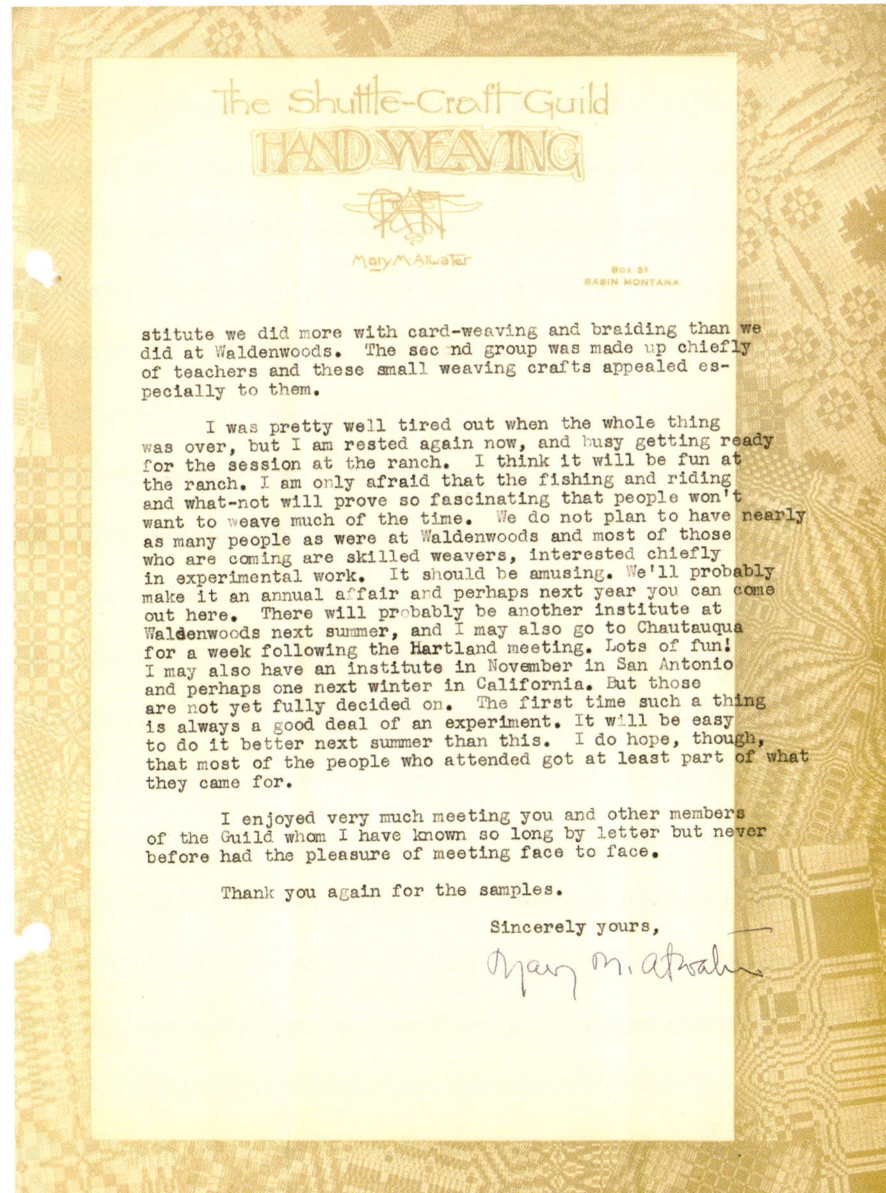

The Shuttle-Craft Guild
HAND WEAVING
Mary M. Atwater
BOX 31
BASIN MONTANA

stitute we did more with card-weaving and braiding than we
did at Waldenwoods. The second group was made up chiefly
of teachers and these small weaving crafts appealed es-
pecially to them.

I was pretty well tired out when the whole thing
was over, but I am rested again now, and busy getting ready
for the session at the ranch. I think it will be fun at
the ranch. I am only afraid that the fishing and riding
and what-not will prove so fascinating that people won't
want to weave much of the time. We do not plan to have nearly
as many people as were at Waldenwoods and most of those
who are coming are skilled weavers, interested chiefly
in experimental work. It should be amusing. We'll probably
make it an annual affair and perhaps next year you can come
out here. There will probably be another institute at
Waldenwoods next summer, and I may also go to Chautauqua
for a week following the Hartland meeting. Lots of fun!
I may also have an institute in November in San Antonio
and perhaps one next winter in California. But those
are not yet fully decided on. The first time such a thing
is always a good deal of an experiment. It will be easy
to do it better next summer than this. I do hope, though,
that most of the people who attended got at least part of what
they came for.

I enjoyed very much meeting you and other members
of the Guild whom I have known so long by letter but never
before had the pleasure of meeting face to face.

Thank you again for the samples.

Sincerely yours,

Mary M. Atwater

Figure 6. Letter from Mary M. Atwater, page 2.

From Miss Hayes' handwritten notes of this first conference, we learn that on June 7: "After luncheon the program was draft-writing at which I was the only one who knew much about it, and as Mrs. Atwater was absent from her class a good part of the time I was teacher rather than pupil."[17]

At the 1939 conference, Miss Hayes' notes indicate that she sold $23.50 worth of weaving and that she took orders for a number of her small woven objects—e.g., thimble holders and "cigarette pack cases." A postcard from Miss Hayes to a friend during this conference says, "I had an exhibition of my work today and sold nearly everything I had. My original drafts are selling for a quarter each. I tried to give them away and they wouldn't hear of it." We have no way of knowing how many of each pattern she wove, inserted in her sample cards, and sold or gave away. Miss Hayes herself says she sold them at the conferences, but these would not have been complete sets. In addition, she welcomed mail orders for her sample cards.[18]

After the 1939 conference, Bertha Hayes pasted a note from a fellow conference participant into her Conference Journal:

> My Dear Miss Hayes:
>
> I have mailed a little package that will I hope make a few little black noses, there was not as much [as] I thought, as I have used a little from time to time as an accent when making a runner of old stockings.
>
> One thing I meant to say to you and failed to do, that was tell you how clever I thought you were in taking off the designs for the Guatamala [sic] weave, I made some in a very unsatisfactory way, then saw Miss Armstrong's, and gave her the credit for the bright idea, and she said that all the credit was due you. I am only sorry that I didn't catch on sooner, as what I made first will have to be transposed and may not come out well.
>
> I enjoyed the conference more because you were there and hope to see you again.
>
> Very Cordially,
>
> Daisy Strong[19]

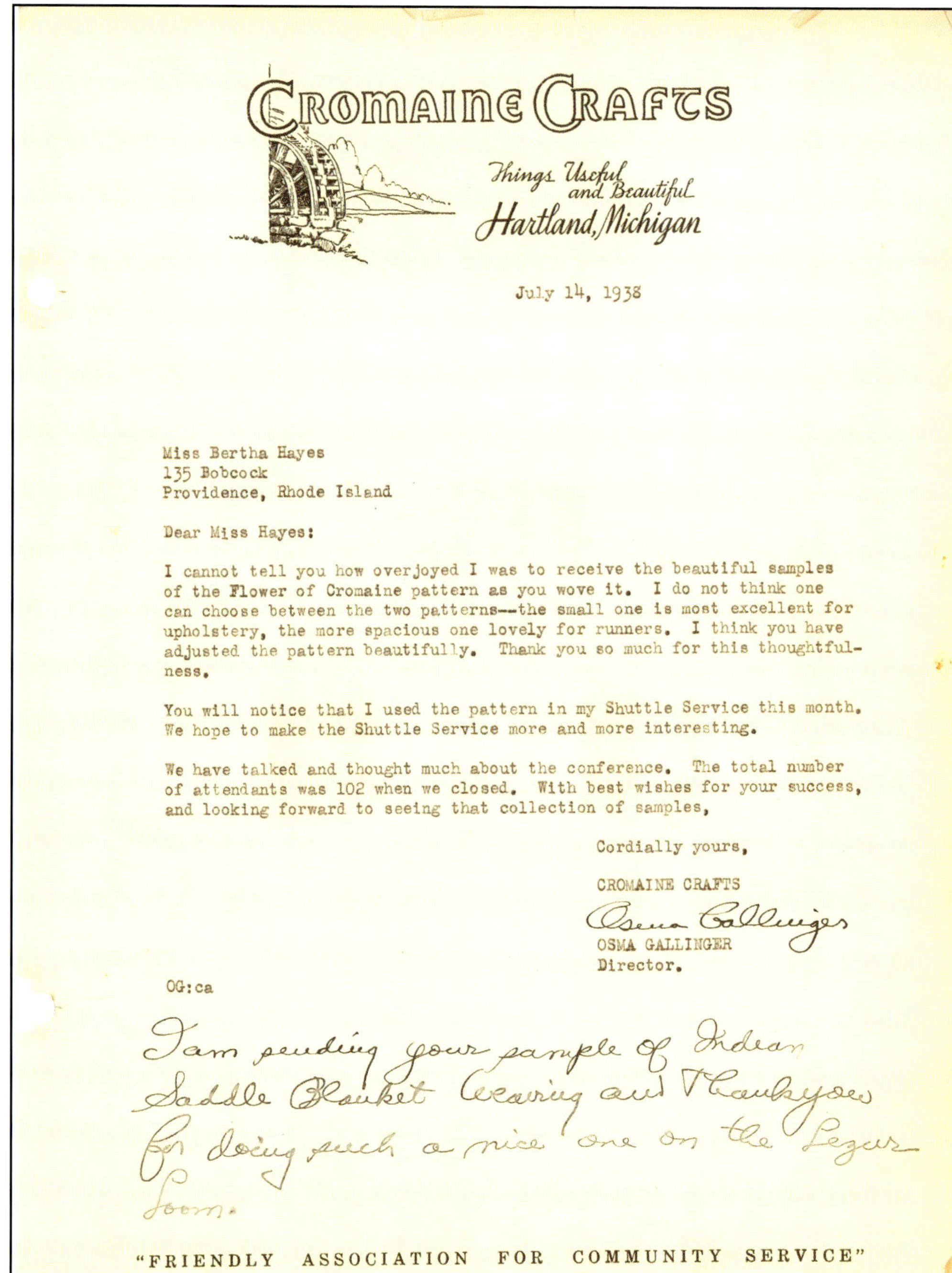

CROMAINE CRAFTS
Things Useful and Beautiful
Hartland, Michigan

July 14, 1938

Miss Bertha Hayes
135 Bobcock
Providence, Rhode Island

Dear Miss Hayes:

I cannot tell you how overjoyed I was to receive the beautiful samples of the Flower of Cromaine pattern as you wove it. I do not think one can choose between the two patterns--the small one is most excellent for upholstery, the more spacious one lovely for runners. I think you have adjusted the pattern beautifully. Thank you so much for this thoughtfulness.

You will notice that I used the pattern in my Shuttle Service this month. We hope to make the Shuttle Service more and more interesting.

We have talked and thought much about the conference. The total number of attendants was 102 when we closed. With best wishes for your success, and looking forward to seeing that collection of samples,

Cordially yours,

CROMAINE CRAFTS

Osma Gallinger
OSMA GALLINGER
Director.

OG:ca

I am sending your sample of Indian Saddle Blanket Weaving and Thank you for doing such a nice one on the Lezur loom.

"FRIENDLY ASSOCIATION FOR COMMUNITY SERVICE"

Figure 7. Letter from Osma Gallinger.

At the 1940 conference, Miss Hayes indicated that one evening she and a friend displayed their work, and she made $27. "I think my drafts took as well as anything." Another evening, Miss Hayes described dinner with the people of the Hartland area. "I had to hold up my sampler before the assembly and name the patterns. Me, to face an audience, but I feel so much at home, I didn't mind it. Mrs. Clark bought a half dozen of my drafts and I autographed them for her." The official log of the 1940 Conference quoted Miss Hayes: "Seems as if I'd been to a new world, taking to the air, the conference and all."[20]

The attendees of this conference are pictured in Figure 8. Those now identified include the following: Osma Gallinger, third from left in front row; Mary Meigs Atwater, fourth from left; Rupert Peters, fifth from left; Harriet Tidball, farthest on right. Fanny C. Crouse, first from left in second row; Bertha Gray Hayes, second from left; Vera Jessup, third from left. J. Robert Crouse, first from left in third row; Grace B. MacAllister, third from left; Josephine Couch, fourth from left; Belle Van Ornum, sixth from left. The hand drawn arrow points to Mrs. Atwater. There are group photos of the first and second annual sessions of the National Conferences in *The Weaver* IV, no. 1 (Jan 1939):24 and V, no. 1 (Jan-Feb 1940):17.

Miss Hayes' *Jitterbug* pattern was published in Mary Meigs Atwater's *Shuttle-Craft Guild Bulletin* after the 1940 conference at Waldenwoods to which Miss Hayes took some of her weavings.

> One of our guild members, Miss Bertha Hayes, of Providence, Rhode Island, brought some attractive 'novelties,' and also a number of woven samples of her original patterns. One of these, which she has named "The Jitterbug," Miss Hayes kindly gave me for the Guild, to be reproduced in the Bulletin. . . . It is a pattern of the 'modernistic' type, and is highly effective for bags and for many other purposes. As all the skips are short it can be used for upholstery and would make very handsome chair seats. As there are so few patterns of the modern type available in the four-harness overshot weave I am sure this pattern will be greatly appreciated. I myself am the proud possessor of a large bag in this pattern, woven by Miss Hayes.[21]

Marguerite P. Davison, in *A Handweaver's Pattern Book*, also recognized Miss Hayes, in the chapter "Overshot Novelties."

> Bertha Gray Hayes excelled in inventing small overshot patterns and left a collection of over sixty of them. Her samples were beautifully woven and mounted in folders, which were marvels of neatness and originality, containing many asymmetrical beauties.[22]

In addition, Miss Hayes' *Superhighway* and *Jitterbug* patterns were published in the 1953 edition of *A Handweaver's Source Book* by Marguerite P. Davison, containing the Laura M. Allen collection of 224 weaving drafts.[23]

In 1957, Creative Crafts published *The Complete Book of Bertha Hayes' Patterns*, and in it Osma Gallinger, who knew Miss Hayes well from the many national conferences she attended and from their correspondence, wrote the following in the preface:

> Bertha Hayes was a creative weaver of New England who spent her spare time weaving samples and designing short Overshot Pattern Drafts of unusual charm and usefulness to the home weaver. Weaving was her sole hobby, her outlet after days in a clerical office. Each evening she returned home to her little collection of 8-in. 4-harness looms, the Structos were favorites, and spent happy hours devising new ways for the pattern notes to take their places on the draft scale. She said that she lived alone and liked it, but we know it was because weaving filled her hours with interest and achievement.
>
> Bertha Hayes was a charter member of the National Conference of American Handweavers, attending eight [sic] successive years. Each fall, as soon as Conference was over, she started her savings in a penny bank, and accumulated them during the year to be able to attend again. She came by any means that she could, by bus, train, car, and once by air. We who were her friends and knew her vibrant, creative personality will never forget her radiant smile which we believe was due to a helpful and optimistic personality, as well as to her true joy in handweaving.[24]

Figure 8. National Conference of American Handweavers 3rd Annual Session. 1940. Bertha Gray Hayes is second from the left in the second row. *Source of photograph unknown.*

The same Creative Crafts book includes a letter from Miss Hayes to Osma Gallinger:

E. Providence, R.I., May 25, 1947

Dear Osma G.,

Enclosed is the folder with the draft of Serenity of Salem dedicated to the Conference. Mrs. T. of Salem is quite pleased with the name. She says her name is Irene which means peace too, so she is going to consider it as her pattern also.

I am sorry that I have no more than the draft to send you, but I was not feeling too well for a couple of months and doing most anything was a task. I am allright now, and feel better than in a long time. I am going to try to find time to make a few pin cushions to send you to sell at the Conference, so there will be a little bit of "me" there.

Now I want to impress upon you that the pattern requires fine yarn to get the effect. For the pattern I seem to get the best results with the enclosed mending wool or fine 2-ply. In experimenting with my pattern Chintz, I used variegated tatting thread for the tabby, and the result was real "Chintzy". So I suggest using tatting thread and mending wool for the samples. One card of wool, and one ball of thread will make about enough for a sample. Each are five cents in the five and ten, (more now of course). To my mind this would be a neat and tidy way for the Conferees to weave the samples. If you want a larger pattern, thread with carpet warp, and use it for tabby. Then for the pattern you can use knitting wool. It is really quite effective.

I have named Jo's pattern "Cheerio", and the other "Daybreak". "Cheerio" somehow fits Jo, and as I do most of my samples in the early morning when most people are still asleep I thought "Daybreak" rather appropriate.

I'm sorry not to be at Conference this year, but I guess it is not possible. O how I wish we could go to Waldenwoods again. I have a perfect memory of our wonderful time there. Last year at Washington was more like it than for a number of years. More "get-to-getherness" and friendliness.

Wishing you all the luck there is in the 1947 Conference, I am

Very truly yours,

Bertha[25]

The following list includes patterns that Miss Hayes designed for the first ten conferences and of the people or places she honored, and one that honored her in 1951. A loom with each year's pattern was set up at each conference for attendees to weave. See page 22.

1938. Design 1. *Flower of Cromaine* was designed at the first national conference, which was organized by Cromaine Crafts and held at the center established by Mr. Crouse and Mr. Tremaine. At Mrs. Atwater's suggestion, this pattern was threaded on a loom for everyone to weave a sample.

1939. Design 2. *Waldenweave* was named for Waldenwoods, a wildlife refuge in Hartland, Michigan, and the location of the conferences for the first years.

1940. Design 4. *The Gallinger Gem* honored Osma Gallinger, Director of Cromaine Crafts.

1941. Design 6. *Meigs Mountain* honored Mary Meigs Atwater who was Director of these Conferences.

1942. Design 7. *Remembrance* was designed for the last conference held at Waldenwoods.

1943. Design 8. *Stars of Victory* was designed for the conference held in Pittsburgh, Pennsylvania.

1944. Design 9. *The Yankee* is a name draft of "Bertha Gray Hayes," designed for the conference in New York City.

1945. Design 10. *Hoosier Tallyho* honored the conference held in Indianapolis, Indiana.

1946. Design 63. *Hazelwood* was named for Hazel Lothrop, an acquaintance. The conference was held in Washington, D.C.

1947. Design 67. *Serenity of Salem* was designed for Thomas McKivergan and the Salem, Oregon, conference.

1951. Design 47. *Stagger* (originally designed in 1938) was chosen to commemorate Miss Hayes, four years after her death.[26]

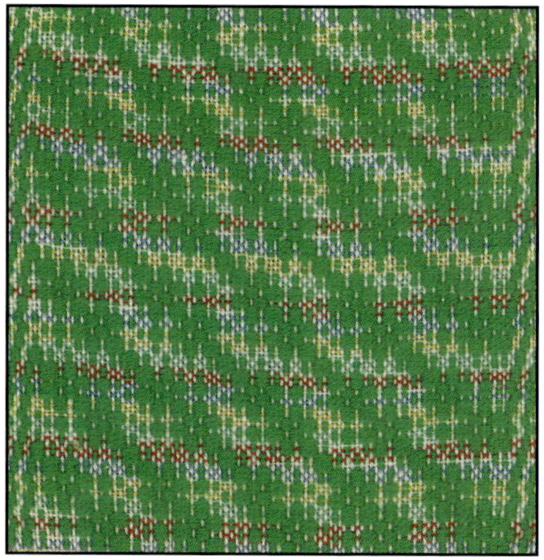

Conference Patterns

2. Bertha Gray Hayes' Weaving

Her Looms

Miss Hayes' notes indicate that she wove on a Structo loom. She referred to the No. 240 loom (an eight-inch four-shaft table loom), as well as No. 420 (fourteen inches) and No. 600 (twenty inches). Although her seventy-two samples were woven four inches wide, she also wove other projects up to twenty inches wide. In our collection are samplers seven inches and twelve inches in width (Figures 194-201) and notebook covers eighteen and one-half inches and twenty inches in width, (Figure 1), probably woven on her Bernat floor loom.[27] The Structo looms typically came with fifteen-dent reeds, although others could be ordered. And, typically, the reeds were sleyed two threads per dent, for a sett of thirty ends per inch (epi). A four-inch-wide reed with a sett of 30 epi accommodated 120 warp ends, and an eight-inch reed would allow for 240 warp ends, suggesting the numbering system for these looms.

The Thompson Manufacturing Company was founded in Freeport, Illinois, in 1907, "to manufacture and sell structural building sets for boys (commonly known now by the phrase coined by the A. C. Gilbert Company: 'erector sets')." In 1912 it was incorporated and renamed Structo Manufacturing Company.[28] By 1919 they had a full line of metal cars and trucks, toys that bore the label "Structo Toys Make Men of Boys." In 1921, the Structo Company held a competition to design a toy for girls. A small metal loom was the winning entry.[29] Using parts designed for their erector sets, Structo developed its first toy loom and, by 1922, they were manufacturing two styles of all-metal blue and black enameled table looms (Figure 9). In 1965 the King-Seeley Thermos Company bought the Structo Company, and in 1972 Dick Blick bought the loom business.[30] In 1930, Mary Meigs Atwater wrote the "Manual of Instructions for the Structo Artcraft Looms: Nos. 240, 420, 600," drafting thirty-two weaving patterns for four shafts and six for eight shafts. Atwater also sold Structo looms through her Shuttle-Craft Guild.

Hexagonal warp beams and pre-wound warp spools for the Structo looms became available in 1932, and Miss Hayes used those spools containing a ten-yard warp of sixty warp ends of 20/2 mercerized bleached or unbleached cotton. It appears that Miss Hayes, and other weavers of that time, designed their threadings for exactly 240 (or 420 or 600) warp ends, that is, multiples of sixty. Therefore, Miss Hayes would determine how many pattern repeats, plus the number of ends needed to balance the pattern, would fit into 240 ends. Extra ends were threaded straight draw at each selvedge (margin). If there were still one end left over, she would thread two ends in the last heddle. See Figures 11 and 17 for examples. She also wound carpet warp on these spools to use on her Bernat loom.[31]

Her Unique Patterns and How She Named Them

Although we know that Miss Hayes took a class at the National Conference of American Handweavers in 1940 with Josephine Estes on miniature overshot patterns, she had already been designing her own small motifs. Her technique differed from that of Miss Estes, who chose traditional overshot patterns having large pattern blocks and then eliminated certain threads to shrink or miniaturize the design. Miss Hayes, in contrast, chose to draft small pattern blocks because she was designing original miniature patterns, usually from name drafts.

Miss Hayes' Workbook pages, one for each of her seventy-two designs, include the threading and drawdown, and often a skeleton drawdown having no half tones. A skeleton drawdown is made by working with overshot blocks rather than individual threads to give a quicker presentation of the overall pattern. Miss Hayes used the term 'skeleton drawdown' for what we more commonly think of as a profile draft.

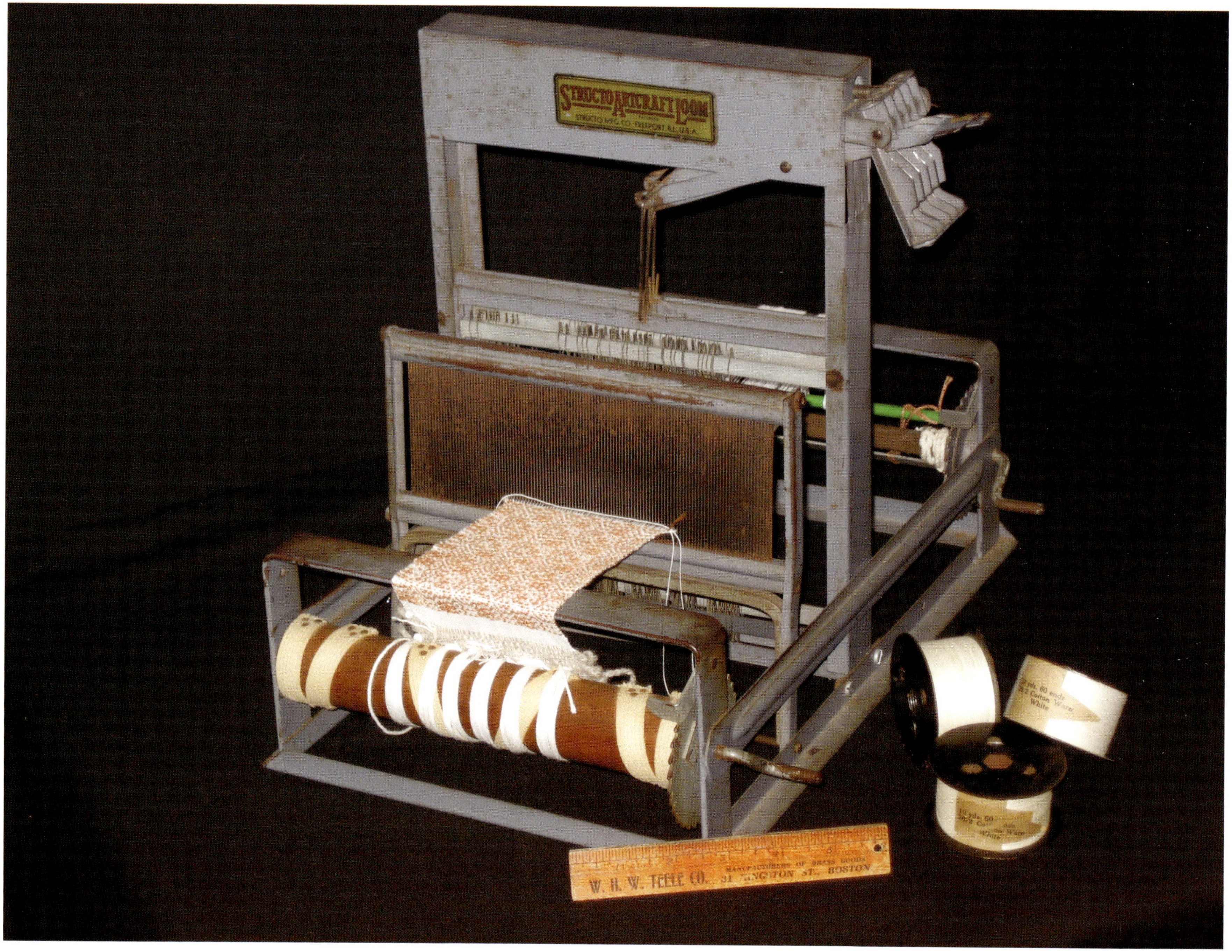

Figure 9. No. 240 Structo Loom of the type Miss Hayes used, and pre-wound warp spools of 20/2 mercerized unbleached cotton. Six-inch ruler to show scale. *Dexter Training Ground 2* **(Design 74) on loom woven by Gretchen White.** *Photograph by Robert Schelleng.*

The names of many of Miss Hayes' patterns reflect the World War II years—*Parachute*, *Bomber Flight*, *Victory*, and *Peace-1945*. Two of the unwoven drafts found in her Workbook, *Dexter Training Ground 1* and *Dexter Training Ground 2*, refer to an area in Miss Hayes' neighborhood in Providence. The Dexter Training Ground adjoins the Rhode Island State Armory on Cranston Street and was a site of patriotic parades during World War II. Some of the patterns have popular song, dance, or movie titles – *Balaliaka* [sic], *Fascination*, *Stormy Weather*, *Tangerine*, *Gone with the Wind*, *Jitterbug*. Others—*Domino*, *The Olive*, and *Butterfly*—reflect their visual image. A few patterns use new 1940s words—*Superhighway* and *Turntable.*

Miss Hayes' last numbered pattern is *Pinwheels*, a name draft of "Susan Sherburne." She wove the samples and also fabric for an upholstered doll's chair with pillow, a pin box, and a thimble holder, all of which she sent to Susan Sherburne of Monrovia, Indiana.[32] Although Miss Hayes did not feel well enough to weave her new design, *Serenity of Salem*, in the spring of 1947, when she was diagnosed with "gastric ulcer carcinoma," her health improved enough for her to design and weave during that summer and fall. She wove *Auld Lang Syne* for a 1947 Christmas present for Nina Lillian Thomas. *Hooks and Eyes* was "designed to take to Rockport, Massachusetts. Edna Bardwell, where I spent a week — August 1947."[33] So although she was not able to attend the tenth National Conference in Salem, Oregon, in 1947, she continued to weave and correspond with weaving friends until close to her death.

We know little of her woven pieces, other than the four-inch samples that she produced from these designs. Most of her overshot samples were woven "as drawn in." One exception is *Bomber Flight* (Design 14), one of the few for which she included treadling directions. Another is *Theme Song* (Design 51) for which she wove a series of three treadlings. *Theme Song* is unusual for another reason. Typically, overshot is threaded in twill fashion, with warp ends alternating on odd and even shafts, which gives a regular plain weave ground. In *Theme Song*, Miss Hayes chose to use a broken twill threading as a part of her design. Three times in each repeat her threading progresses from shaft one to shaft three to shaft one. This provides vertical or warp stripes in the plain weave areas, as well as the asymmetrical motif she wanted. Her first treadling of *Theme Song* she called "Victory." "This combines the three dots and a dash of the Morse code with the V for victory." This is not to be confused with *Victory* (Design 57).

One of the most unusual aspects of Miss Hayes' designs is her use of asymmetry. She often created her patterns with the name draft technique, designing in one direction and omitting the mirror image. She worked this out on graph paper with the diagonal line of the pattern drawn from upper right to lower left. She usually wove the diagonal in the reverse from lower right to upper left. Sometimes she designed asymmetrical elements within the larger motif. See examples in *Mosaic* (Design 35), a symmetrical pattern, and in *Ring Around A Rosey* (Design 62) and *Daybreak* (Design 65), both asymmetrical.

Selected Pages from the Workbook

Figures 10 to 17 are eight pages from Miss Hayes' Workbook. These examples were chosen for their visual impact and are representative of the collection. They show the development of her designs. For example, Figure 11 shows a variation in the pattern of what would become *Gallinger Gem - miniature* (Design 5). Weaving "as drawn in" produces the pattern on her sample card. This work sheet uses the same threading as the sample card, however, a slight change in treadling interrupts the diagonal line and alters the pattern.

A design technique she may have used was to develop a skeleton drawdown from an earlier one, as a way to create an entirely new design. Her work sheet for *Blossom* (Design 13) includes a skeleton drawdown for *Blossom* plus one for *Filigree* (Design 26). This is presented in Figure 12. She may have started with an idea from *Blossom*, but the result in *Filigree* is quite different. This work sheet also has graphed motifs she used for her greeting cards, to be woven in the inlay technique, dukagang.

For several of these workpages, she enhanced the motifs with colored pencils. One can only imagine the pleasure she must have gotten from coloring the bombers and primroses, as she was planning designs for her small

Figure 10.

Figure 11.

Figure 12.

Figure 13.

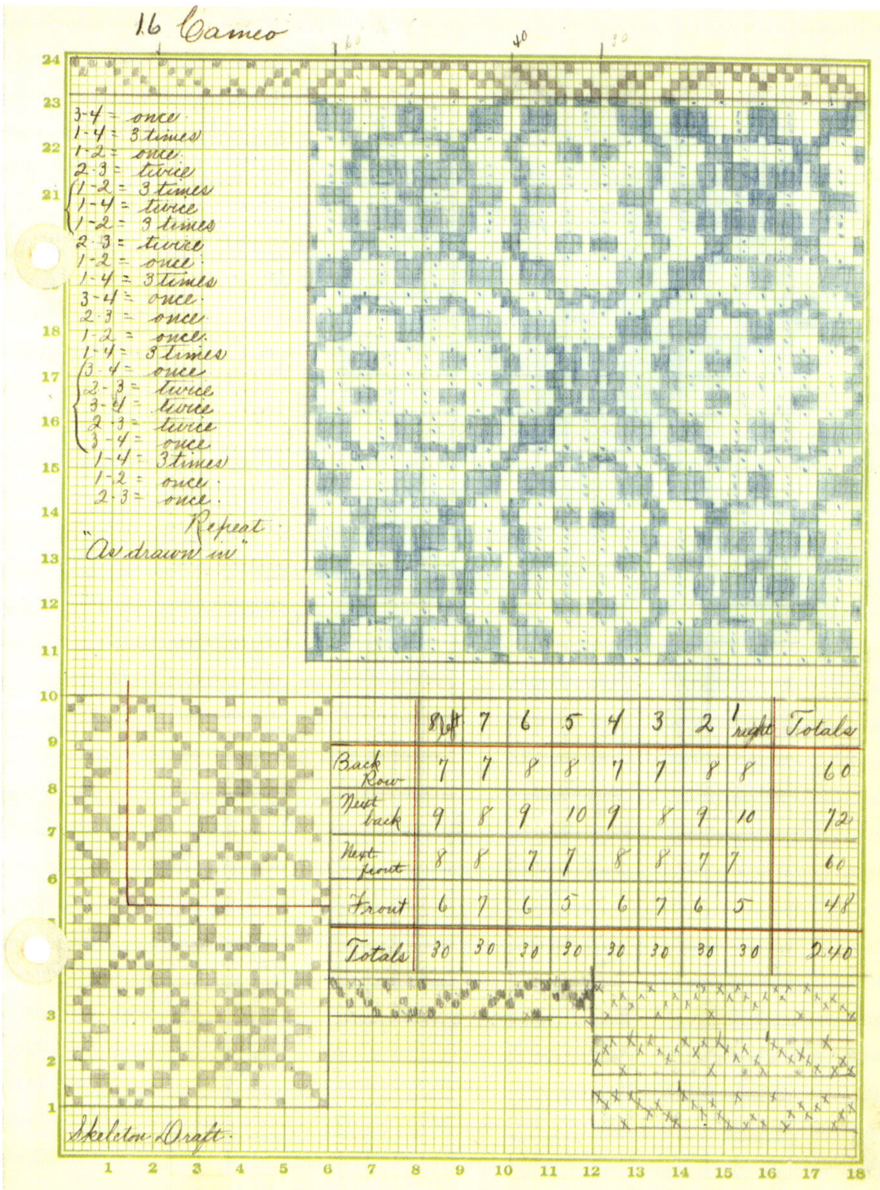

Figure 14.

Figure 15.

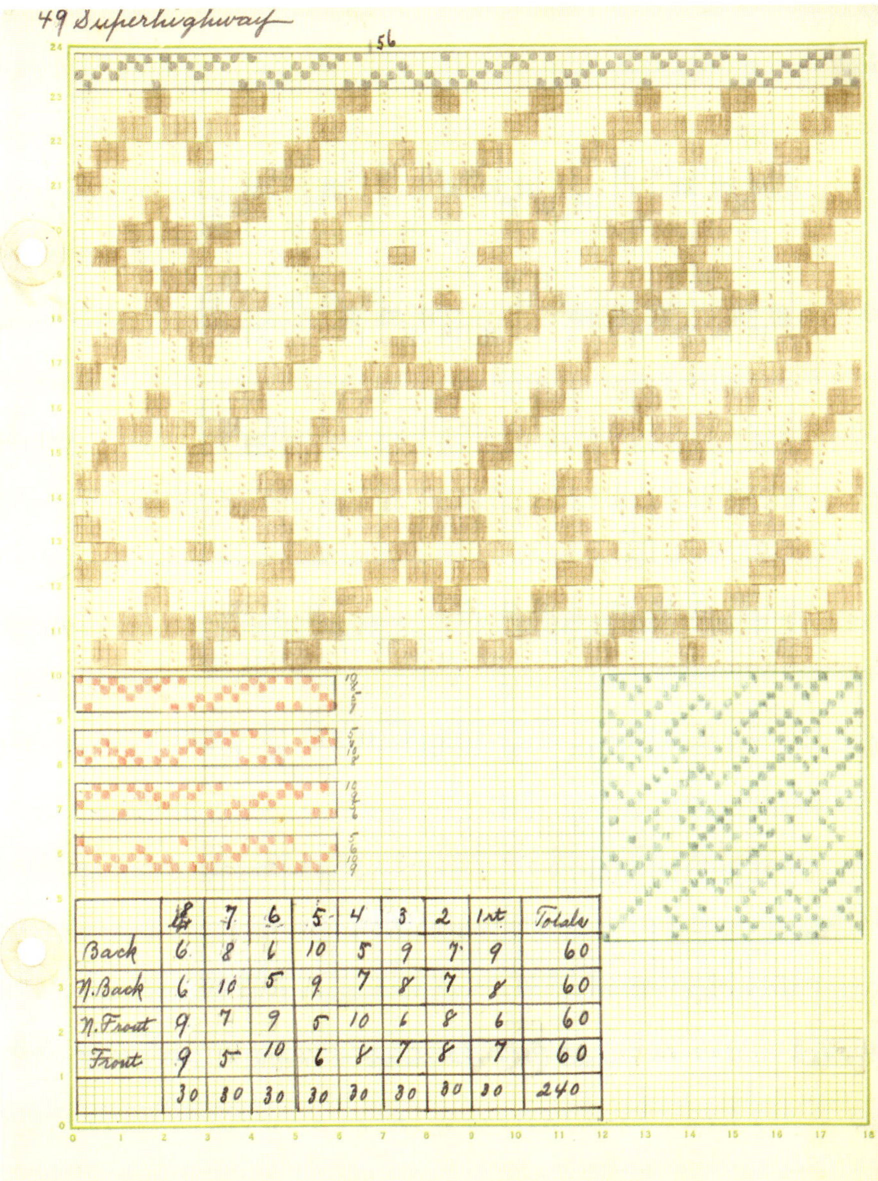

Figure 16.

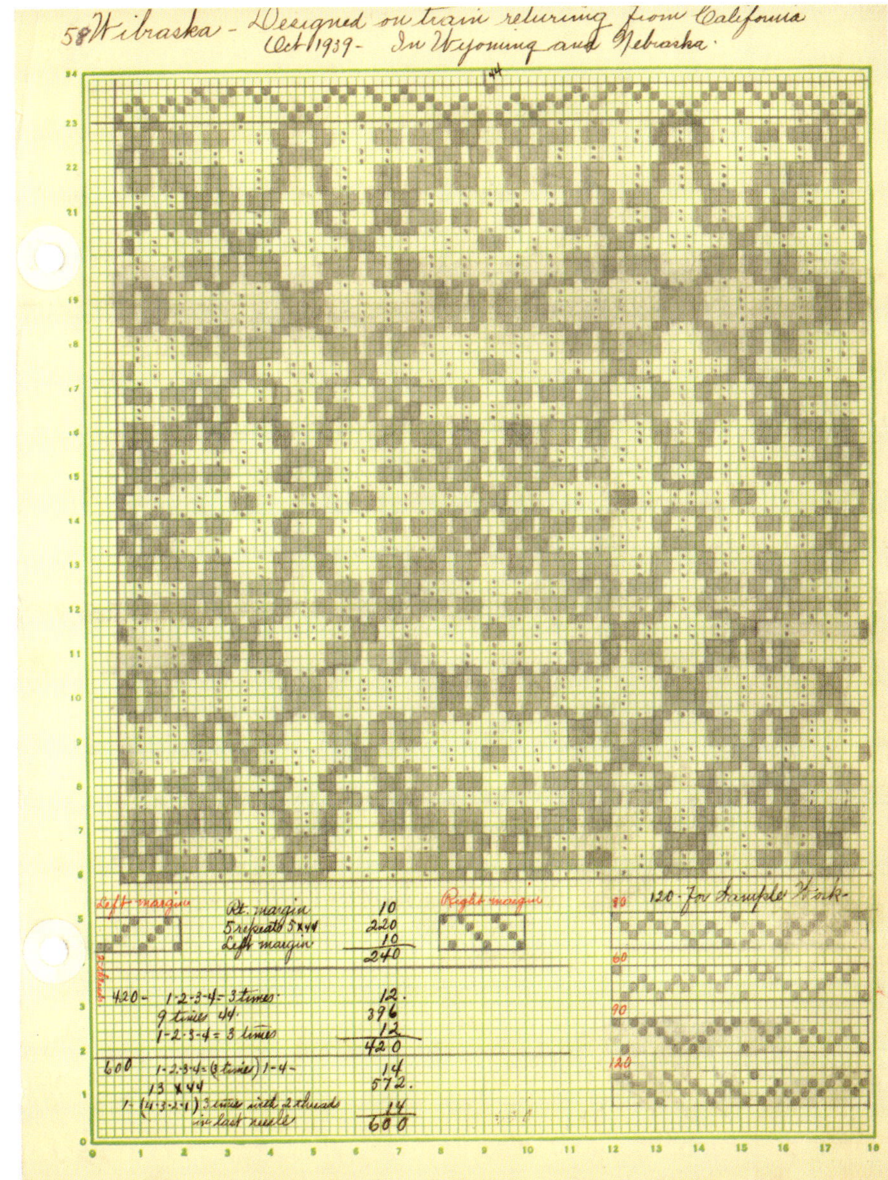

Figure 17.

woven projects. (Figures 13 and 15.) Some patterns are unique. *Wibraska* was "designed on train returning from California Oct 1939 – In Wyoming and Nebraska" (Workbook). Because Miss Hayes had the leisure of a cross-country journey through this unfamiliar landscape, we are the fortunate recipients of this complex-looking, hand-drawn name draft design.

For many patterns, Miss Hayes' design process began with a name draft. She then worked out the threading and made a drawdown, and last of all, a skeleton drawdown, if she wished, as for *The Yankee* (Design 9). With other patterns, she may have begun with a skeleton drawdown that was reminiscent of the visual effect she wanted and from that developed the threading and drawdown, as in *Domino* (Design 21) and *Superhighway* (Design 49). (See Figure 16.)

Oddments of a Weaver at Work

In our collection is a box of twenty-one small samples woven in a variety of techniques. Miss Hayes wove some of them while at the National Conferences. All weavers paid for the samples they wove. For example, she paid thirty cents for a five-inch sample of Flossa Rug Weave. Another sample is finely woven, with several rows of single and double leno and a leno tree motif. Most are neatly hemmed. There are many examples of Indian braid in two or more colors of wool, approximately ten inches long, displaying several patterns. Mrs. Atwater taught her this technique, and Miss Hayes then taught others at the first two conferences.

Although Miss Hayes kept very neat and organized weaving notebooks, she also jotted notes on the backs of discarded Providence Gas Company file cards. These notes were to remind her of topics that interested her, including references to the source of the information.

Included in the material from Miss Hayes is a small (four and one-half inches high by six inches wide) handmade book (Red and White Album, see Figure 1). It is covered in a red and white overshot weave, tied together with a green ribbon, and lined with a commercial red fabric. The fifty-four pages are in varied pastel colors, and the book reminds one of the autograph albums from long ago. Each of the fifty-four pages has a typewritten number and pattern name. The names are those we are familiar with, but the numbers are not those she has used elsewhere. Fifty-three of the fifty-four patterns are the same as those in her sample cards, and the additional one is *Rosette*, that we know of only because one of the brown envelopes has that name and draft.

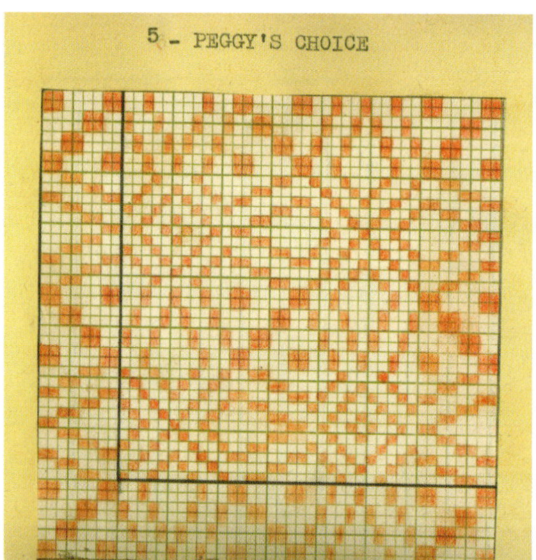

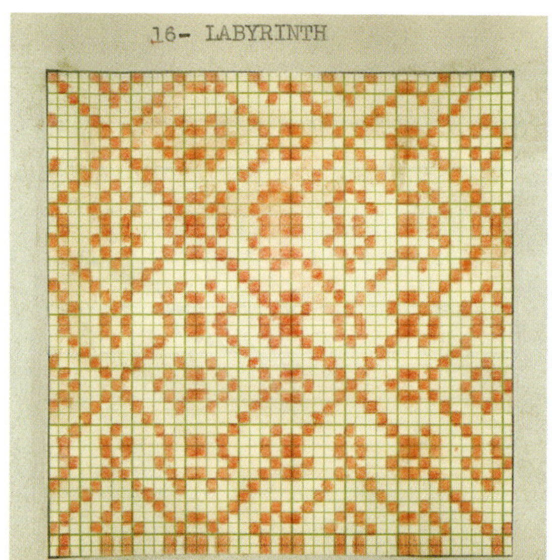

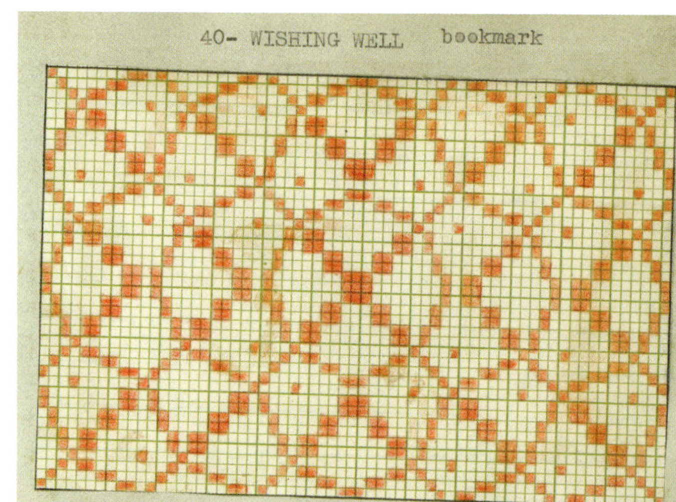

Figure 18. Selected skeleton drawdowns from Red and White Album.

Pasted onto each page of this handmade book is a skeleton drawdown on graph paper, drawn in various shades of red pencil. (See Figure 18.) She adapted several of her threadings to make narrow bookmarks. Five times she has added a drawdown to be used for this purpose. Four of the five have only a slight variation from the original (*Waldenweave*, *Estrellita*, *Wishing Well*, and *Fantasia*). If the warp in the draft for the bookmark *Wishing Well* runs horizontally, then this is not a different threading, but is a treadling variation, producing an effect reminiscent of ripples in water. The fifth bookmark is quite different in appearance from the original draft, because she reversed the threading to make it a symmetrical pattern. It has been given its own number, Design 90. This is *Meigs Mountain-bookmark*.

A manila envelope contains forty-seven small (two and one-quarter inches by three inches) graphed motifs suitable for greeting cards. Miss Hayes wrote an article for *The Weaver* describing Christmas card weaving.[34] She gave very complete and specific directions for weaving one's own cards and offered to provide "color charts and finished cards" if requested in writing. Illustrations in this article include six finished woven examples each with a reverse image graphed design. The design is laid-in and woven upside down, dukagang fashion, on a rosepath threading. As with her seventy-two woven samples, she wove her motifs four inches wide (120 warp ends sett at 30 epi), using a 240 Structo loom, 20/2 cotton warp and weft for the plain weave, and a wide assortment of heavier weft pattern yarns. Her graphed designs for the greeting cards are worked out in colored pencils, and all but one in our collection are positive images (see Figure 19). She worked out her designs first and then converted them to reverse images for weaving.

Name Drafts: Bertha Gray Hayes' "Personalized Designs"

A few things especially stand out in Miss Hayes' work. First, her very meticulous work is seen in the detailed drawdowns she made for each of her seventy-two (and more) patterns and in the skeleton

Figure 19. Selected greeting card designs.

drawdowns of fifty-four patterns contained in the Red and White Album. (Refer to Figure 18.) Secondly, she sought many ways to treadle a given pattern. (See the samplers in Figures 195, 196, 198, 200, and 201.) Treadling variations are found on many of her workbook pages. (See Figure 188.) She once gave a friend an eight-sided sewing basket, lined with fabric having a different treadling on each panel, highlighting her creative designing ability. A handwoven thimble holder was tucked into the basket. Thirdly, Miss Hayes created most of her overshot patterns using a method now called "name drafting." Thus, most of her designs were both unique and personalized.

Miss Hayes wrote to Mrs. Gallinger in 1944:

> I have a new idea suggested to me by a correspondent in California. I am not sure whether I have her idea, but all the better if I haven't, for it will be all the more original. I call it "Personalized Design". The draft is worked out by using the letters of one's own name, and in doing this for others, I make the finished weaving into an original folder for their ration books or tokens. I've had a lot of fun doing them as gifts for my friends, and have sold some too. This draft is my own name but I am calling it "The Yankee" for I AM A YANKEE. I dedicate it to the conference. [35]

A name draft uses a code that is a device to create an original threading, most often in the overshot technique. Variations of this code involve different arrangements of the twenty-six letters of the alphabet. Miss Hayes often gave her patterns names other than the words used in creating her threadings. She designed *Cheerio* from the name "Josephine Couch" and *Ring Around A Rosey* from the name "Middleborough," her birthplace.

Miss Hayes appears to have been consistent in her use of the following sequence for her name drafts, taken from the work page shown in Figure 164.

Shafts	Letters						
4	D	H	L	P	T	X	
3	C	G	K	O	S	W	
2	B	F	J	N	R	V	Z
1	A	E	I	M	Q	U	Y

After assigning letters to shafts, one chooses the appropriate words or phrase that one wishes to commemorate and selects the shafts where those letters fall. For example, Bertha Hayes created the pattern *The Yankee* (Design 9) from her own name. It is a symmetrical pattern with the threading reversing at thread twenty-two to give a pattern repeat of forty-three threads. She wrote her code and threading working from right to left.

S E Y A H Y A R G A H T R E B

This represents a starting point to develop the threading, which then needs to have more threads added to create a proper overshot threading, as in the following.

S _ E _ Y _ A H Y _ A R G _ A H _ T _ R E B
3 1 1 1 4 1 1 2 3 1 4 4 2 1 2

To provide the plain-weave ground for overshot, threads on even shafts must always alternate with those on odd shafts. Four-shaft overshot is a pattern weave threaded on four blocks, i.e., 1-2, 2-3, 3-4, 4-1. The smallest overshot block is composed of two warp ends, threaded on adjacent shafts. The larger the pattern block, that is, the more repeats of a two-thread unit, the longer the weft floats will be. Therefore, when the name draft suggests two odd or two even adjacent threads, additional threads are added to maintain the odd-even sequence, creating a good weave structure, a pleasing motif, and the desired size blocks. Once one is familiar with the overshot technique, one determines whether to create larger or smaller pattern blocks. These two possible options show this process.

Option 1: 3 4 1 4 1 4 1 4 1 4 1 2 3 4 1 4 1 4 1 2 1 2

Option 2: 3 2 1 2 1 4 1 4 1 2 1 2 3 2 1 4 3 4 3 2 1 2

Here Option 1 produces extra long blocks on shafts 1and 4 with pattern floats over 10 and 6 warp ends, (here underlined). Option 2 produces smaller blocks on shafts 1 and 4, and on 3 and 4 with weft floats over 5 and 4 warp ends, respectively. Because Miss Hayes was designing miniature overshot patterns, she often chose to use smaller pattern blocks.

B E R _ T _ H A _ G R A _ Y H A _ Y _ E _ Ŝ _ E _ Y _ A H Y _ A R G _ A H _ T _ R E B

2 1 2 3 4 3 4 1 2 3 2 1 2 1 4 1 4 1 2 1 2 3̂ 2 1 2 1 4 1 4 1 2 1 2 3 2 1 4 3 4 3 2 1 2

Miss Hayes used Option 2, reversing her name draft of twenty-two ends at the S (^) to make a symmetrical pattern of forty-three threads for *The Yankee*.

To increase the size of the motif and to make it symmetrical, which is the most traditional form of overshot, the threading is reversed at the last thread. However, Miss Hayes designed many asymmetrical patterns for her miniature overshot motifs. Twenty-five percent of her seventy-two samples are asymmetrical. This appears to be unique to her in the 1940s.

Publications

Miss Hayes published three articles in *The Weaver*, and others have described her work in numerous weaving magazines and newsletter articles. Two of her articles were about the weaving and construction of tote bags.

In *The Weaver* (Volume VI, Number 1, 1941) she described a bag that she had woven, exhibited at the 1940 Conference, and given to Mary Meigs Atwater. (See quotation from Atwater cited in the section on The National Conferences of American Handweavers.) "A Bag in Featherstitch Technique" describes her overshot treadling variation that she named "featherstitch effect." The threading Miss Hayes chose for Atwater's bag and this article was *Jitterbug* (Design 31). She eliminated the tabby weft between unlike pattern shots. In other words, tabby shots are alternated between like pattern shots, but not woven between unlike pattern shots. This variation, described in her article, also is written on the back of a Providence Gas Company file card stapled onto the draft page for *Jitterbug* in her Workbook

In addition, because she wanted to weave a bag of patriotic colors, she used blue wool pattern weft on a white warp, and inlaid red knitting yarn in each of the "eyes" of the motifs. The blue weft floated under the "eye" warps. These two pattern rows were woven using a stick shuttle. She finished her bag with woven handle straps and red pompoms attached to the zipper. The result is eye-catching, literally, because of the color contrast within the irregular diamond-like motifs and the placement of the "eyes" on the handles.[36]

"Bags for the Woman Who Reads" (published in *The Weaver*, Volume VII, Number 1, 1942) illustrates Miss Hayes' personality and sense of humor.

> If you are one of those people who like to read on bus or train, this is just the bag which will appeal to you. With just room enough for the latest "best seller," a time table or two, your Handkerchief and change purse, together with your bi-focals, if need be, it can be carried on the arm with very little inconvenience.
>
> For a long time I have eyed the tops of my cast off semi-service hose, and wondered if they might not be put to some use. Finally my Scotch thrift got the better of me, and I grabbed the scissors and cut off the offending tops. Then I cut the seam open and pressed out the result into a double flat oblong shape, which I proceeded to cut the long way into quarter inch strips. Taking hold of each strip by either end, I gave it a long stretch, and the result, a soft tubular cord, with the cut edges conveniently curled inside.[37]

Continuing with her patriotic sensibility and a few months into World War II, Miss Hayes dyed those strips red and blue for pattern weft in what she called a "simple" crackle threading on a white warp. She chose *Meigs Mountain in Crackle Weave* (Design 89) for these bags. Her third article, "Christmas Card Weaving," appeared in *The Weaver* (Volume VI, Number 4, 1941.) (See a description of this in the section Oddments of a Weaver at Work.)

3. The Sample Cards

Bertha Hayes created note cards for the samples she designed and wove. Folded in half, they measure four and one-half inches wide by three and three-quarter inches high. The front of the cards has her printed logo (her initials over a stick shuttle and ball of yarn), plus a handwritten number and the name of the sample with her signature. A look at the seventy-two sample cards will show that she generally used the same colored pencils to color her logo and to record the threading on the inside. Sometimes she used several colors within a logo and its accompanying threading. (See 72 Sample Cards.)

Inside the card on the left is a four-shaft threading grid. She had a stamp made for this purpose, allowing for up to 120 ends, although few threadings were that long. The longest threading, *Waldenweave - enlarged* (Design 3), of 122 ends, has two extra ends added at the lower left. (See Figure 22.)

Apparently Miss Hayes had two different stamps made for her threading grid. Close scrutiny of her patterns reveals that most, but not all, of her cards were divided into five-thread units. While Mrs. Atwater divided her overshot threadings into groups of ten ends, Miss Hayes divided hers into groups of five ends. The threading grid has a small vertical line marking every fifth thread. However, eighteen of her sample cards have this vertical line after ends 4, 9, 14, 20, 25 and 30, and the grid is slightly smaller. This appears to be an error, and it must have been in the stamp itself. Miss Hayes compensated in all cases, counting out her warp ends by fives. Again, this is an example of her meticulous work. *Stars of Victory* (Design 8) and *Blossom* (Design 13) are examples of this discrepancy.

Included with the collection of seventy-two sample cards are matching envelopes, one for each design, plus an additional one for Lambeth Walk, on which Miss Hayes wrote "use next time I weave the draft." This may refer to a treadling variation such as we see in the sampler, Figure 199. The name and number of each design is written in one corner, as well as the number of samples contained in the envelope (usually 1, 2 or 3, although there is only one sample card for each envelope in our collection.) On five of the envelopes are names Miss Hayes used in their name drafts: John Baird (Daybreak), Jo Couch (Cheerio), Thomas McKivergan (Serenity of Salem), Jane McKivergan (Sweet and Lovely), and Mary Ruth (Parquetry).

Samples were stapled inside the cards on the right. They measure three and three-eighths inches in width and usually three and one-quarter inches in height, although that ranged from two and three-quarters to three and three-quarters inches. She threaded her samples four inches wide in the reed. She used 120 ends of 20/2 mercerized unbleached cotton sett at 30 epi. She often refers to a "120 loom." The plain weave weft was usually the same as the warp yarn, but occasionally she used a colored yarn, such as for *Meigs Mountain* (Design 6), *Chintz* (Design 17), and *Cretonne* (Design 19), which she wove with a red, green, yellow, and blue variegated tatting thread.

Pattern weft yarns were often fine cotton (such as 10/2), heavier than the warp, in mercerized and unmercerized cotton, fine wool, and, several times, lustrous rayon. Miss Hayes used many colors for her pattern wefts, including shades of red, rose, lilac, blue, green, and even black on a bright green plain weave. Thematic samples woven in stripes of red and white plain weave with a blue pattern yarn for the patriotic *Stars of Victory* (Design 8), in black on white, *Domino* (Design 21), and in blue on white *Peace-1945* (Design 39), indicate that her color choice was sometimes influenced by the inspiration for her sample. Handwritten on the cards for *Bomber Flight* (Design 14) and *Theme Song* (Design 51), beneath the samples, are treadling directions that are shown on the back covers of those cards.

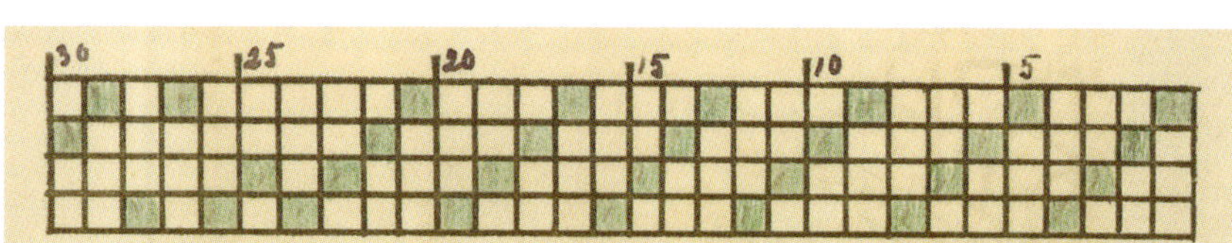

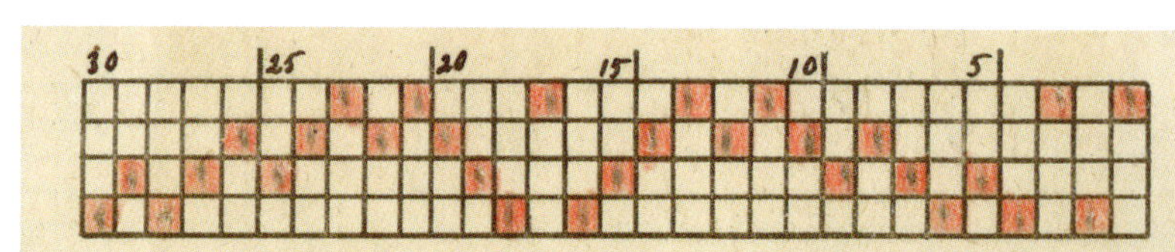

Another point of interest in her samples is that three of them (*Bomber Flight*, *Estrellita*, and *Treasure Island*) have been mounted on her cards with what we think of as the reverse side up; the diagonal line is white ground rather than pattern, and one can assume that this was a conscious design decision on her part. However, she worked them out in her Workbook with the diagonal line in the pattern. Her pattern repeats vary in length from fourteen ends (*Needlepoint*) to 122 ends (*Waldenweave - enlarged*), with eighty percent of them being between twenty-four and sixty ends. Patterns *Bagatelle* through *Zigzag* are arranged alphabetically in her Workbook. She may not have woven these chronologically, because her working notes were in a two-ring binder, and she could have inserted pages in any order. Most of Miss Hayes' threadings begin on either shaft one or shaft four, with just one beginning on shaft two and three on shaft three.

The hand-drawn threadings on a few of her sample cards have minor errors. By comparing them with her working drafts, one sees the original correct version. In the written threading for *Waldenweave*, thread fifty-four should be on shaft one, not three, to make this weave symmetrical. In *Gone with the Wind*, thread one should be on shaft four. For *Jitterbug - enlarged*, where there is no sample card, and it appears there is a threading block missing in her draft, we chose to make the drawdown the way we think Miss Hayes meant it to be. There is a discrepancy of eight threads between Miss Hayes' sample threading for *Zigzag* and that in her Workbook. Her sample is woven from the Workbook threading, which is also used in the drawdown, p. 156. A few of the woven samples in our collection have treadling errors, seen by the break in the diagonal pattern line. They were graphed correctly in the drawdowns found in her Workbook. These errors do not detract from the overall charm of the collection, but point out that they were made by human hand.

Miss Hayes neatly hemstitched her samples in groups of four warp ends, with fringes cut very short. Samples were missing from some of her cards and have been woven by Tony Kormos to replace Designs 10, 25, 35, 48, 61, 65, 66, and 71 and by Sandra Reynolds to replace Design 36. The front and the back of each sample card are shown at actual size in Figures 20 to 91.

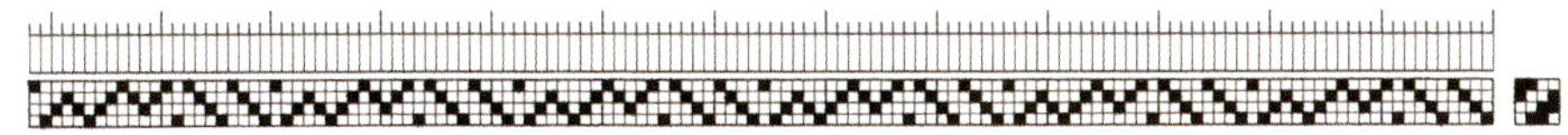

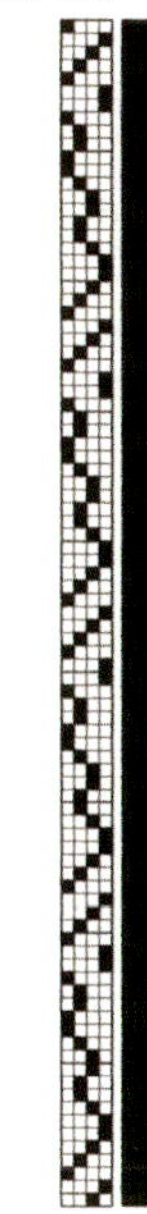

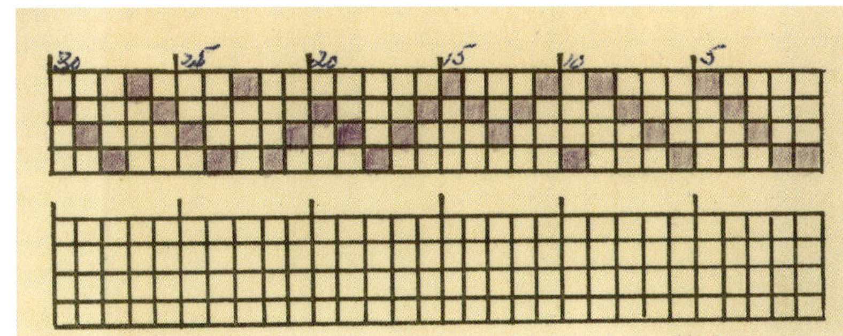

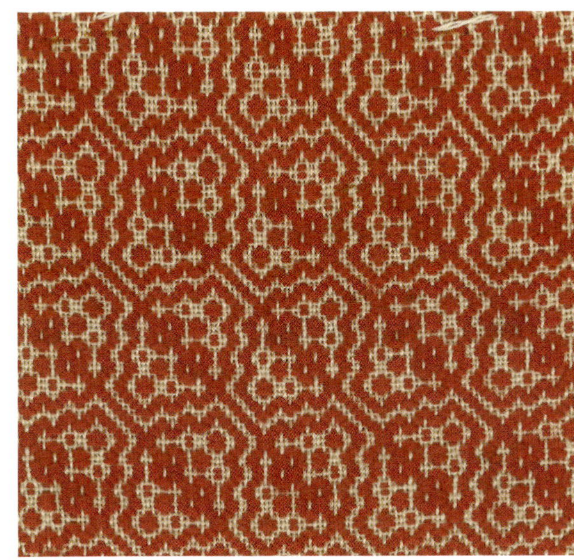

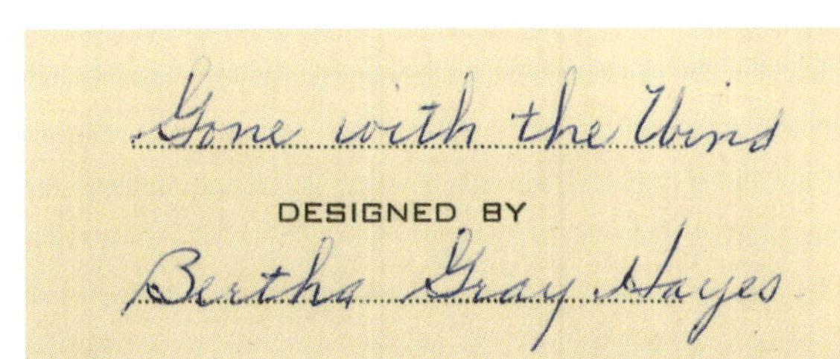

Miss Hayes' List of Sample Cards

1. *Flower of Cromaine*
2. *Waldenweave*
3. *Waldenweave - enlarged*
4. *The Gallinger Gem*
5. *The Gallinger Gem - miniature*
6. *Meigs Mountain*
7. *Remembrance*
8. *Stars of Victory*
9. *The Yankee*
10. *Hoosier Tallyho*
11. *Bagatelle*
12. *Balaliaka [sic]*
13. *Blossom*
14. *Bomber Flight*
15. *Butterfly*
16. *Cameo*
17. *Chintz*
18. *Cornerstones*
19. *Cretonne*
20. *Delight*
21. *Domino*
22. *Estrellita*
23. *Fantasia*
24. *Fascination*
25. *Ferns and Flowers*
26. *Filigree*
27. *Flagstones*
28. *Foursquare*
29. *Gone with the Wind*
30. *Honiton*
31. *Jitterbug*
32. *Lambeth Walk*
33. *Labyrinth*
34. *Linoleum*
35. *Mosaic*
36. *Needlepoint*
37. *The Olive*
38. *Parachute*
39. *Peace-1945*
40. *Peggy's Choice*
41. *Petite*
42. *Plaza*
43. *Posey Patch*
44. *Primrose*
45. *Rose O'Day*
46. *Springtime Fancy*
47. *Stagger*
48. *Stormy Weather*
49. *Superhighway*
50. *Tangerine*
51. *Theme Song*
52. *This and That*
53. *Three Times Three*
54. *Treasure Island*
55. *Trellis*
56. *Turntable*
57. *Victory*
58. *Wibraska*
59. *Wild Rose*
60. *Wishing Well*
61. *Zigzag*
62. *Ring Around A Rosey*
63. *Hazelwood*
64. *Queen Anne's Lace*
65. *Daybreak*
66. *Cheerio*
67. *Serenity of Salem*
68. *Sweet and Lovely*
69. *Parquetry*
70. *Auld Lang Syne*
71. *Hooks and Eyes*
72. *Pinwheels*

Alphabetical List of Sample Cards

Auld Lang Syne 70
Bagatelle 11
Balaliaka [sic] 12
Blossom 13
Bomber Flight 14
Butterfly 15
Cameo 16
Cheerio 66
Chintz 17
Cornerstones 18
Cretonne 19
Daybreak 65
Delight 20
Domino 21
Estrellita 22
Fantasia 23
Fascination 24
Ferns and Flowers 25
Filigree 26
Flagstones 27
Flower of Cromaine 1
Foursquare 28
Gallinger Gem 4
Gallinger Gem - miniature 5
Gone with the Wind 29
Hazelwood 63
Honiton 30
Hooks and Eyes 71
Hoosier Tallyho 10
Jitterbug 31
Labyrinth 33
Lambeth Walk 32
Linoleum 34
Meigs Mountain 6
Mosaic 35
Needlepoint 36
The Olive 37
Parachute 38
Parquetry 69
Peace-1945 39
Peggy's Choice 40
Petite 41
Pinwheels 72
Plaza 42
Posey Patch 43
Primrose 44
Queen Anne's Lace 64
Remembrance 7
Ring Around A Rosey 62
Rose O'Day 45
Serenity of Salem 67
Springtime Fancy 46
Stagger 47
Stars of Victory 8
Stormy Weather 48
Superhighway 49
Sweet and Lovely 68
Tangerine 50
Theme Song 51
This and That 52
Three Times Three 53
Treasure Island 54
Trellis 55
Turntable 56
Victory 57
Waldenweave 2
Waldenweave - enlarged 3
Wibraska 58
Wild Rose 59
Wishing Well 60
The Yankee 9
Zigzag 61

The 72 Sample Cards

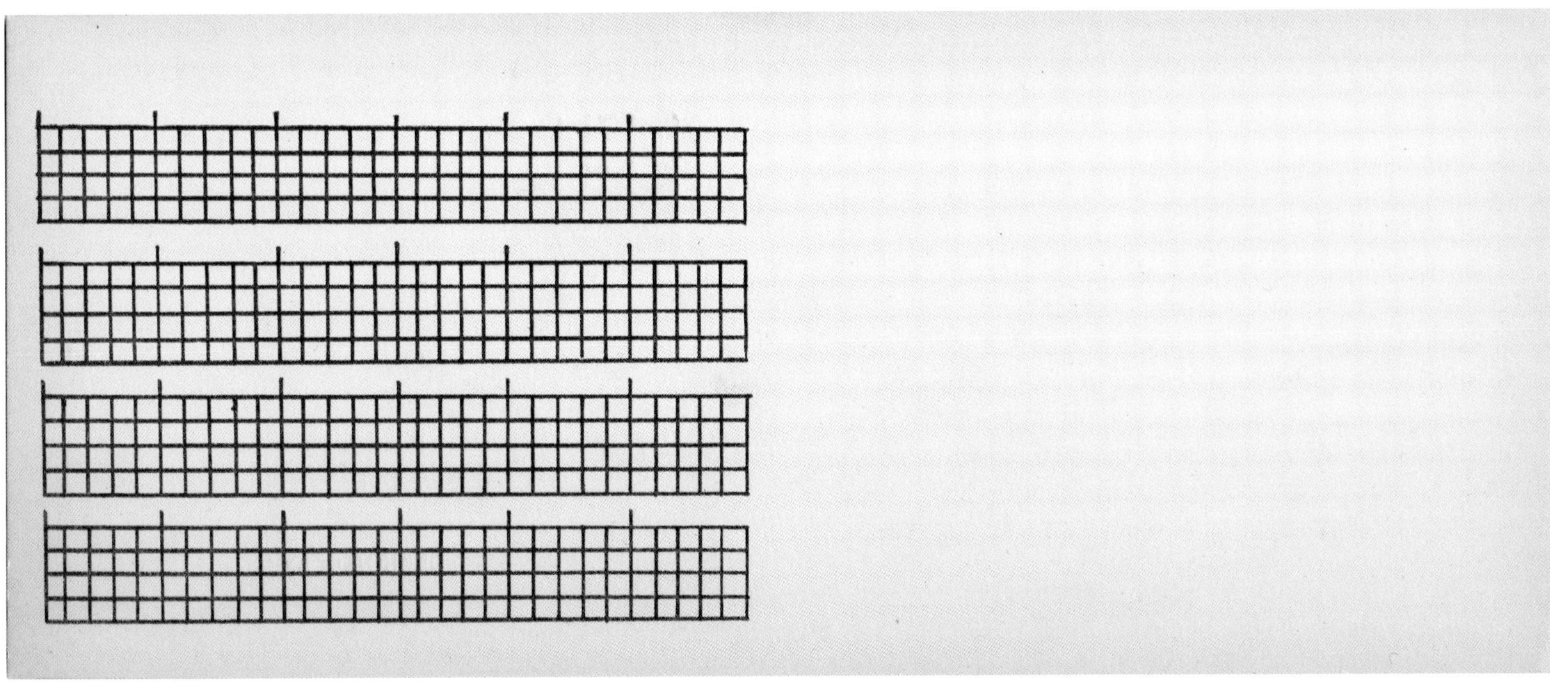

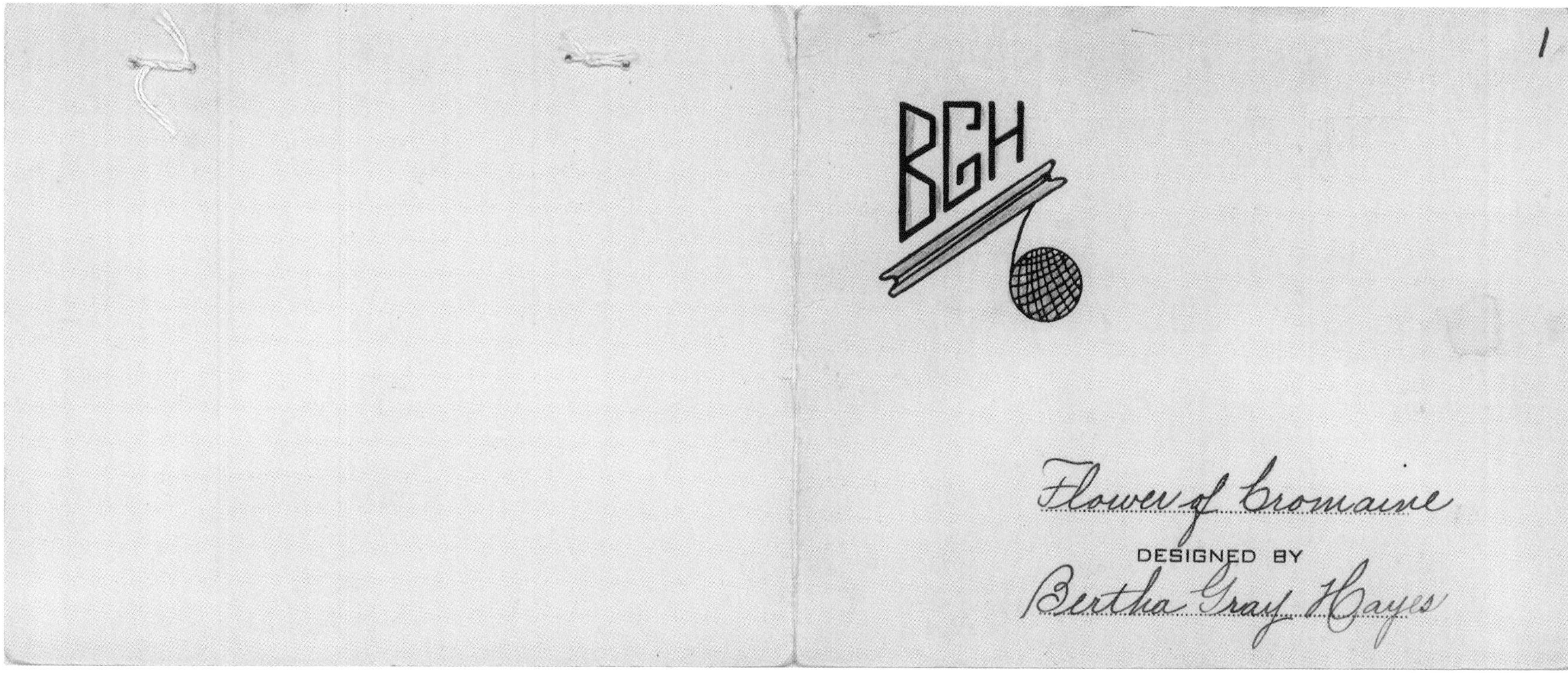
1
BGH
Flower of Cromaine
DESIGNED BY
Bertha Gray Hayes

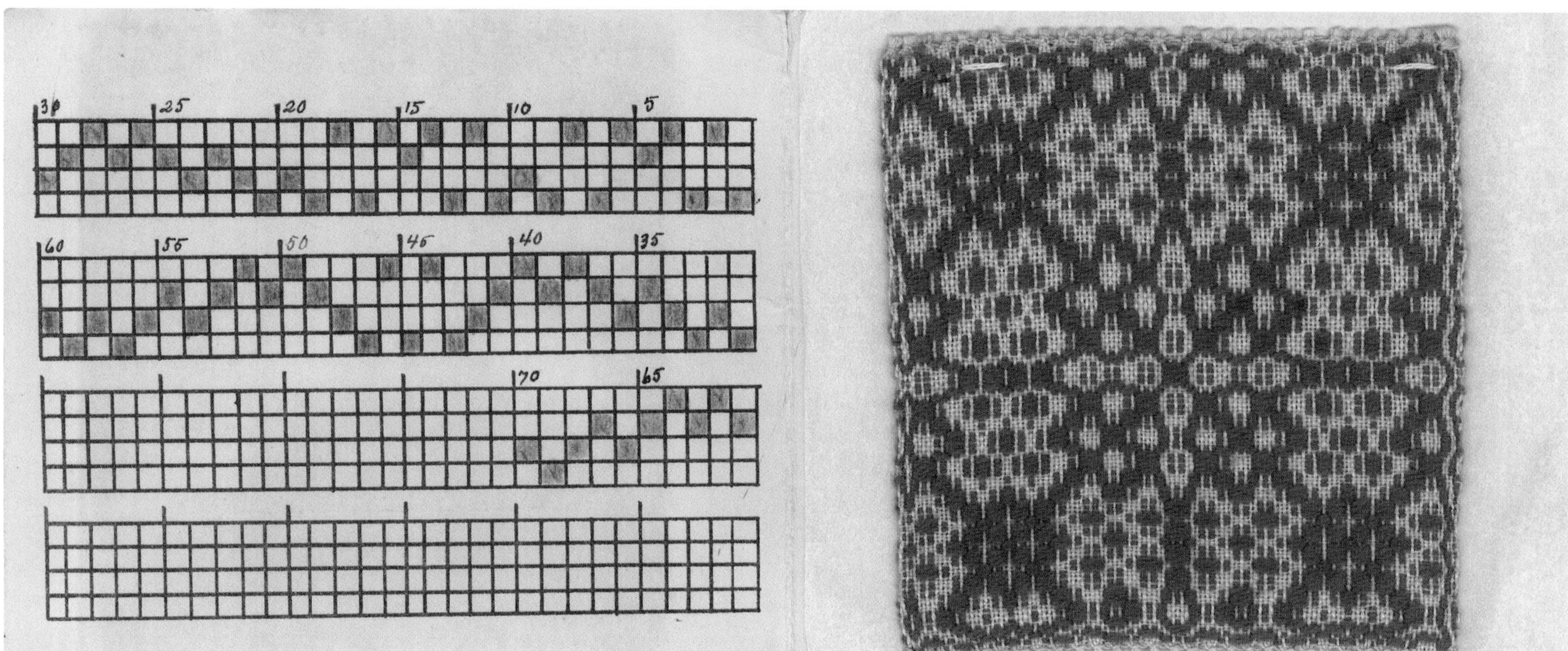
30
25
20
15
10
5
60
55
50
45
40
35
70
65

Figure 20.

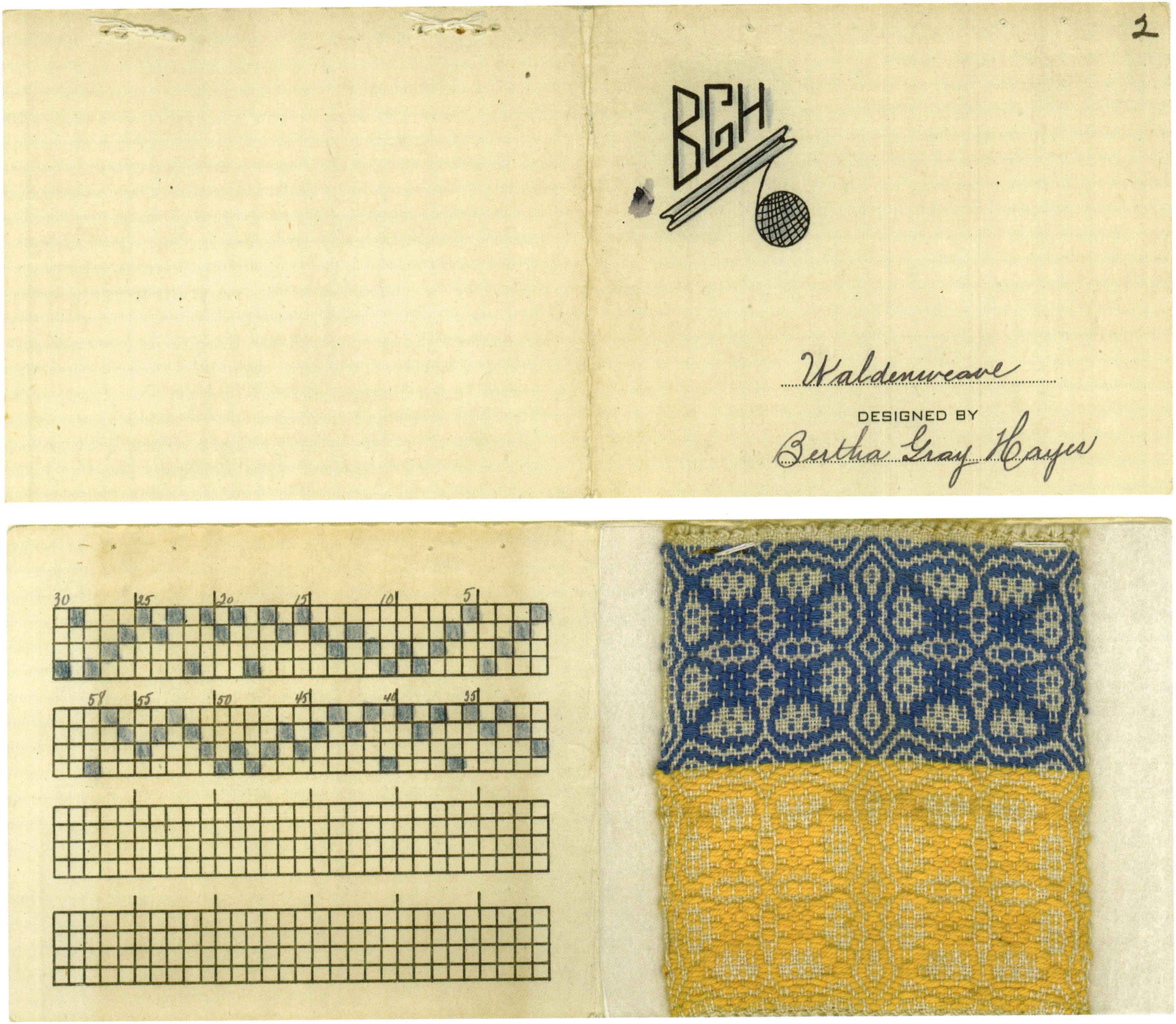
2
BGH
Waldenweave
DESIGNED BY
Bertha Gray Hayes
30 25 20 15 10 5
58 55 50 45 40 35

Figure 21.

Figure 22.

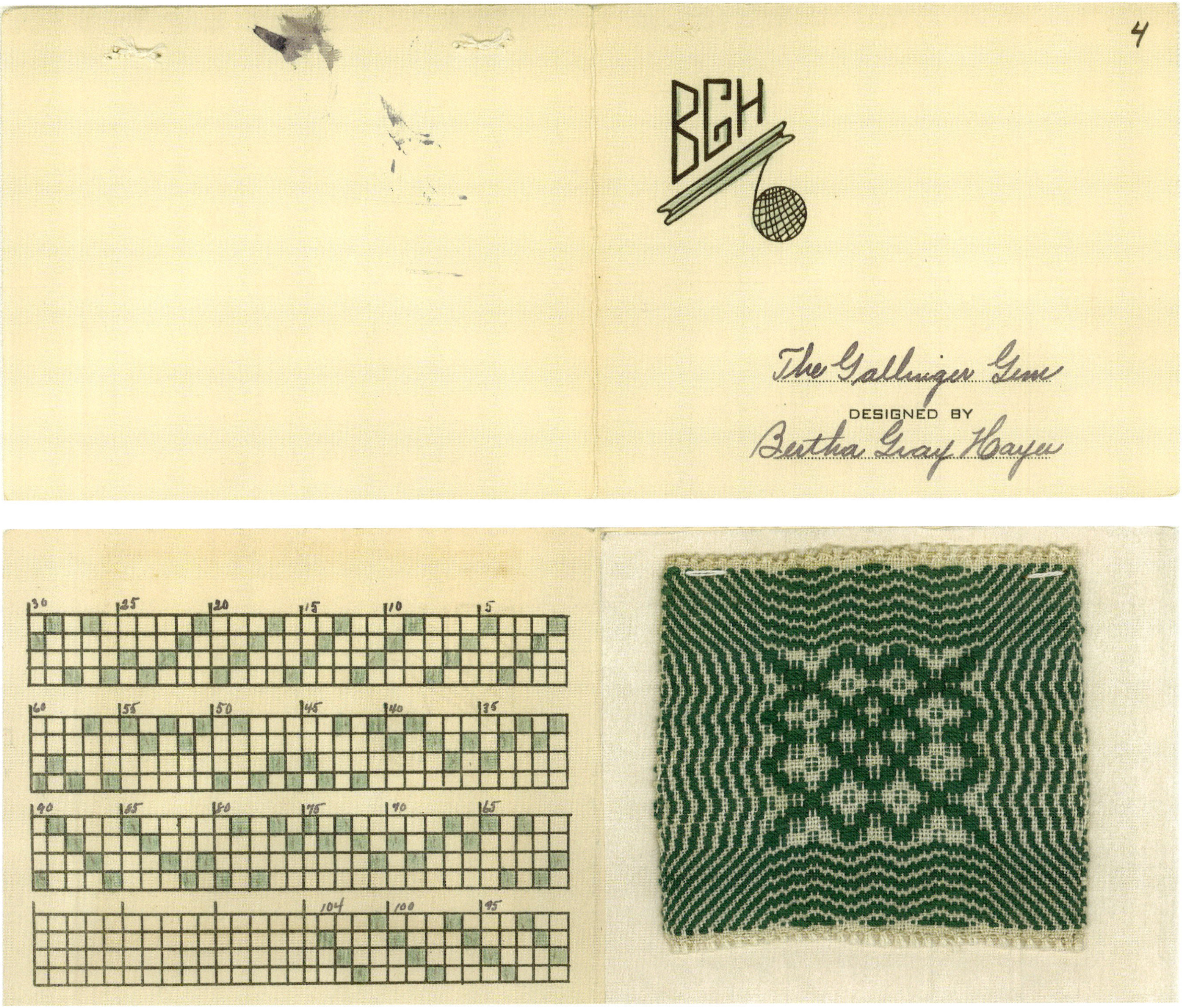

Figure 23.

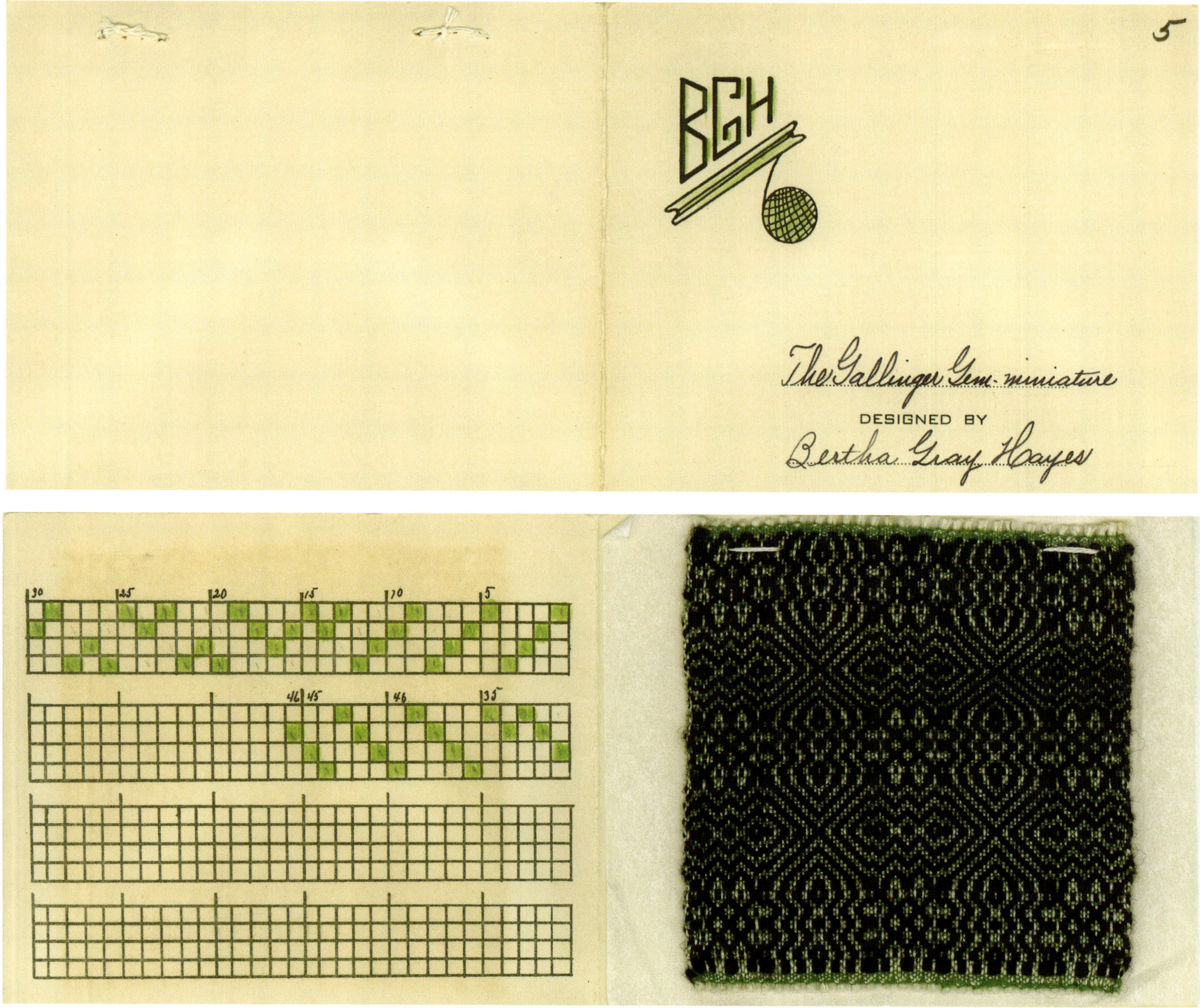
5
BGH
The Gallinger Gem miniature
DESIGNED BY
Bertha Gray Hayes
30
25
20
15
10
5
46
45
46
35

Figure 24.

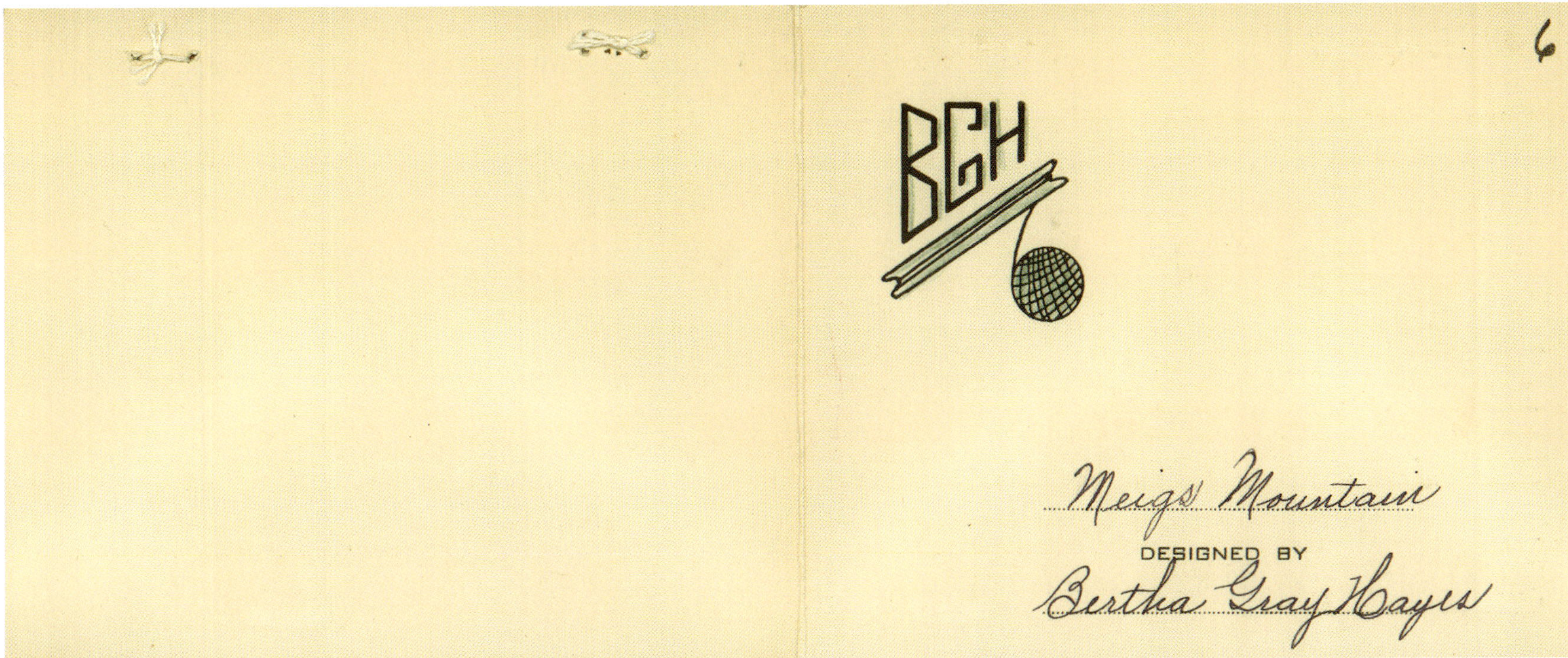

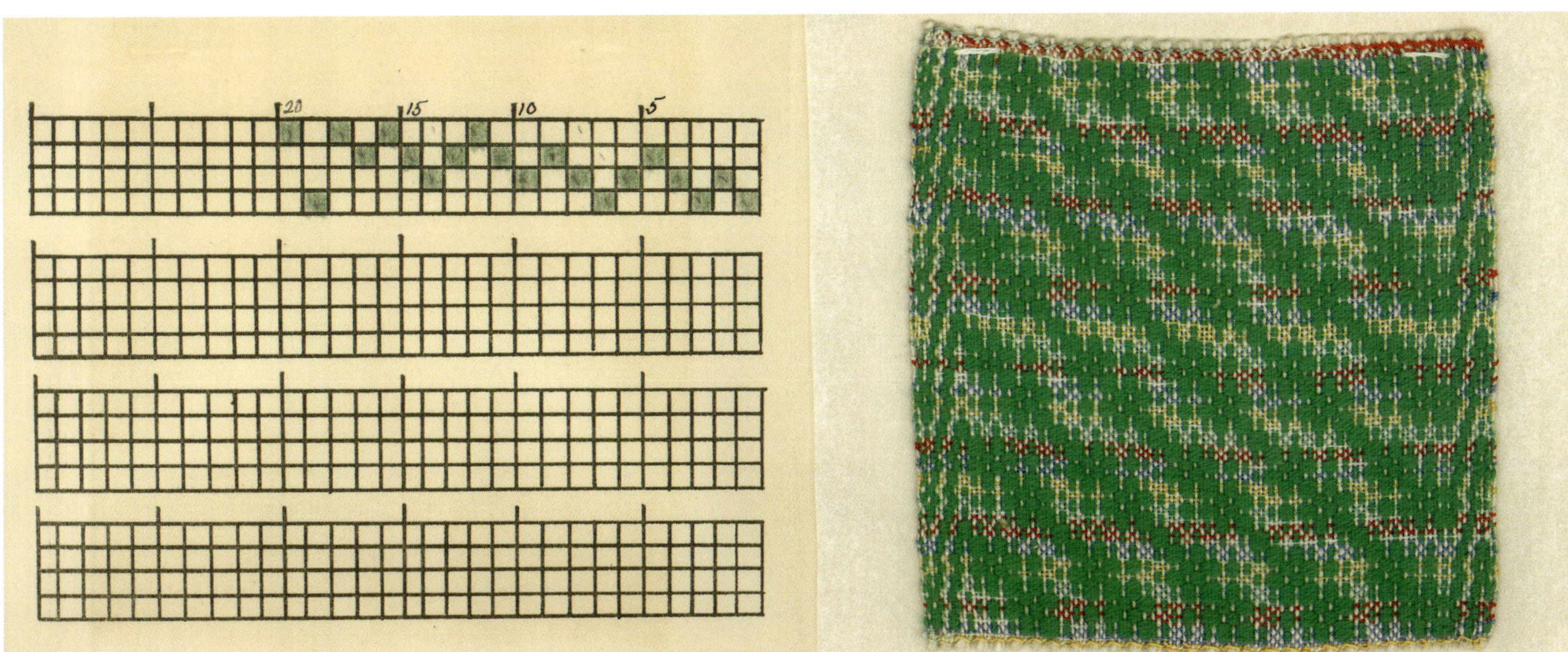

Figure 25.

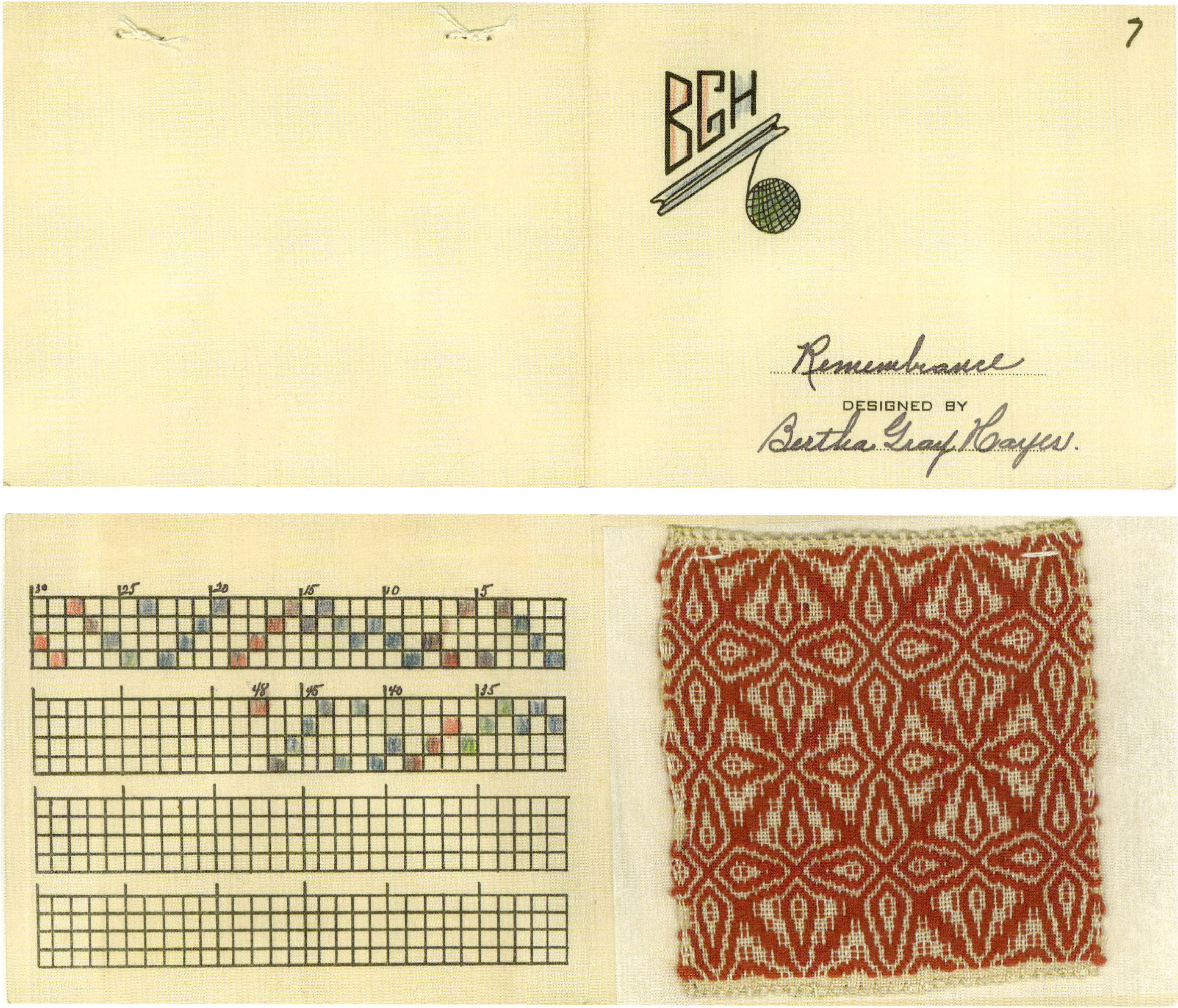

Figure 26.

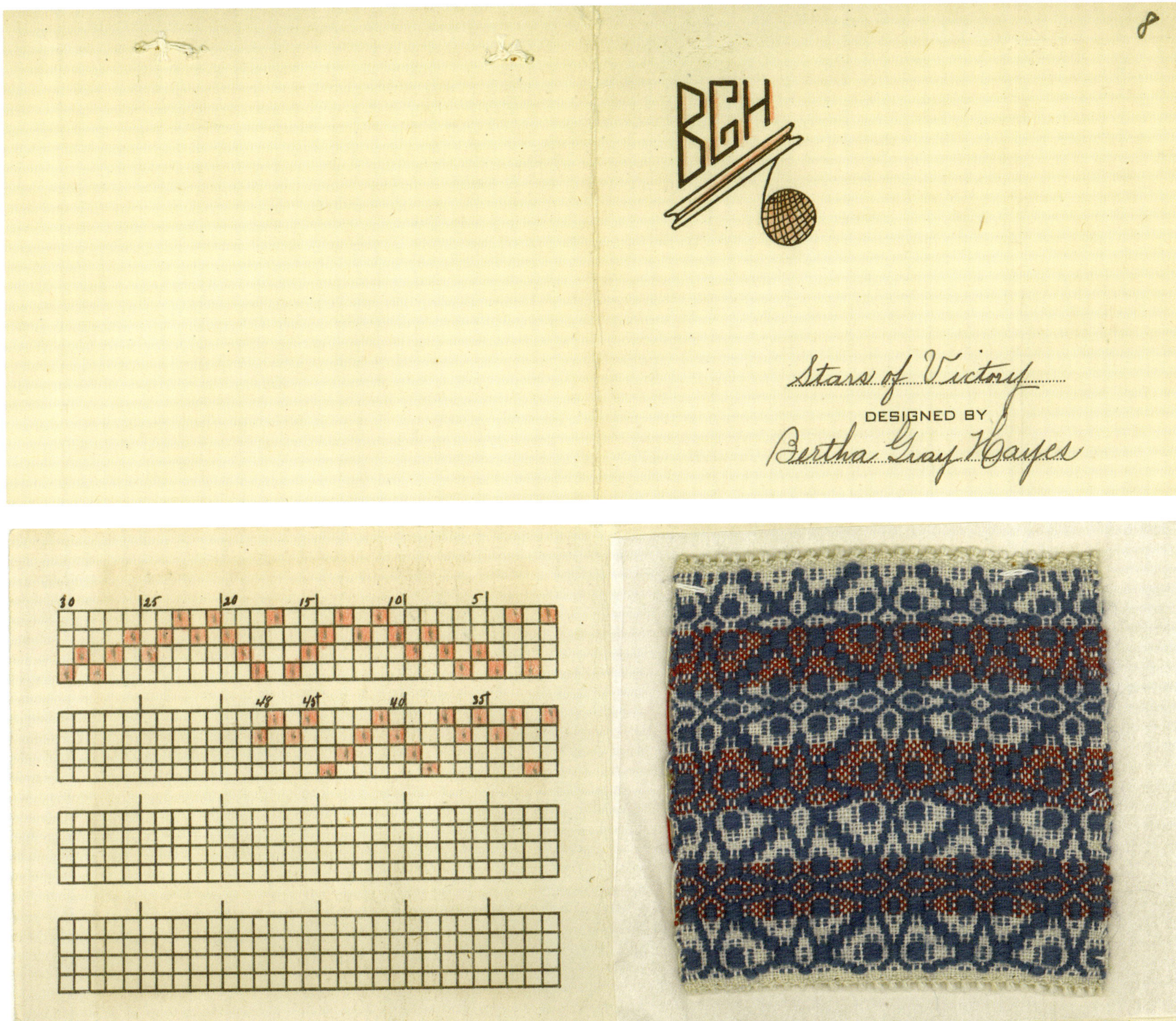
8
BGH
Stars of Victory
DESIGNED BY
Bertha Gray Hayes
30
25
20
15
10
5
48
45
40
35

Figure 27.

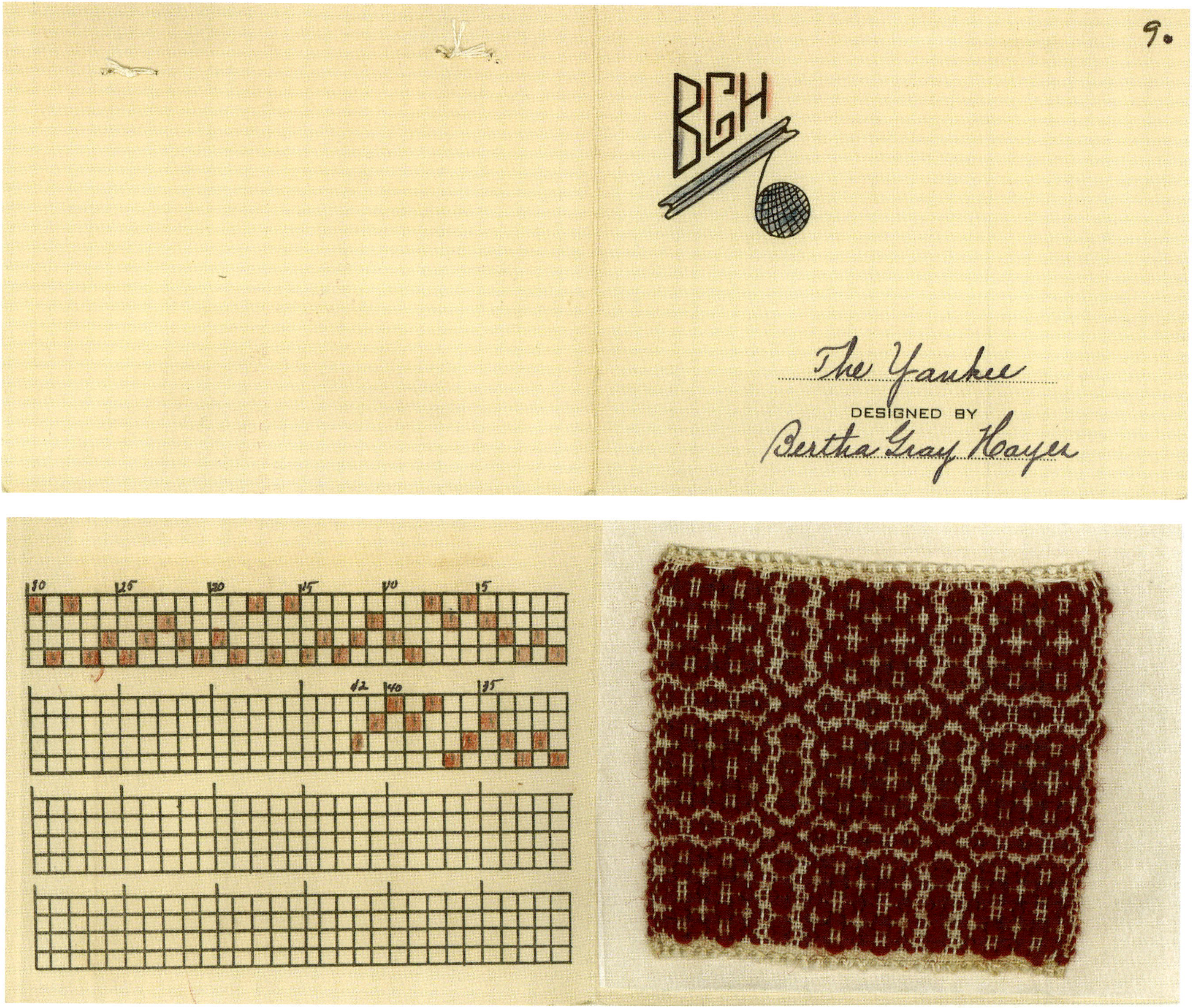
9.
BGH
The Yankee
DESIGNED BY
Bertha Gray Hayes
30
25
20
15
10
5
42
40
35

Figure 28.

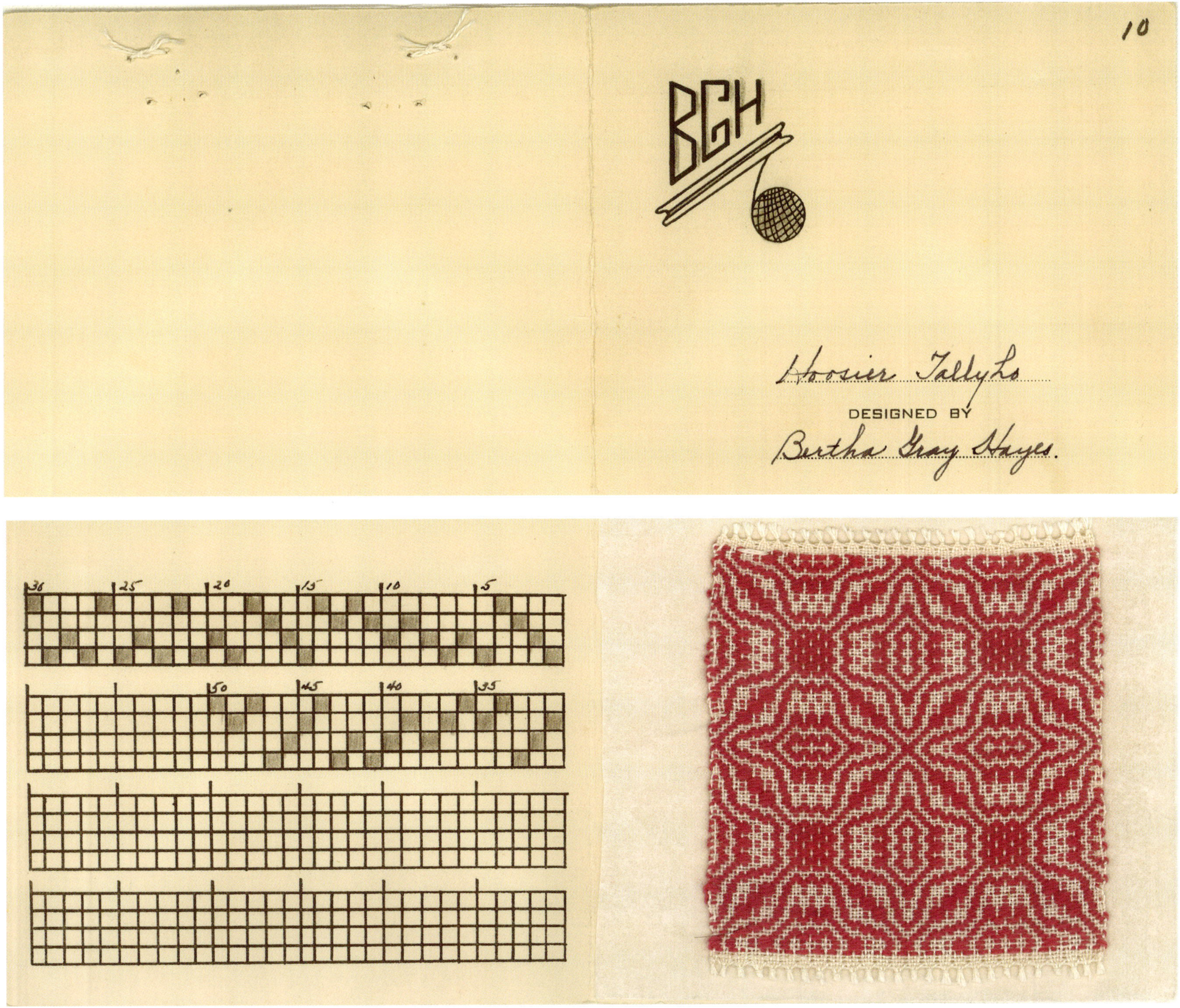
10
BGH
Hoosier Tallyho
DESIGNED BY
Bertha Gray Hayes.
30
25
20
15
10
5
50
45
40
35

Figure 29.

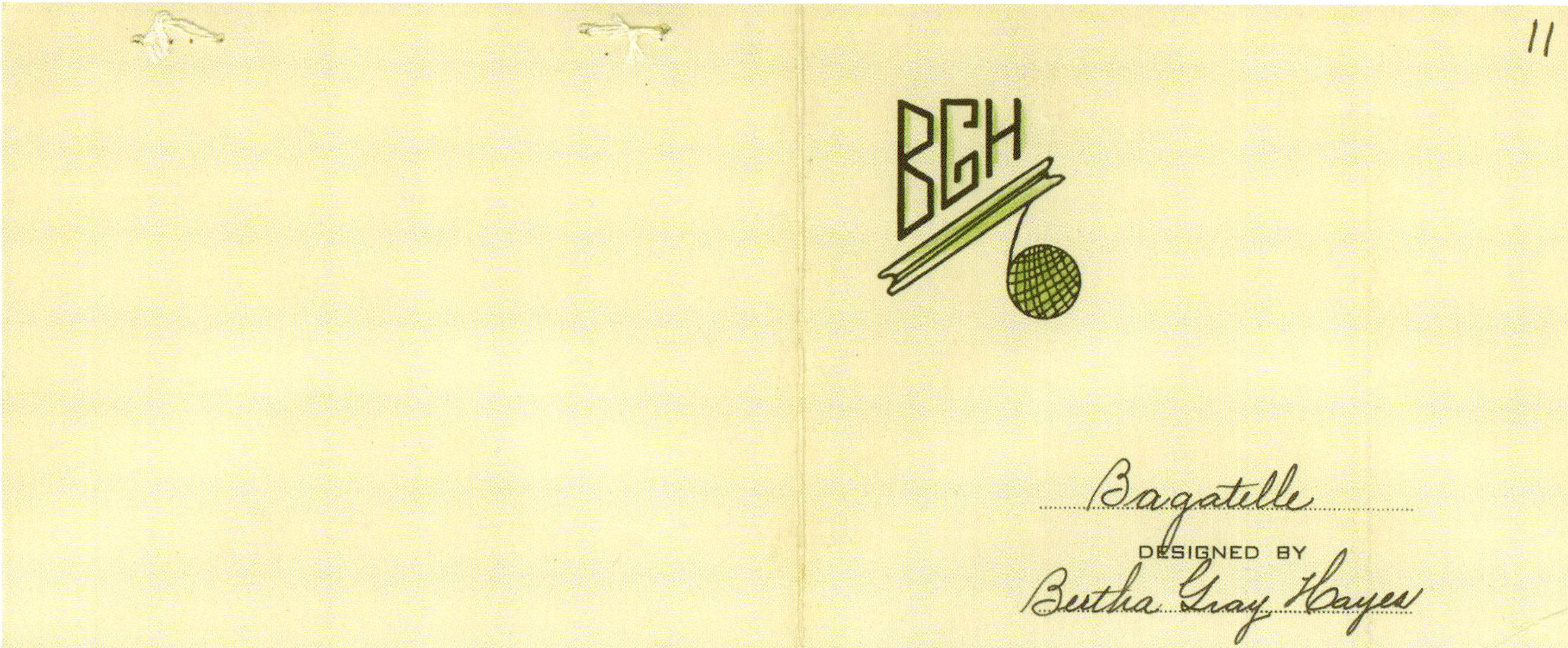

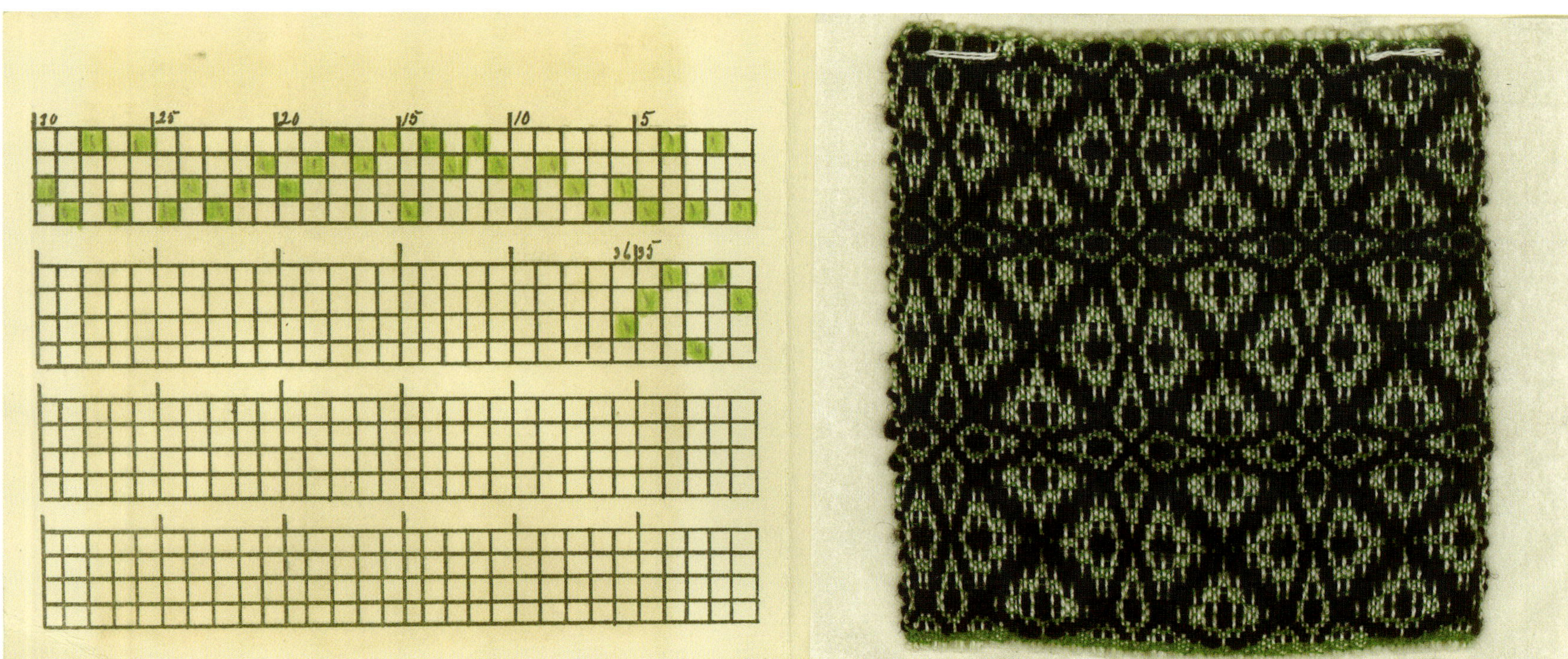

Figure 30.

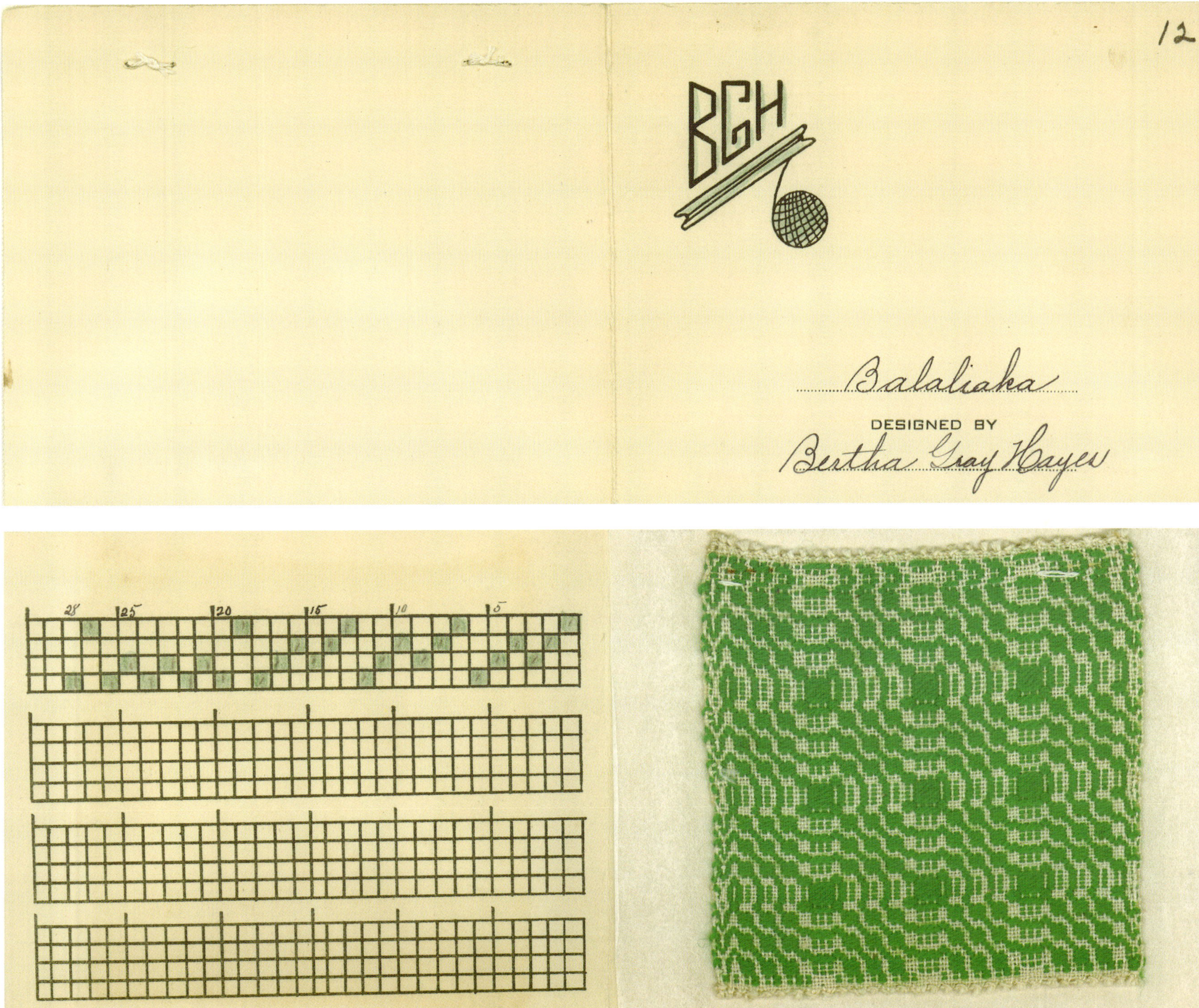
12
BGH
Balaliaka
DESIGNED BY
Bertha Gray Hayes
28
25
20
15
10
5

Figure 31.

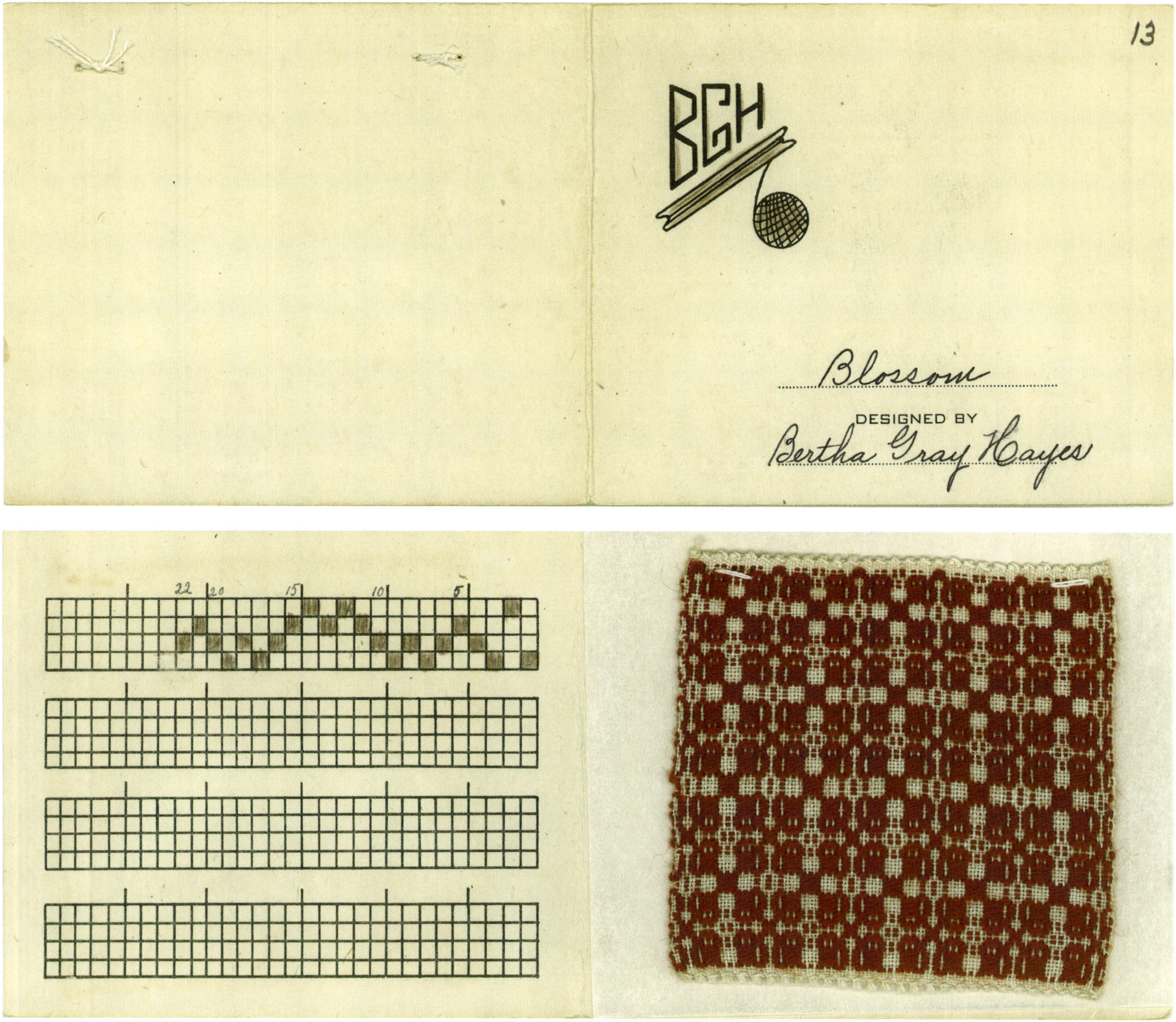

Figure 32.

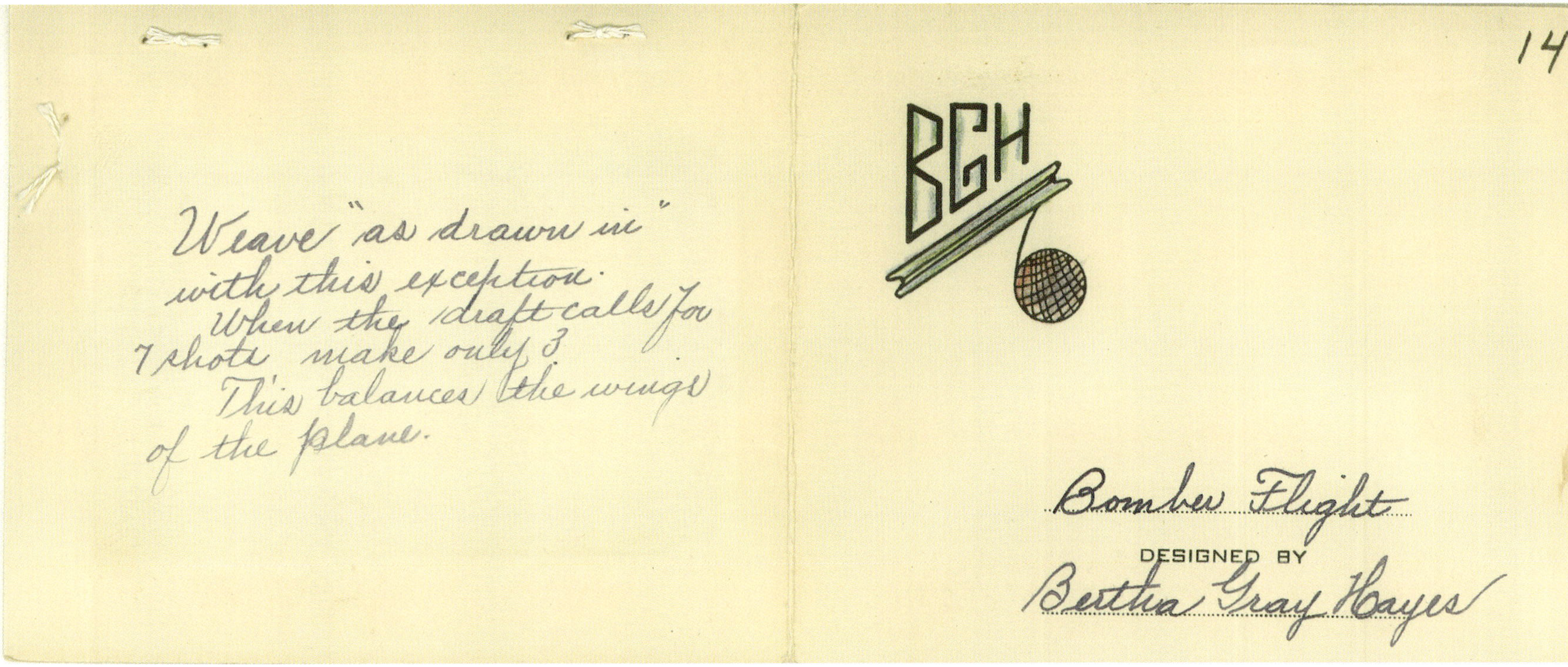
14
BGH
Weave "as drawn in"
with this exception.
When the draft calls for
7 shots make only 3
This balances the wings
of the plane.
Bomber Flight
DESIGNED BY
Bertha Gray Hayes

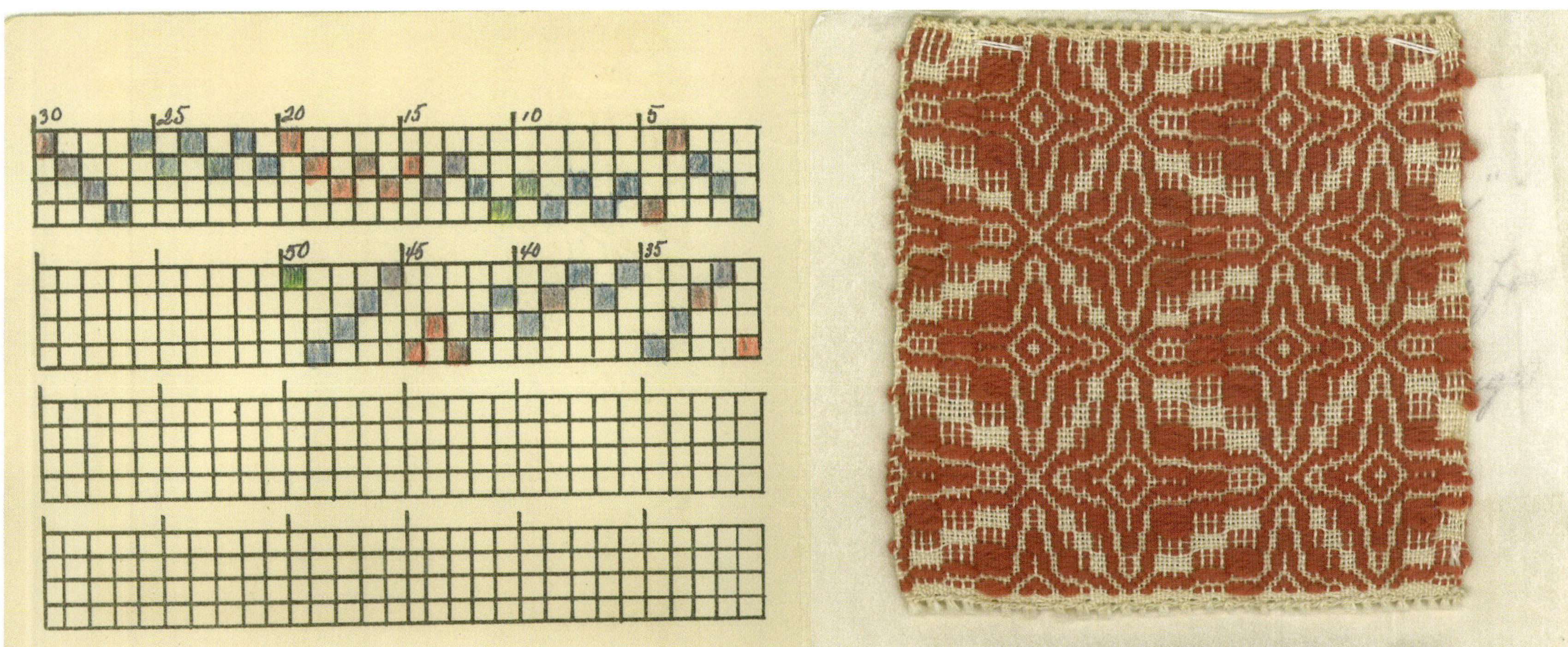
30
25
20
15
10
5
50
45
40
35

Figure 33.

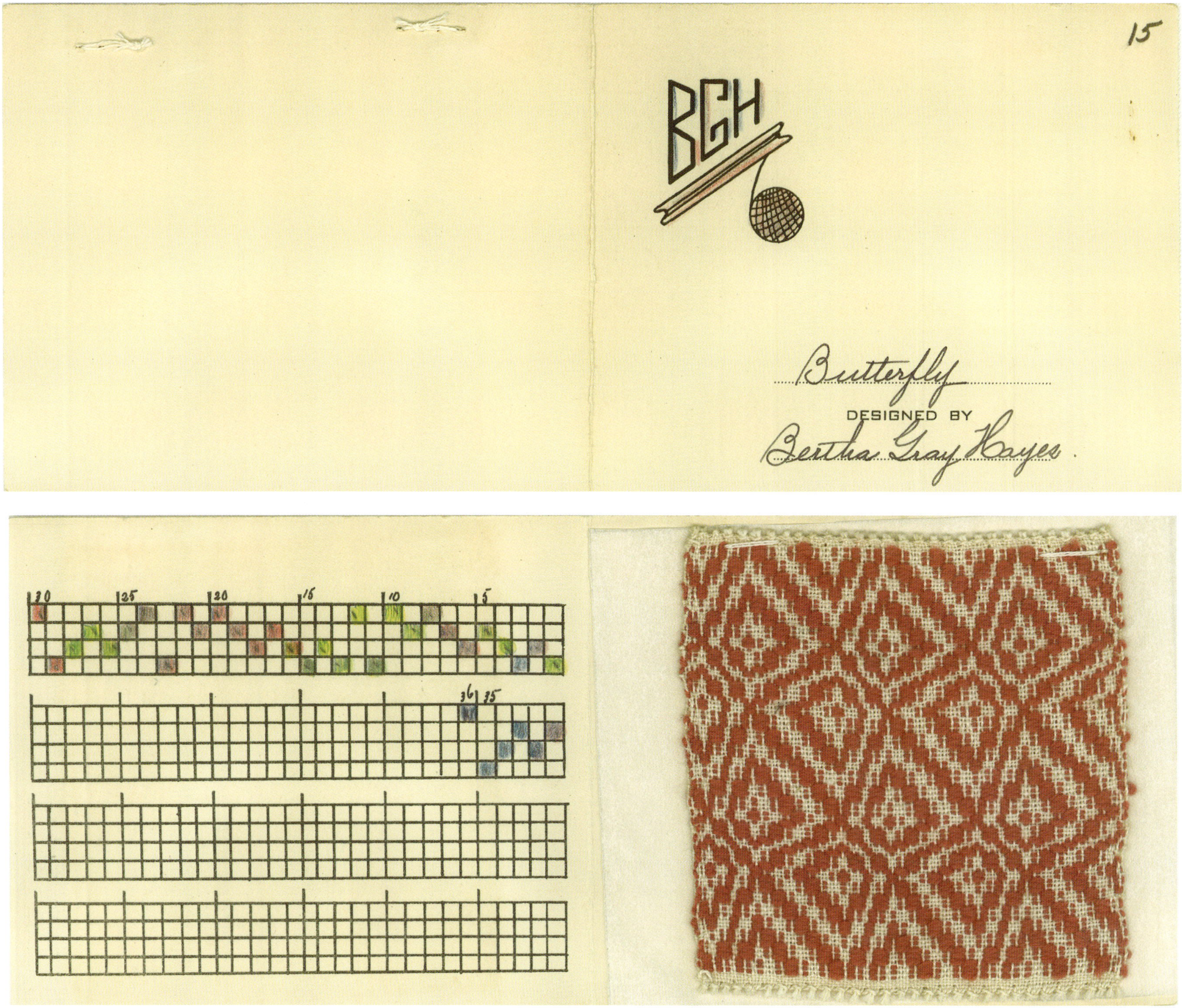
15
BGH
Butterfly
DESIGNED BY
Bertha Gray Hayes
30
25
20
15
10
5
36
35

Figure 34.

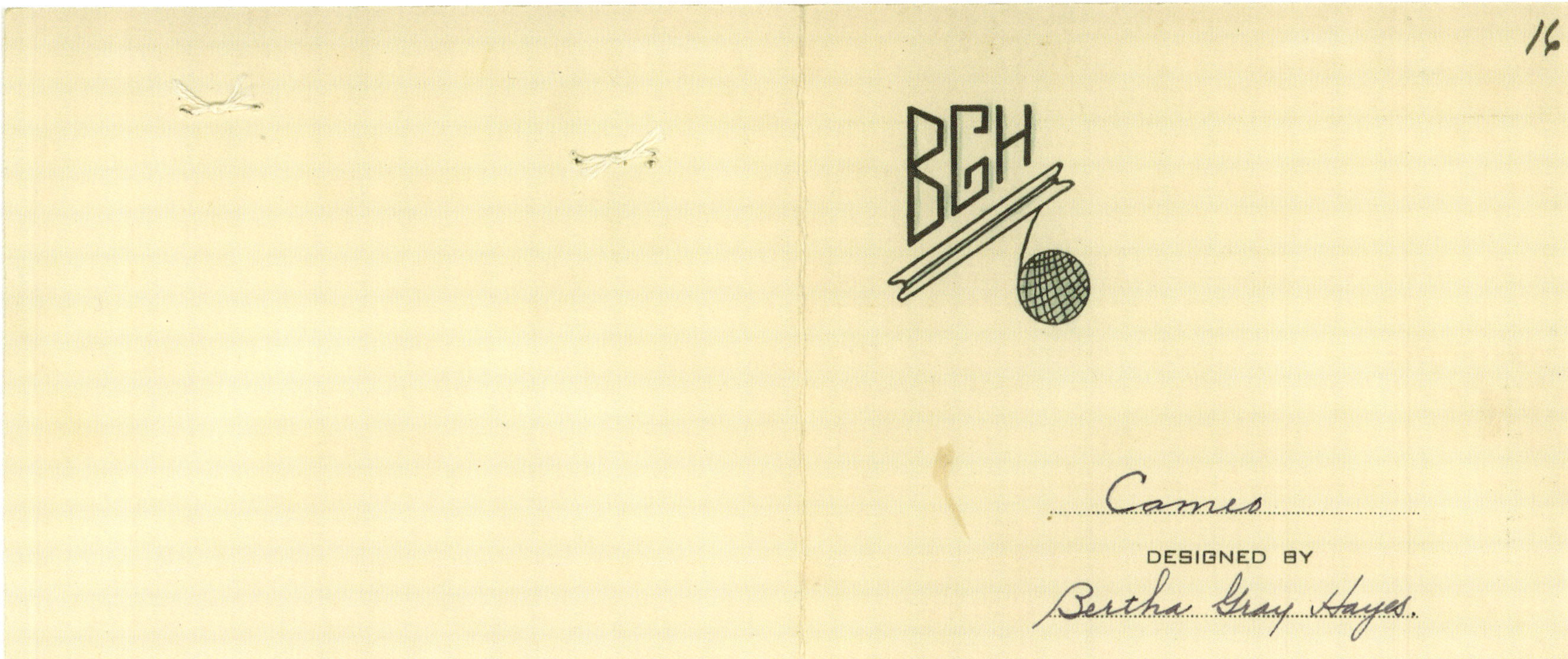
16
BGH
Cameo
DESIGNED BY
Bertha Gray Hayes.

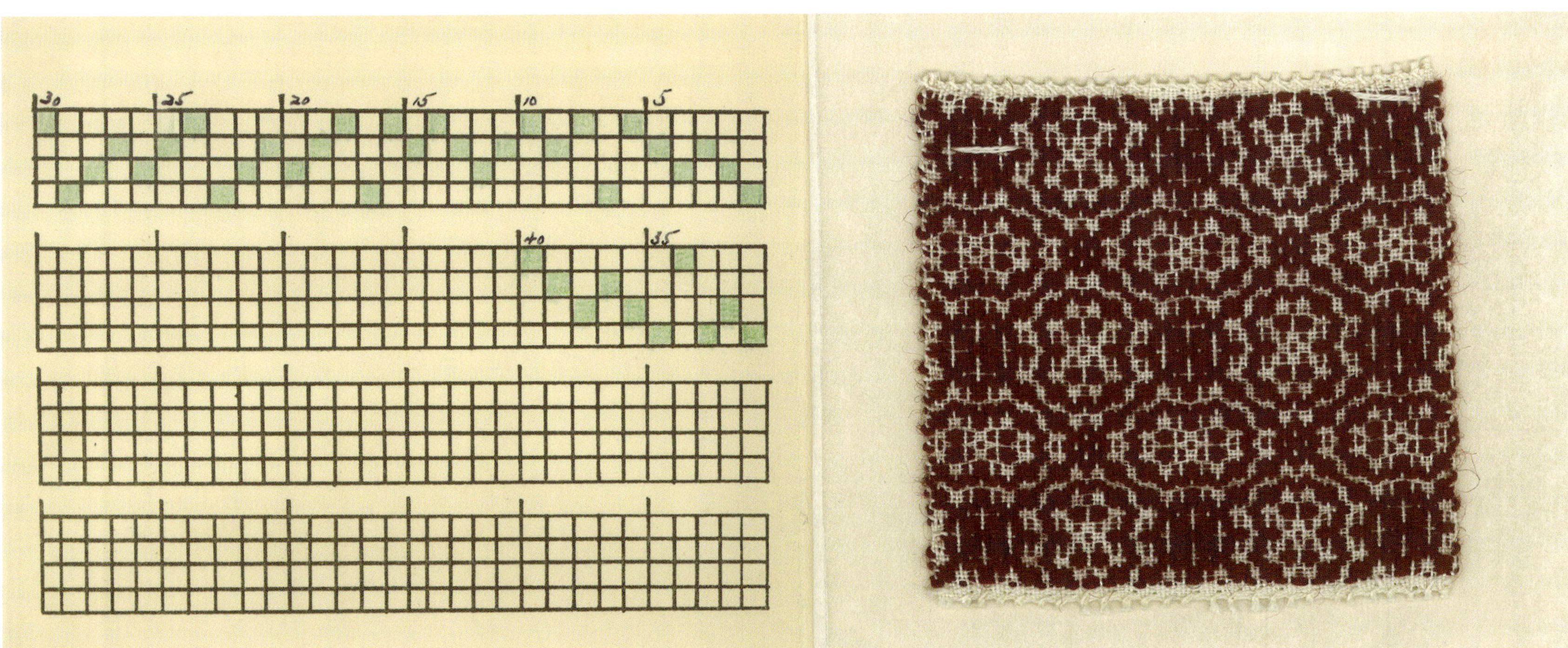
30
25
20
15
10
5
40
35

Figure 35.

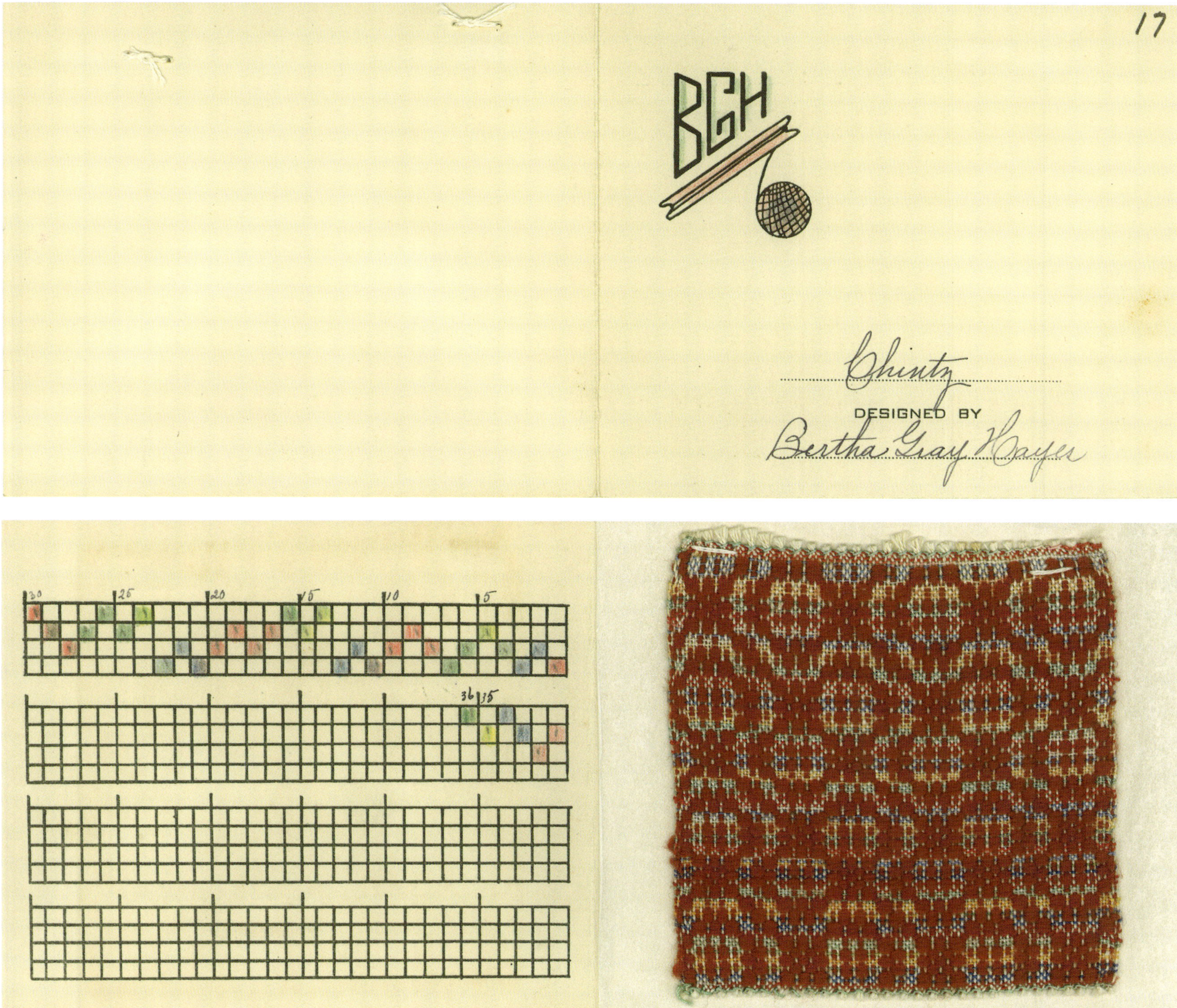
17
BGH
Chintz
DESIGNED BY
Bertha Gray Hayes
30
25
20
15
10
5
36
35

Figure 36.

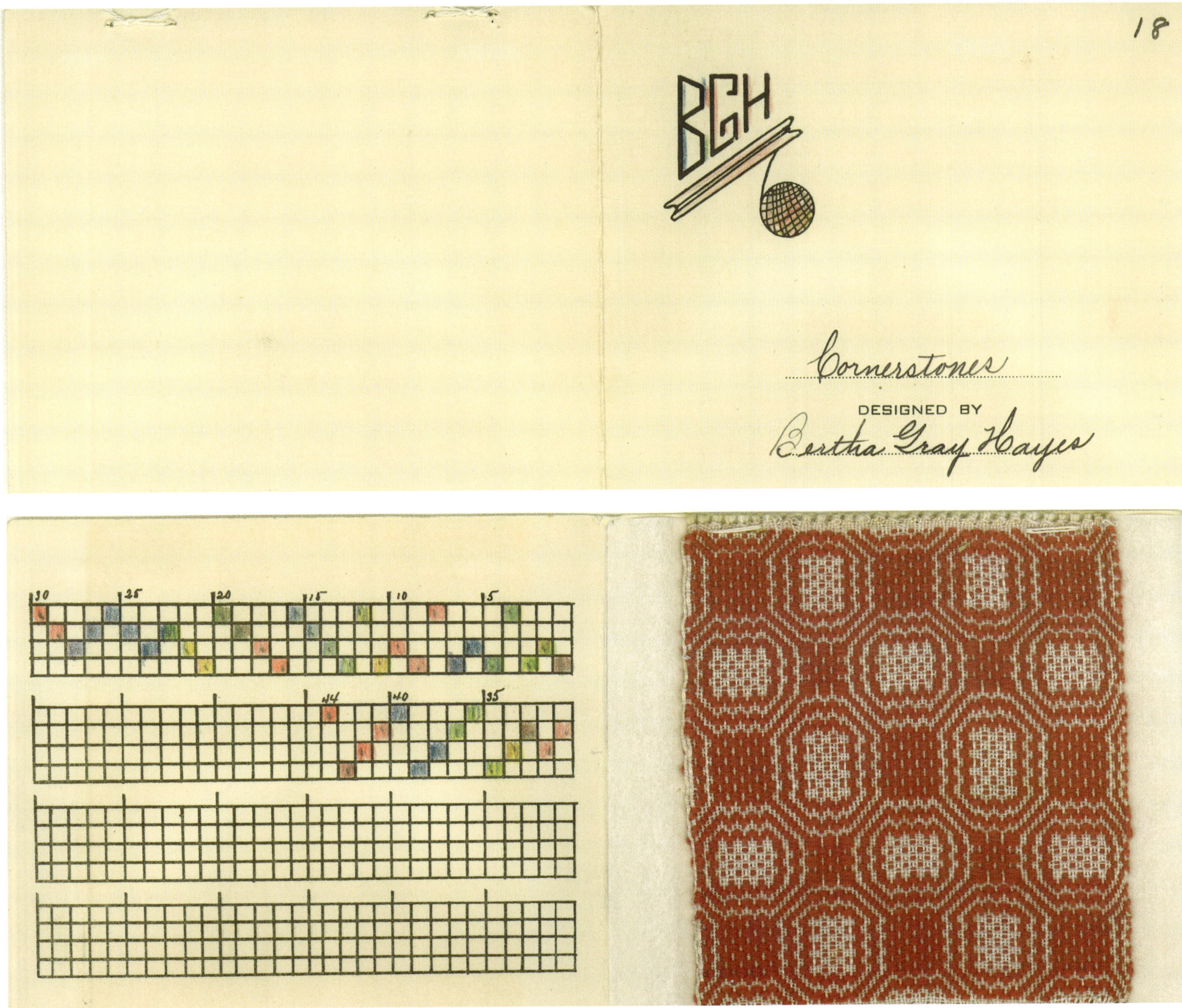
18
BGH
Cornerstones
DESIGNED BY
Bertha Gray Hayes
30
25
20
15
10
5
44
40
35

Figure 37.

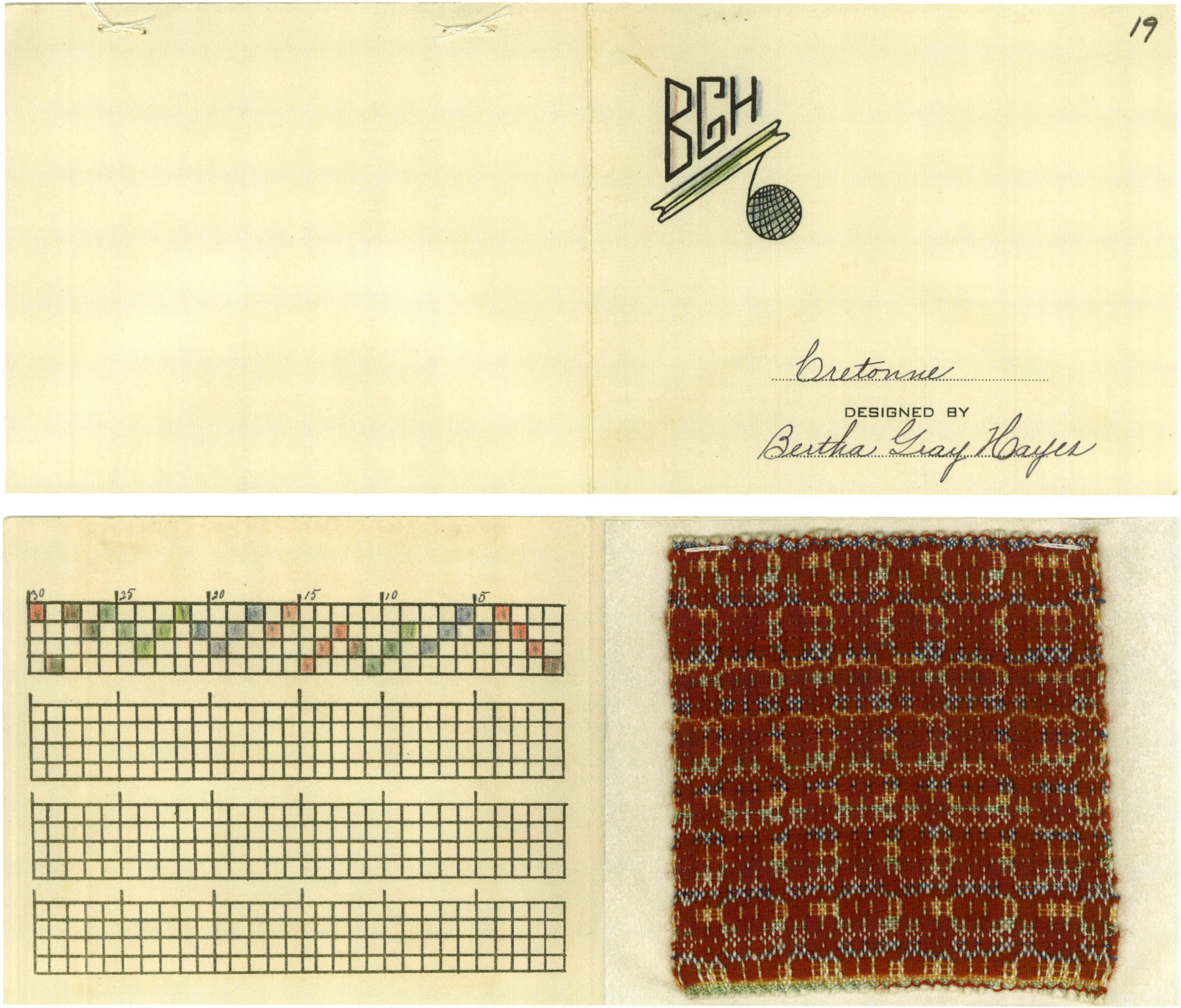

Figure 38.

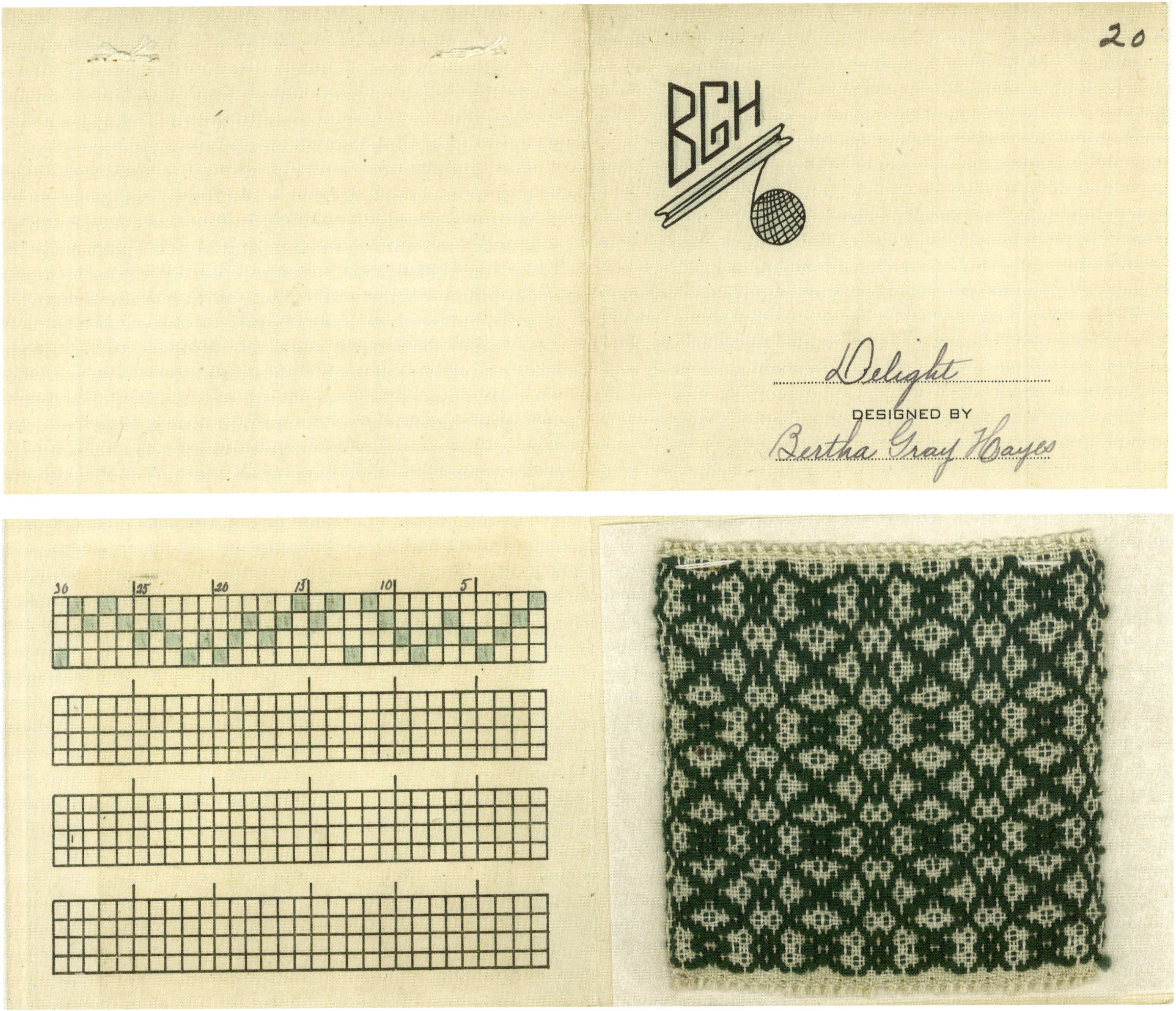

Figure 39.

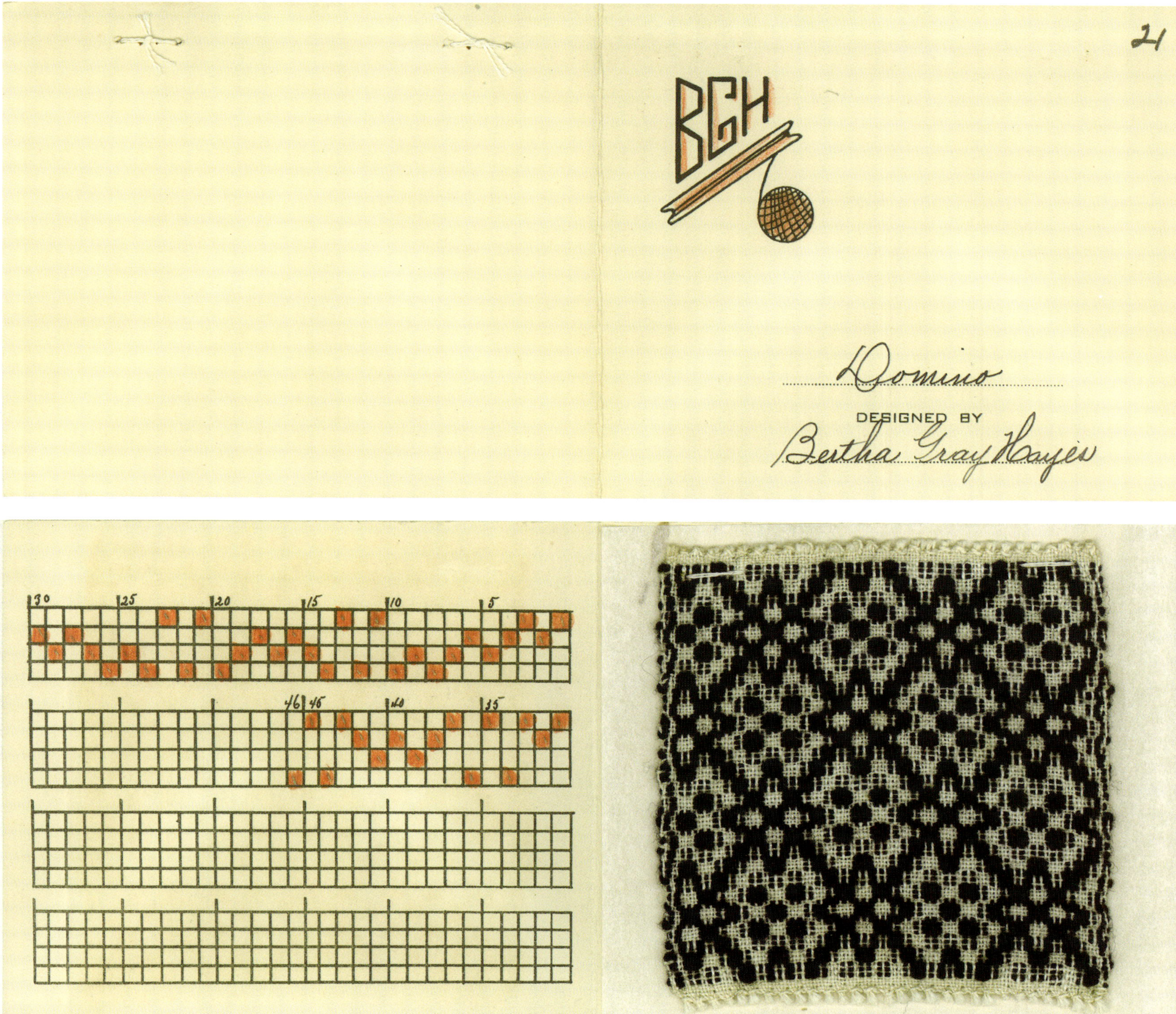
21
BGH
Domino
DESIGNED BY
Bertha Gray Hayes
30
25
20
15
10
5
46
45
40
35

Figure 40.

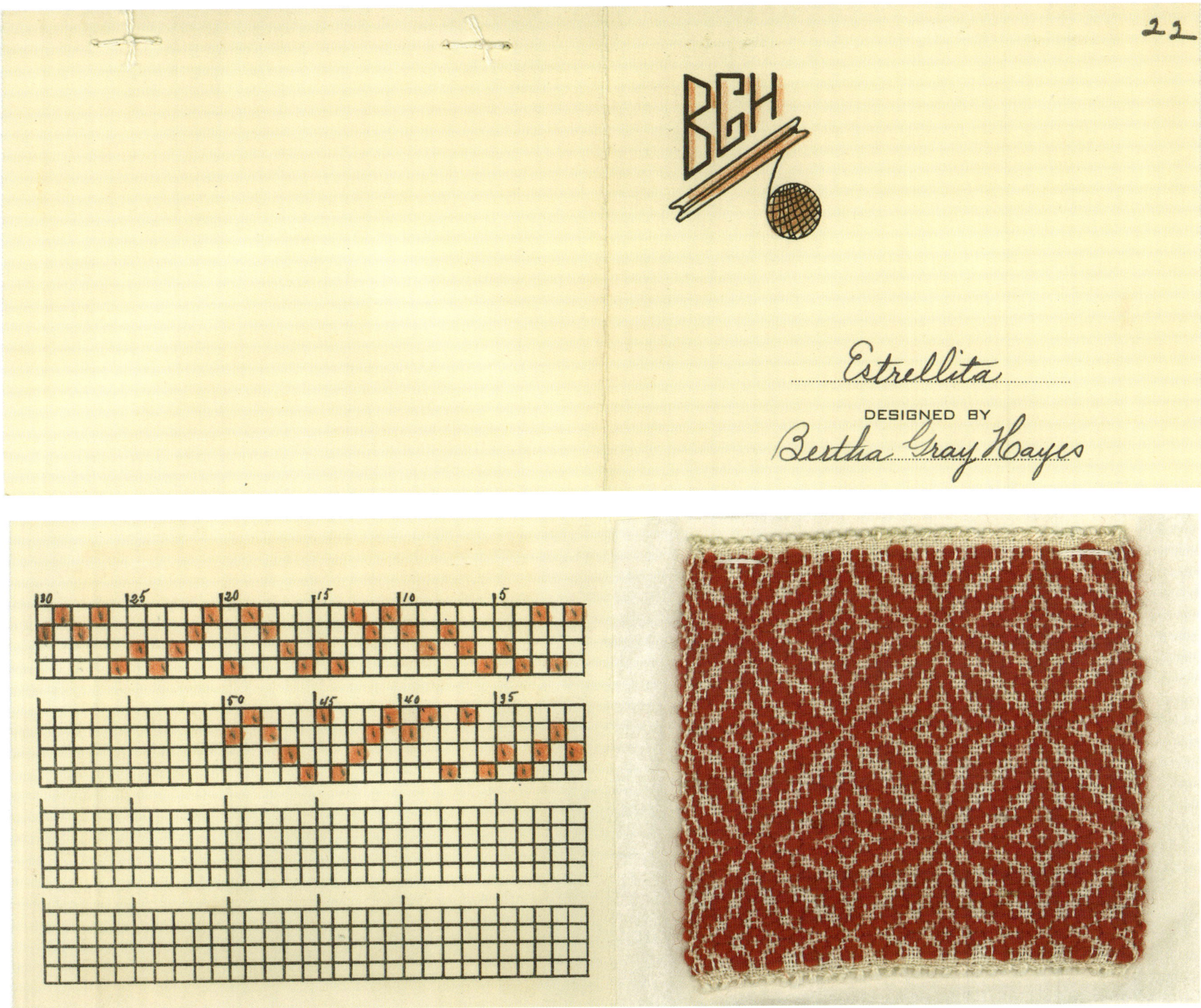
22
BGH
Estrellita
DESIGNED BY
Bertha Gray Hayes
30 25 20 15 10 5
50 45 40 35

Figure 41.

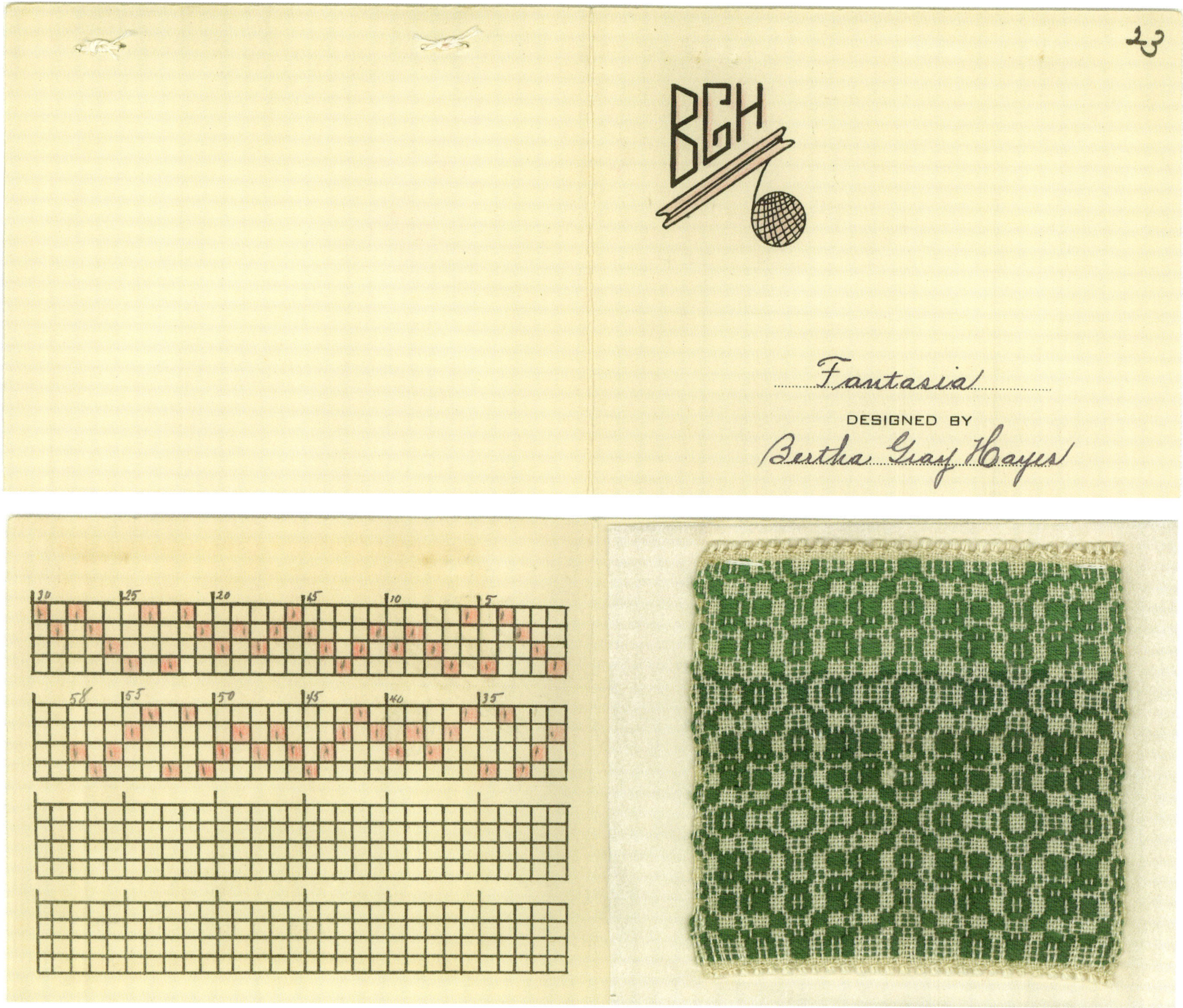
23
BGH
Fantasia
DESIGNED BY
Bertha Gray Hayes
30
25
20
15
10
5
58
55
50
45
40
35

Figure 42.

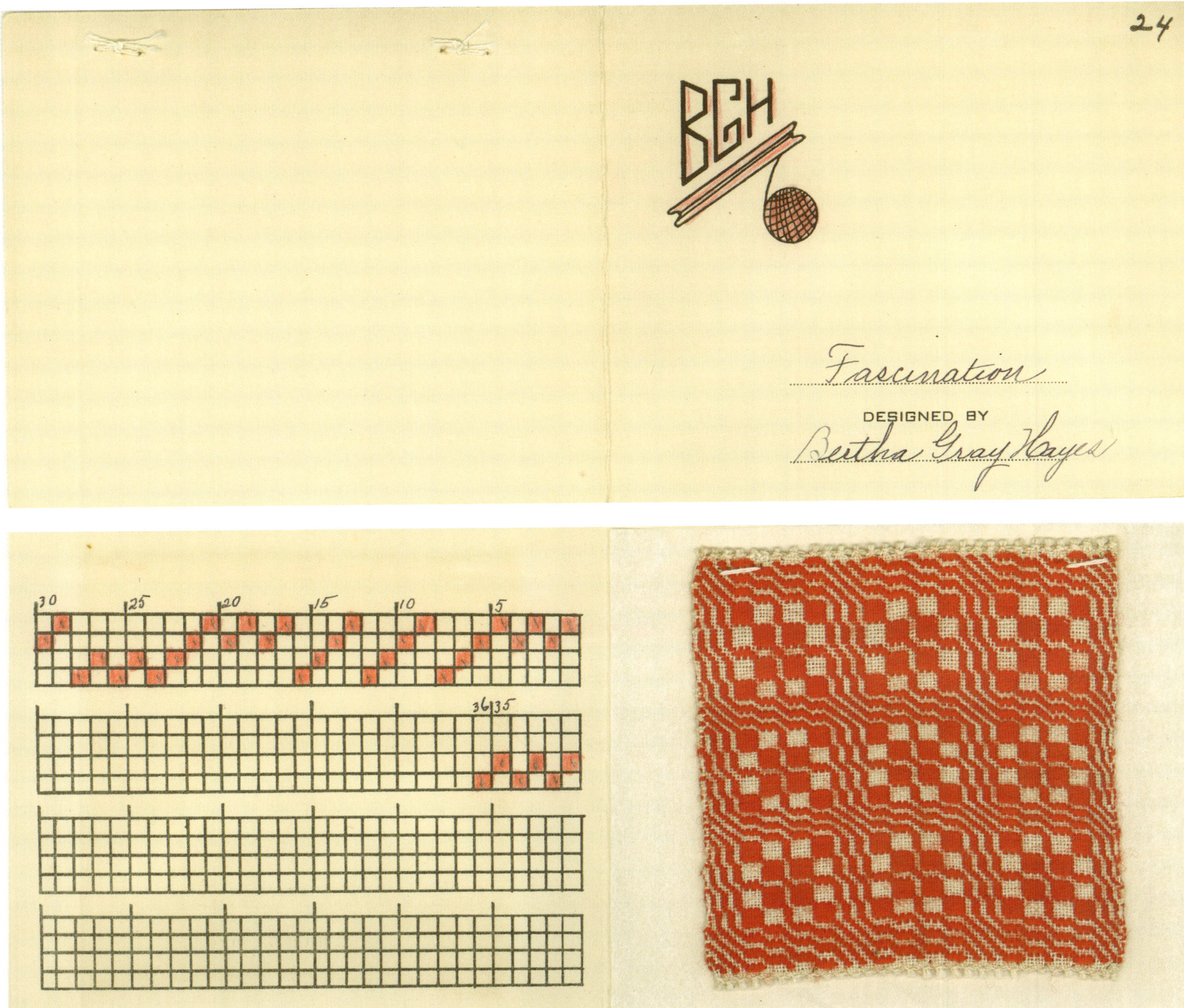
24
BGH
Fascination
DESIGNED BY
Bertha Gray Hayes
30
25
20
15
10
5
36
35

Figure 43.

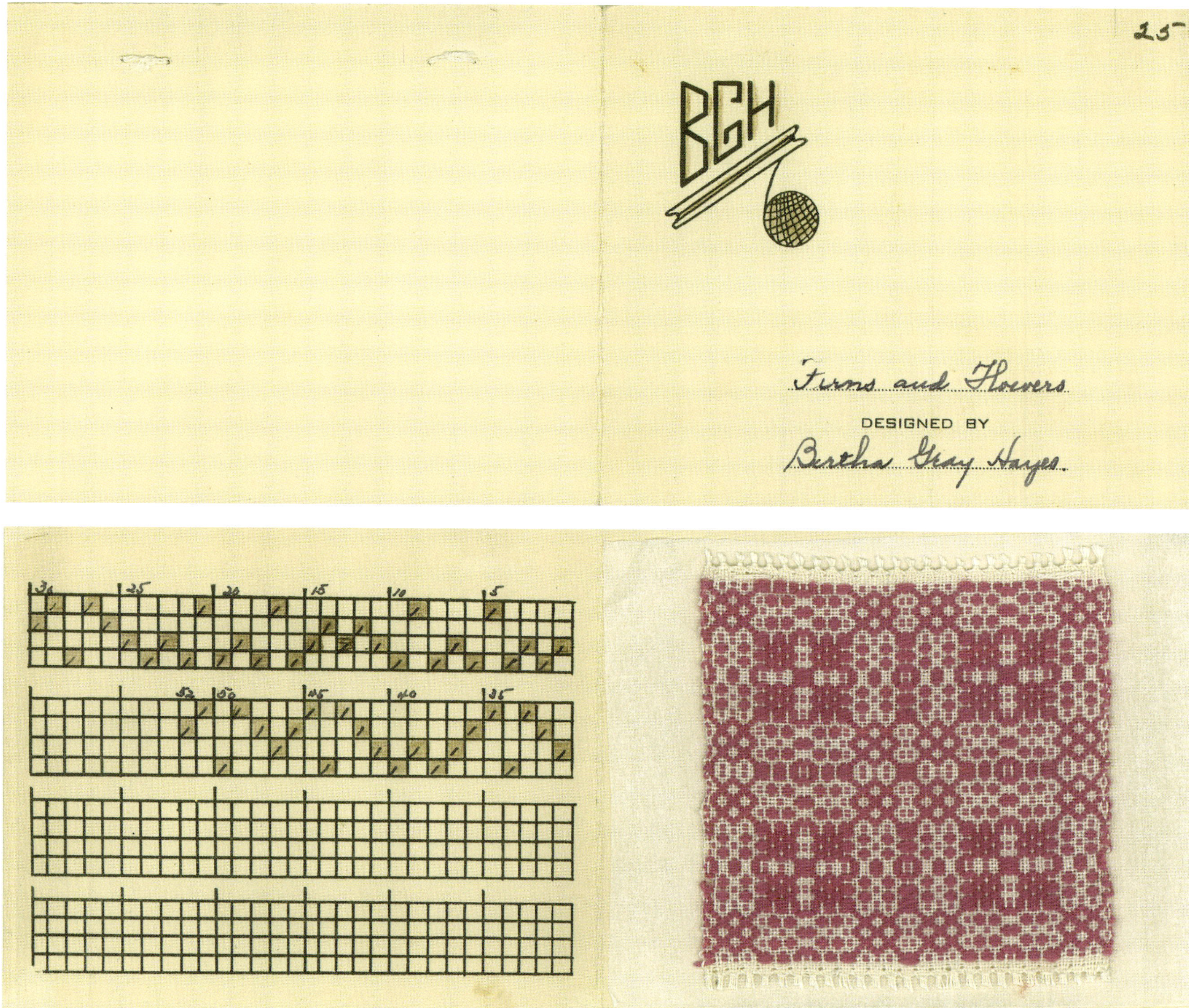

25
BGH
Ferns and Flowers
DESIGNED BY
Bertha Gray Hayes
30
25
20
15
10
5
52
50
45
40
35

Figure 44.

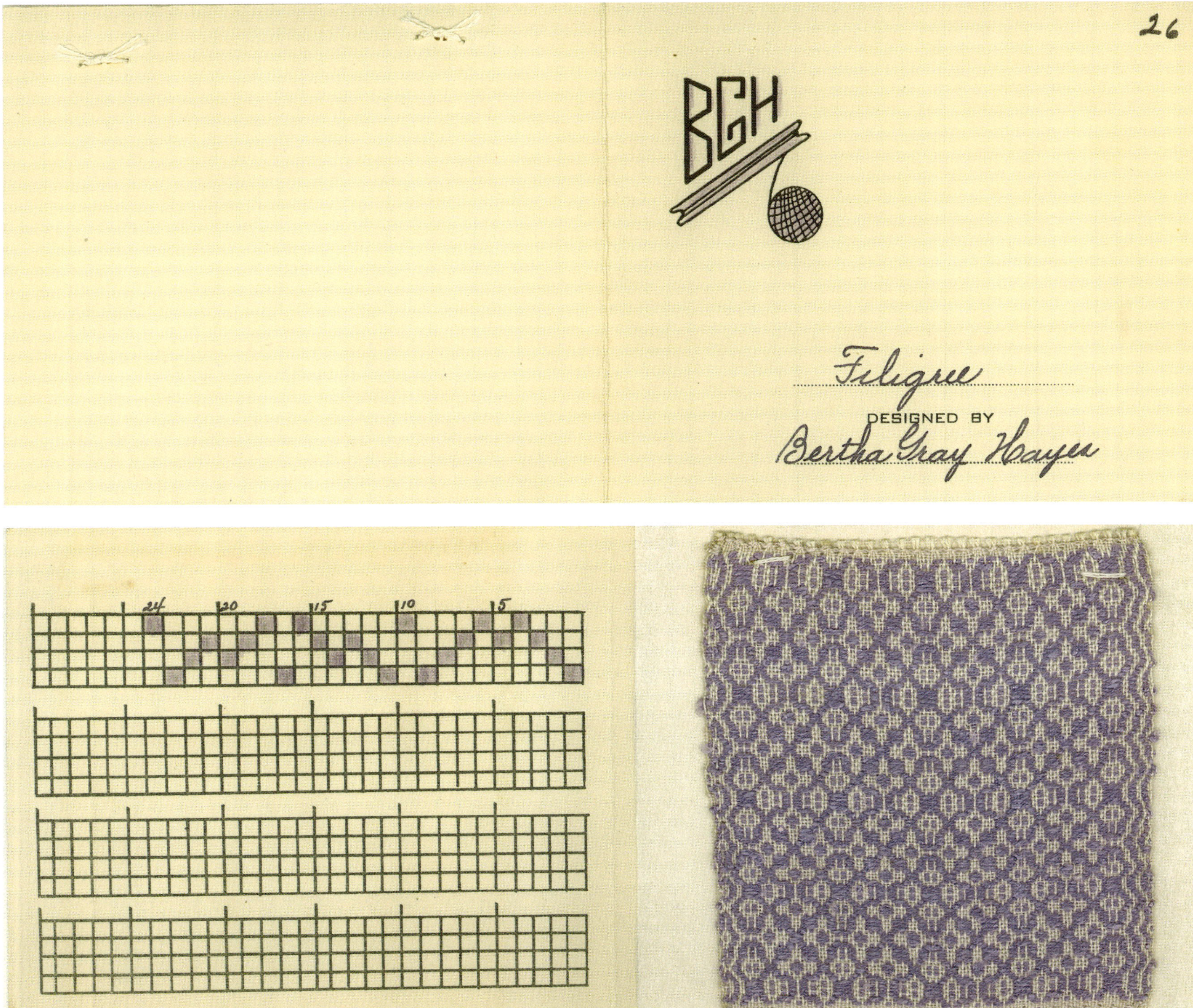

Figure 45.

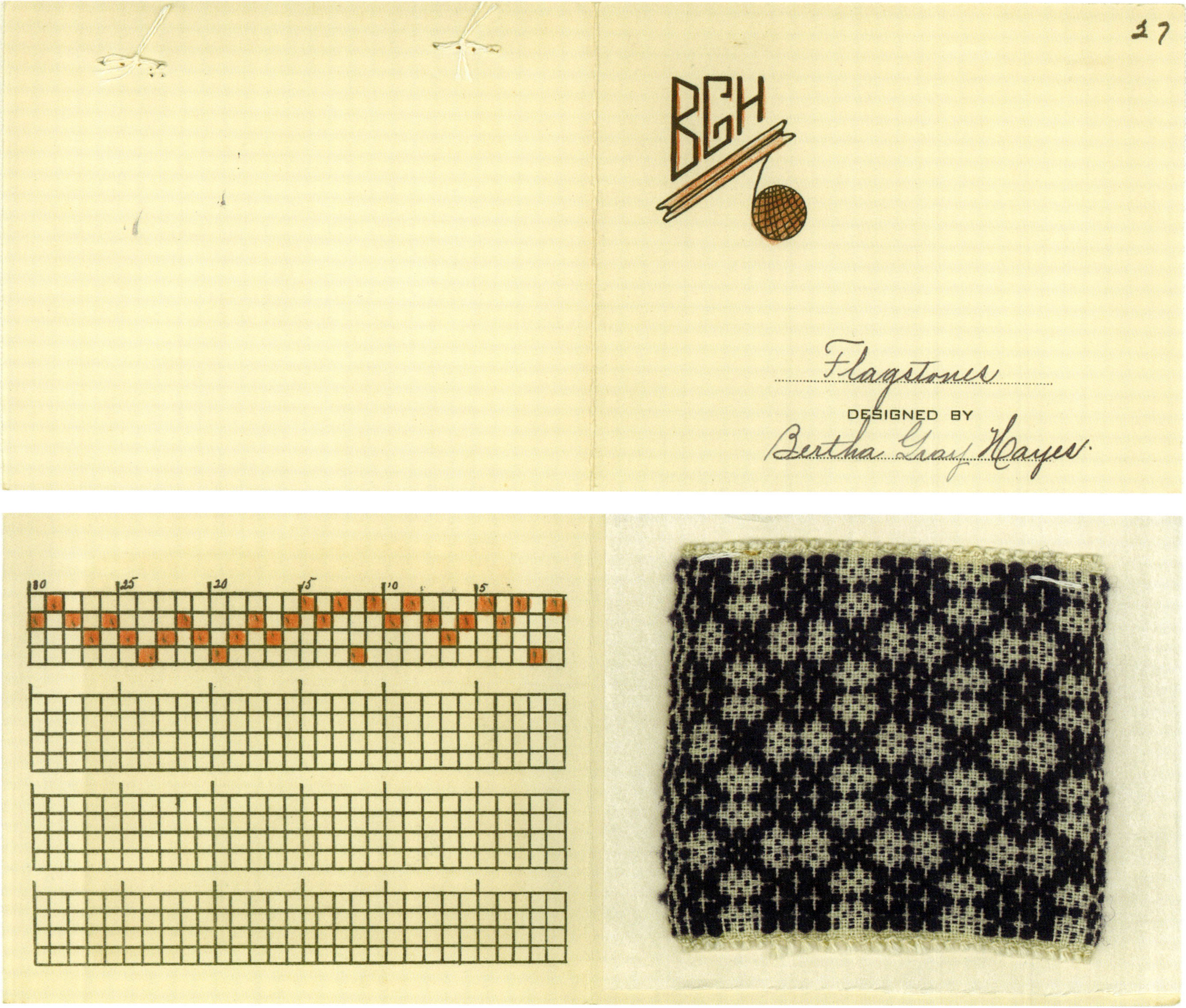
27
BGH
Flagstones
DESIGNED BY
Bertha Gray Hayes
30
25
20
15
10
5

Figure 46.

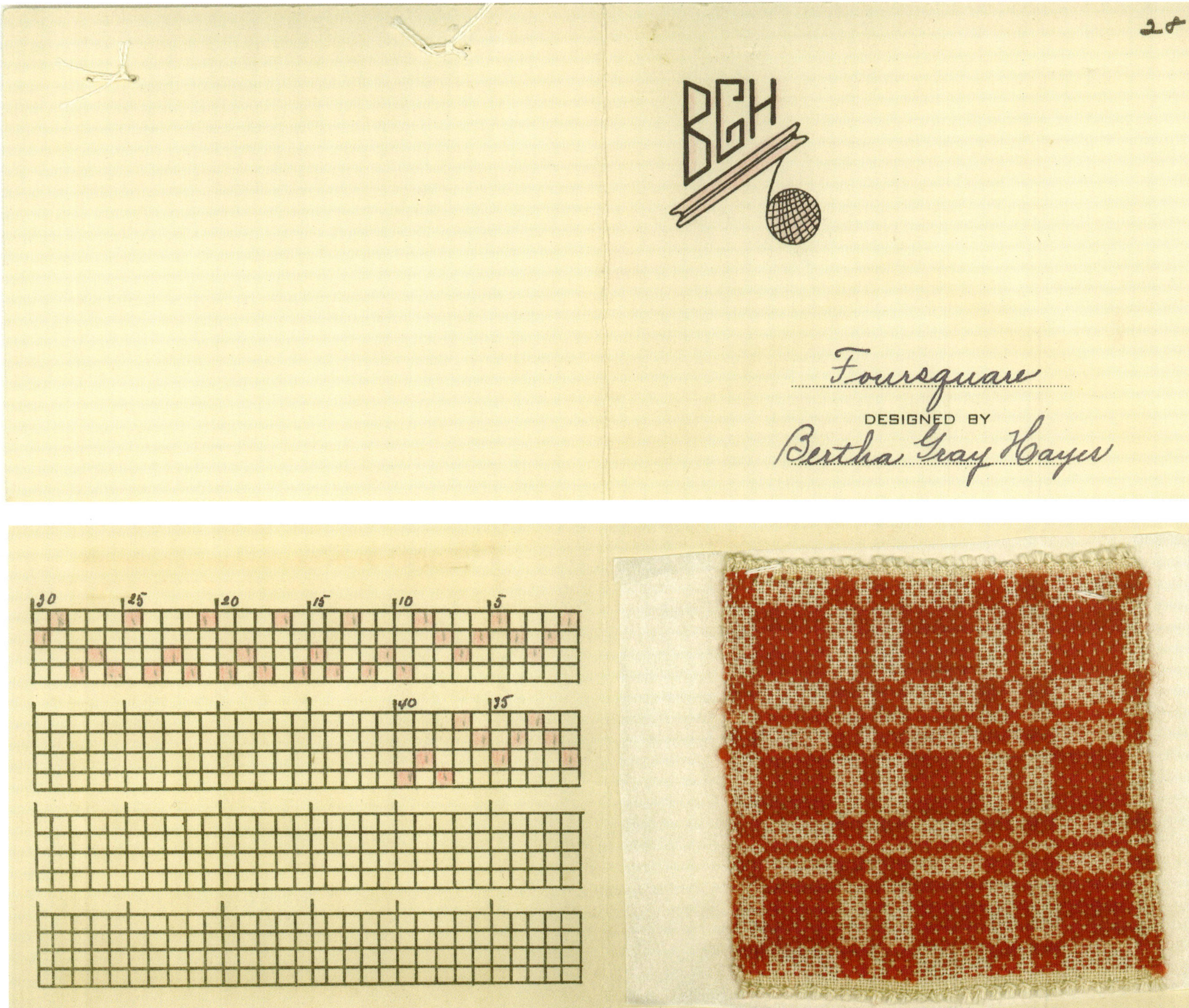
28
BGH
Foursquare
DESIGNED BY
Bertha Gray Hayes
30 25 20 15 10 5
40 35

Figure 47.

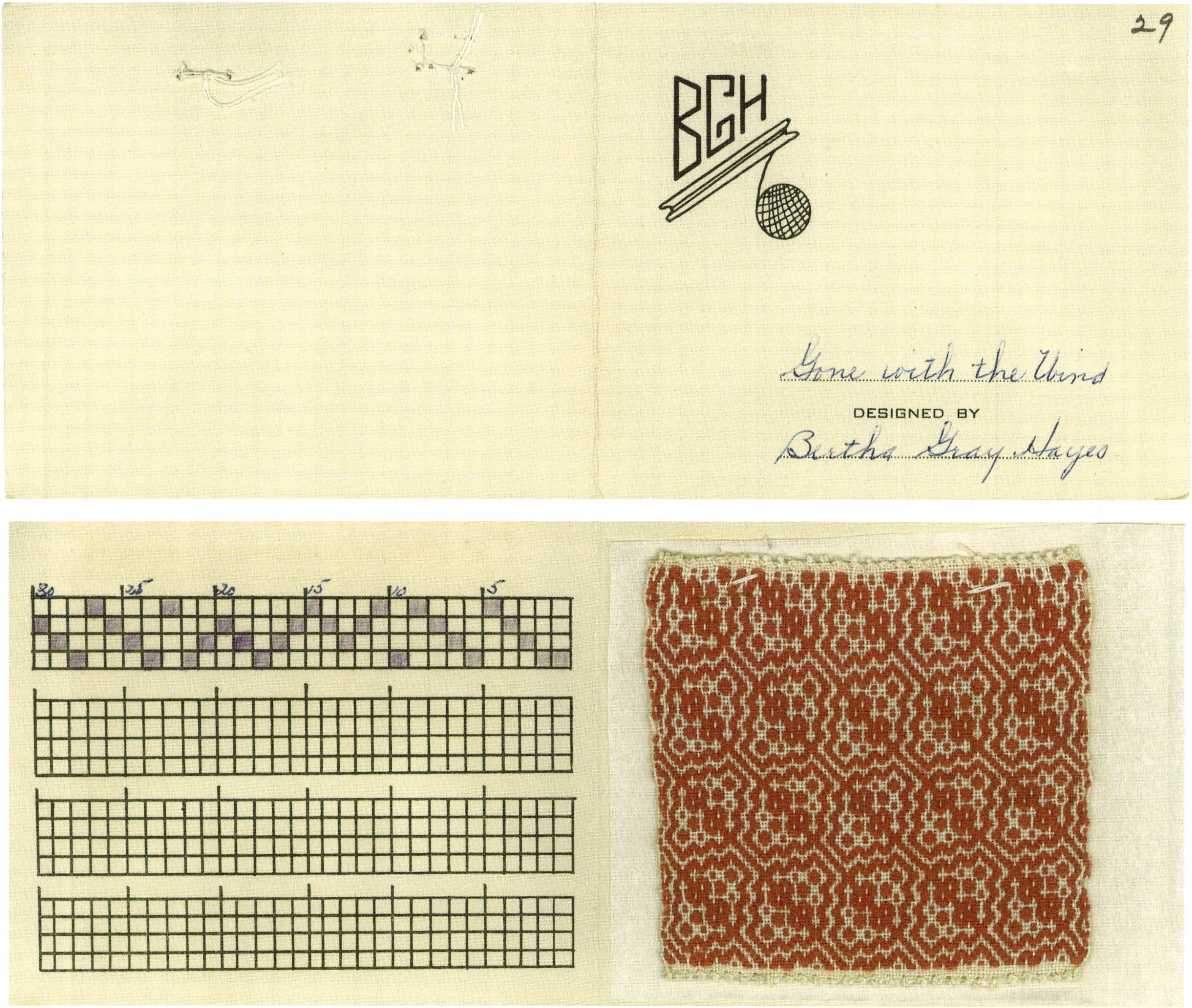
29
BGH
Gone with the Wind
DESIGNED BY
Bertha Gray Hayes
30
25
20
15
10
5

Figure 48.

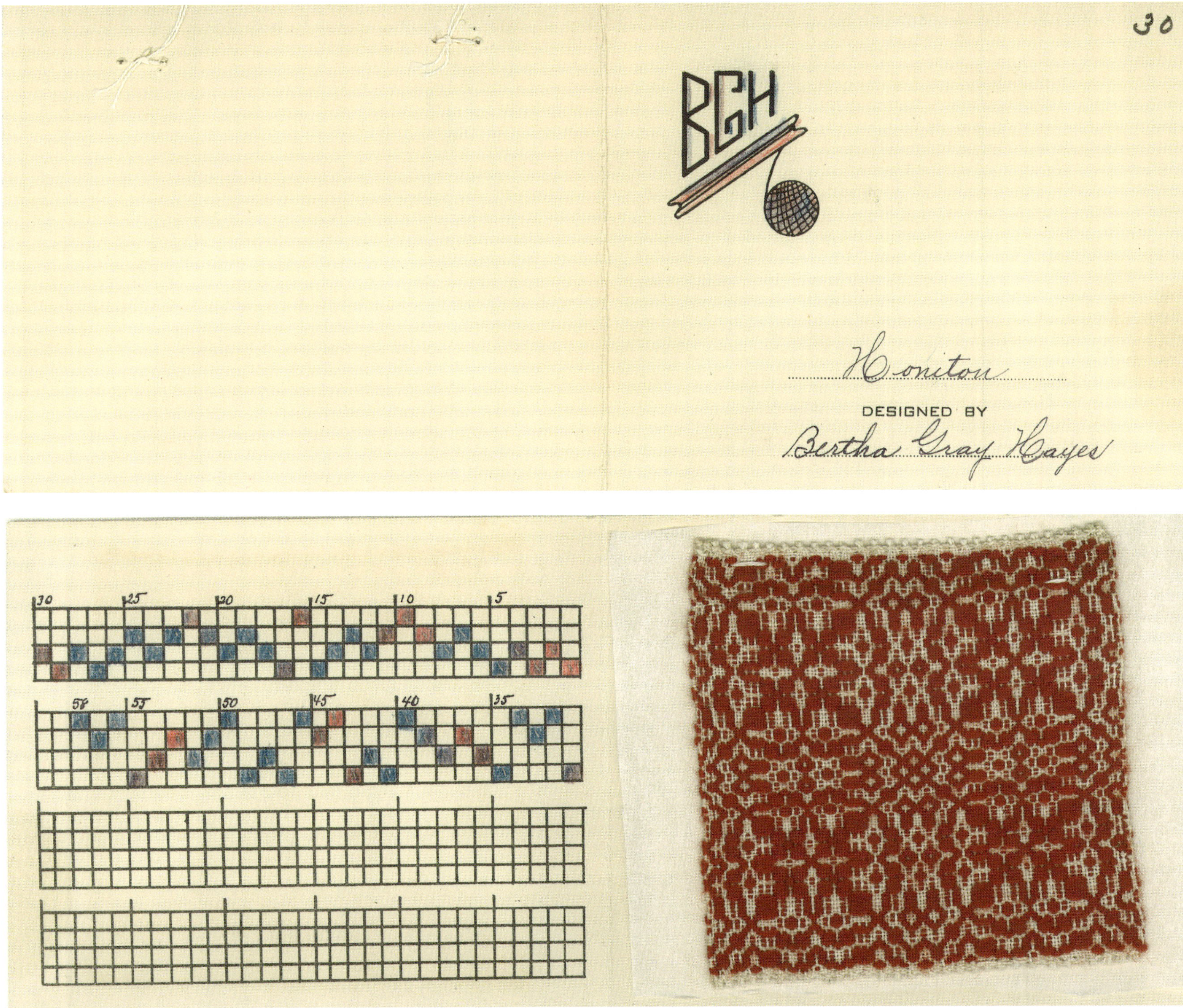
30
BGH
Honiton
DESIGNED BY
Bertha Gray Hayes
30
25
20
15
10
5
58
55
50
45
40
35

Figure 49.

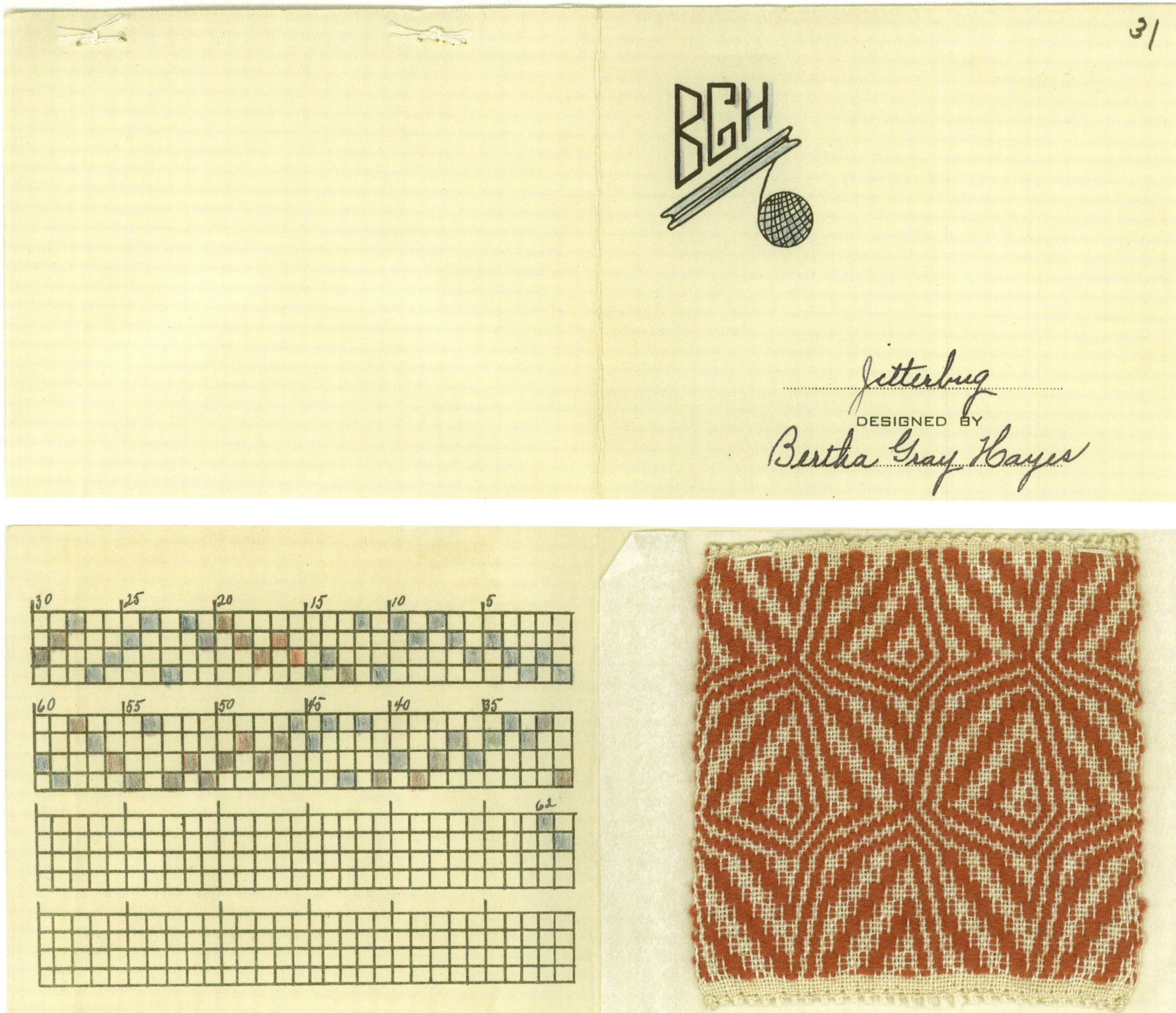
31
BGH
Jitterbug
DESIGNED BY
Bertha Gray Hayes
5 10 15 20 25 30
35 40 45 50 55 60
62

Figure 50.

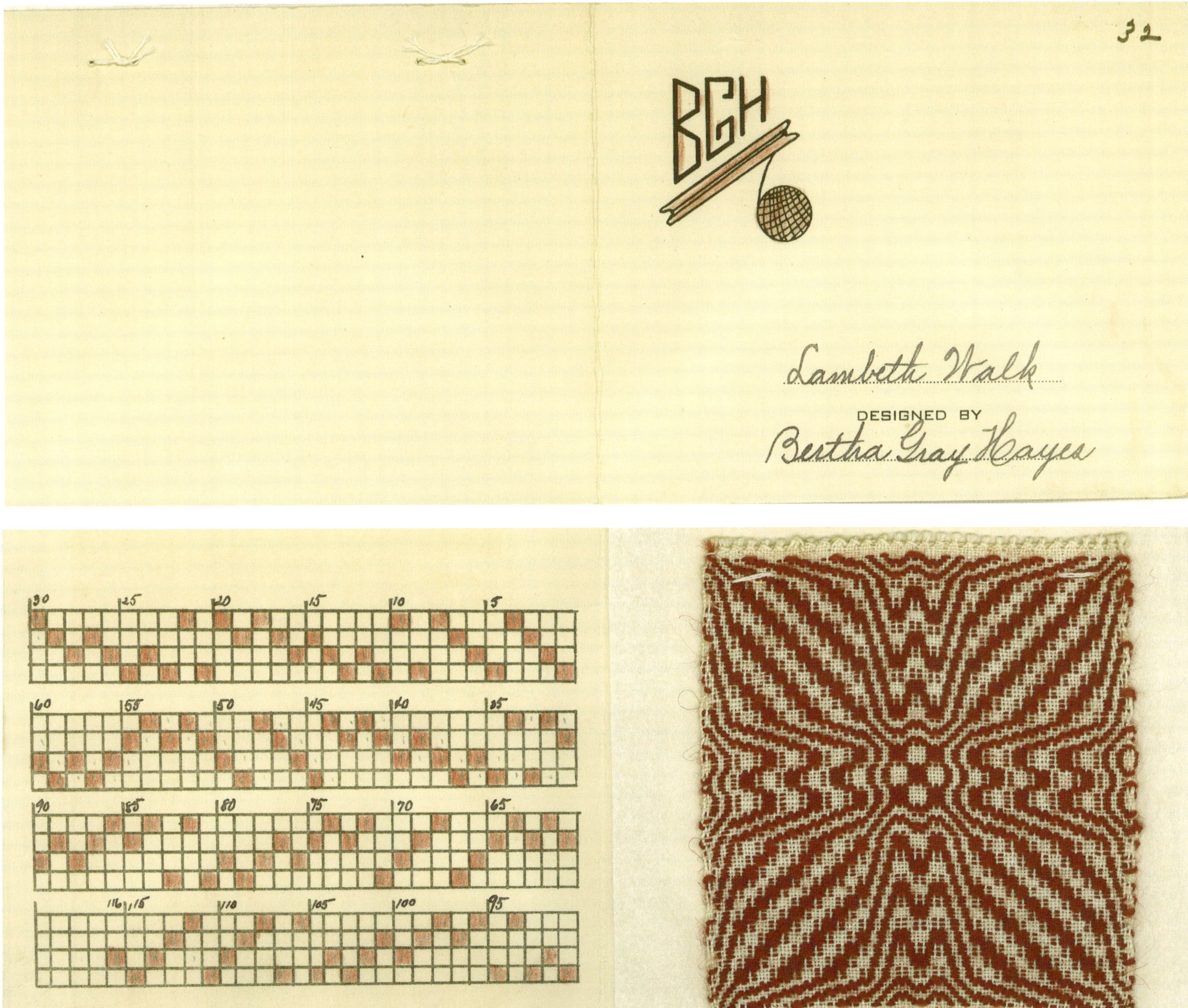
32
BGH
Lambeth Walk
DESIGNED BY
Bertha Gray Hayes
30 25 20 15 10 5
60 55 50 45 40 35
90 85 80 75 70 65
116 115 110 105 100 95

Figure 51.

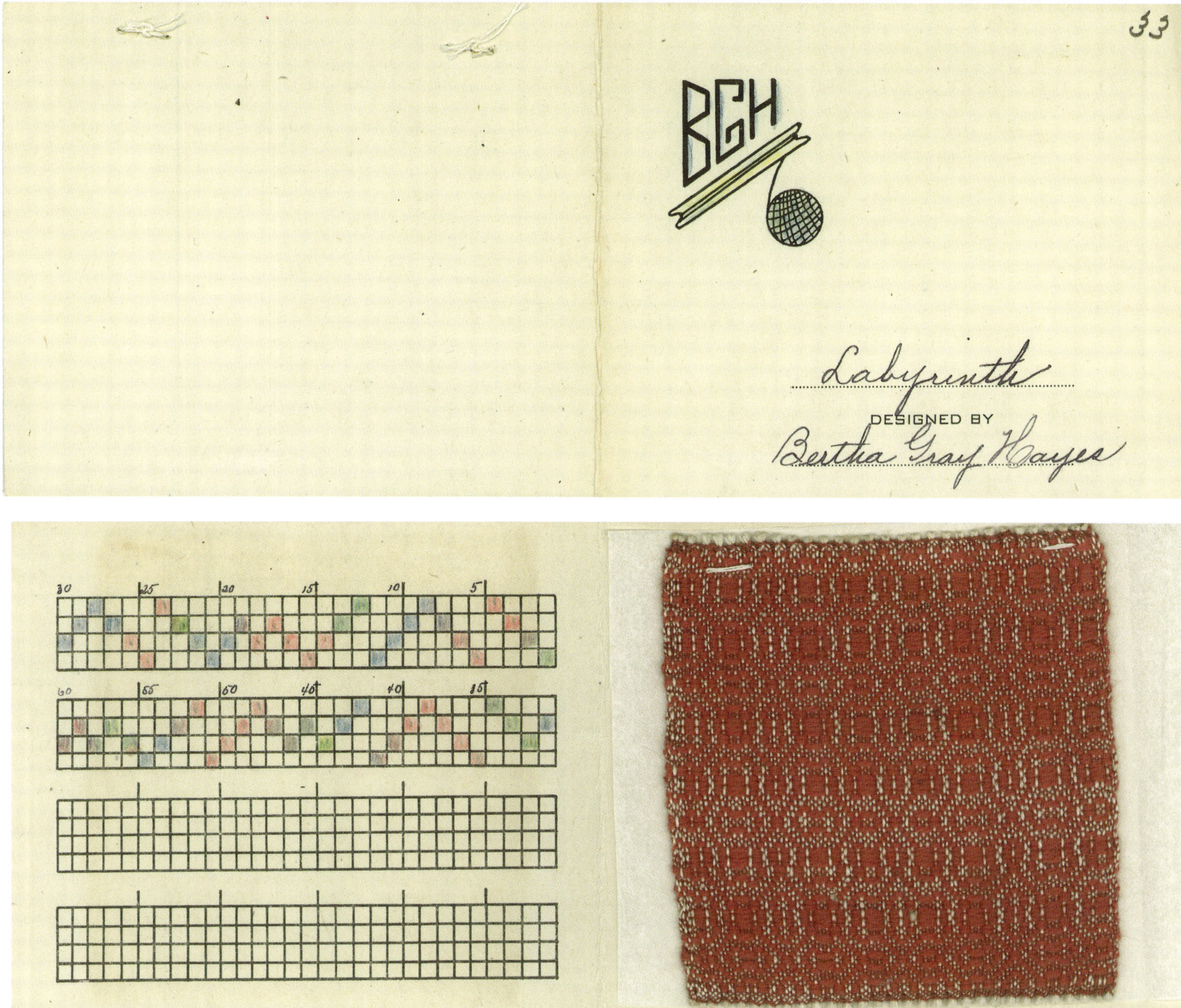

Figure 52.

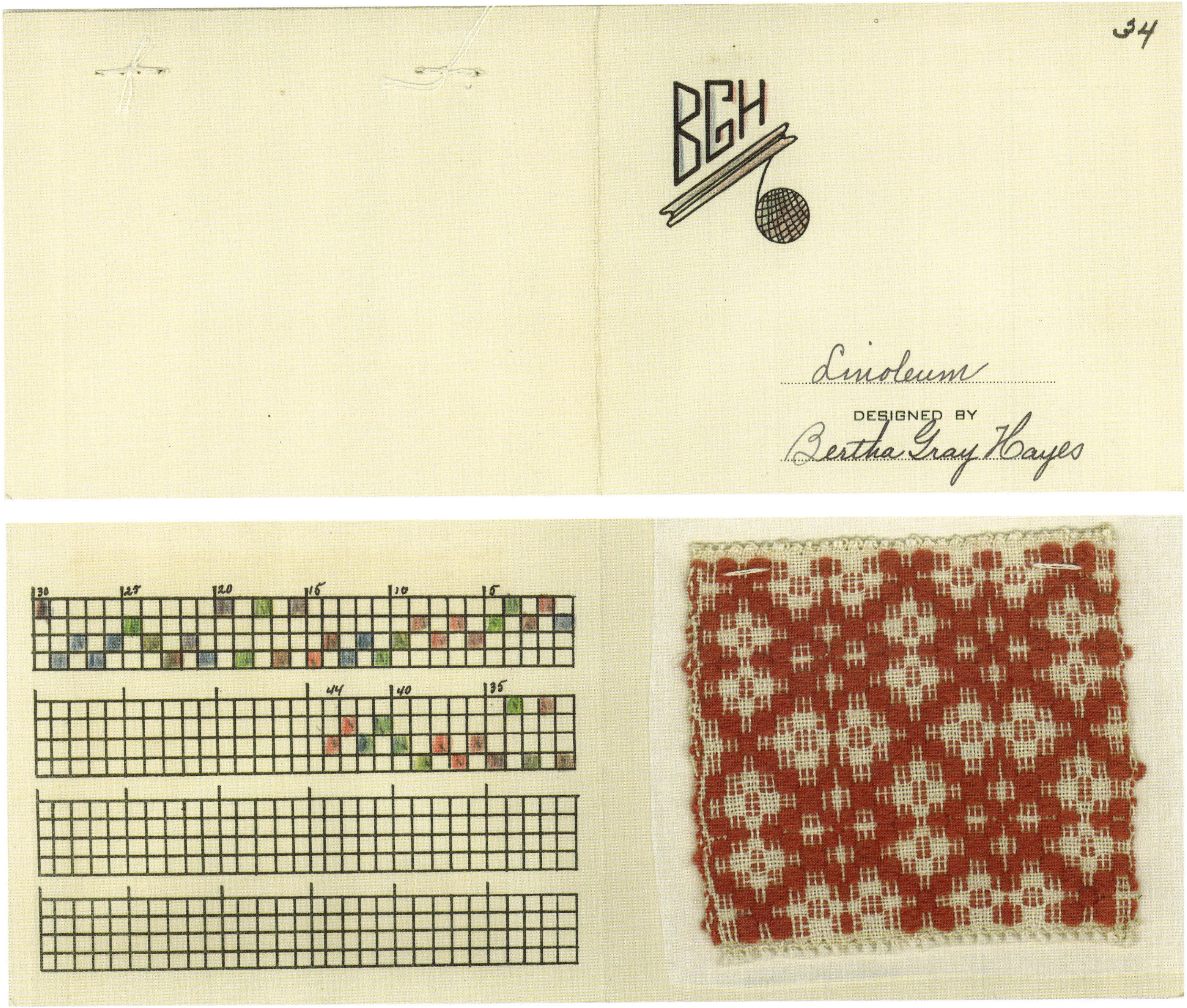
34
BGH
Linoleum
DESIGNED BY
Bertha Gray Hayes
30
25
20
15
10
5
44
40
35

Figure 53.

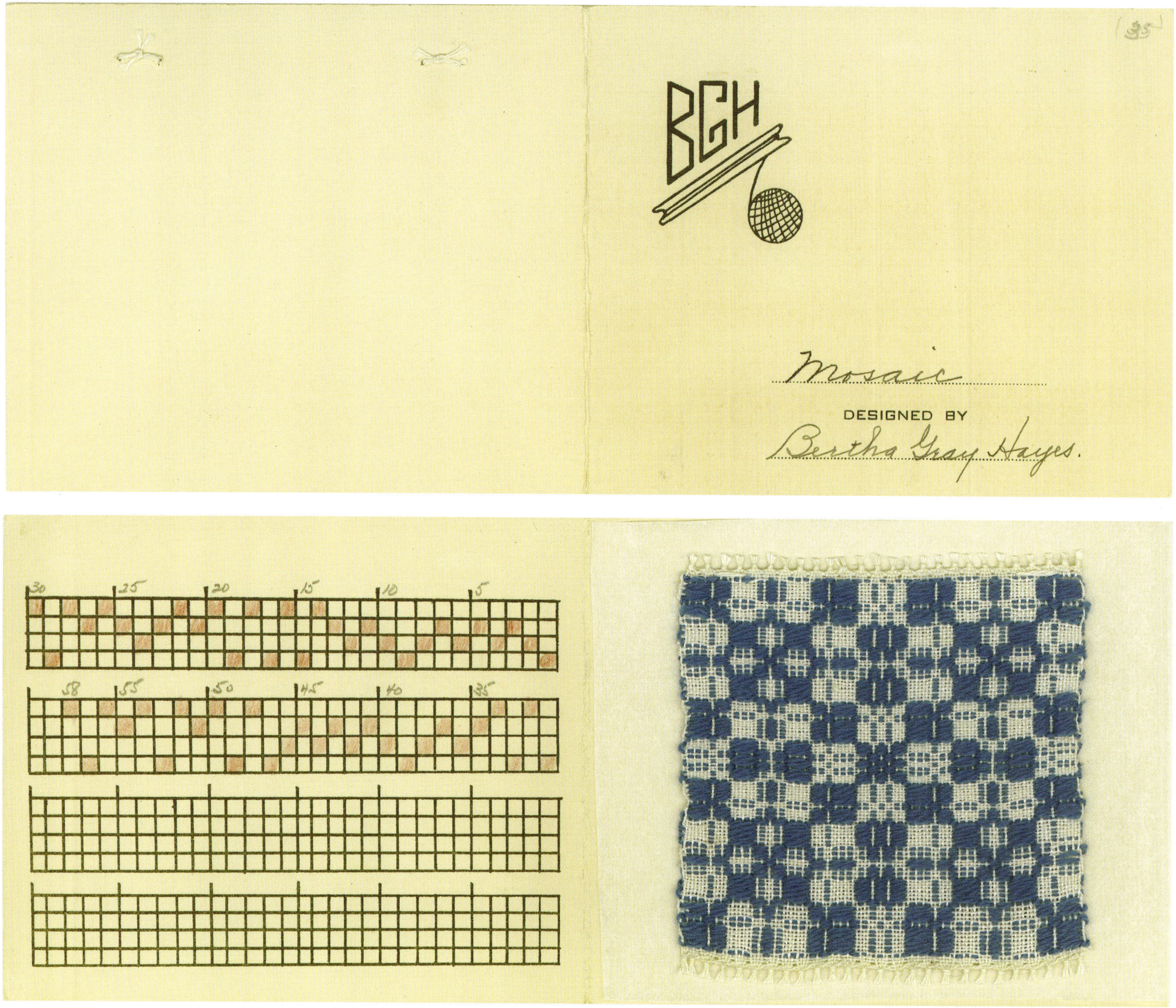
BGH
Mosaic
DESIGNED BY
Bertha Gray Hayes.
30
25
20
15
10
5
58
55
50
45
40
35

Figure 54.

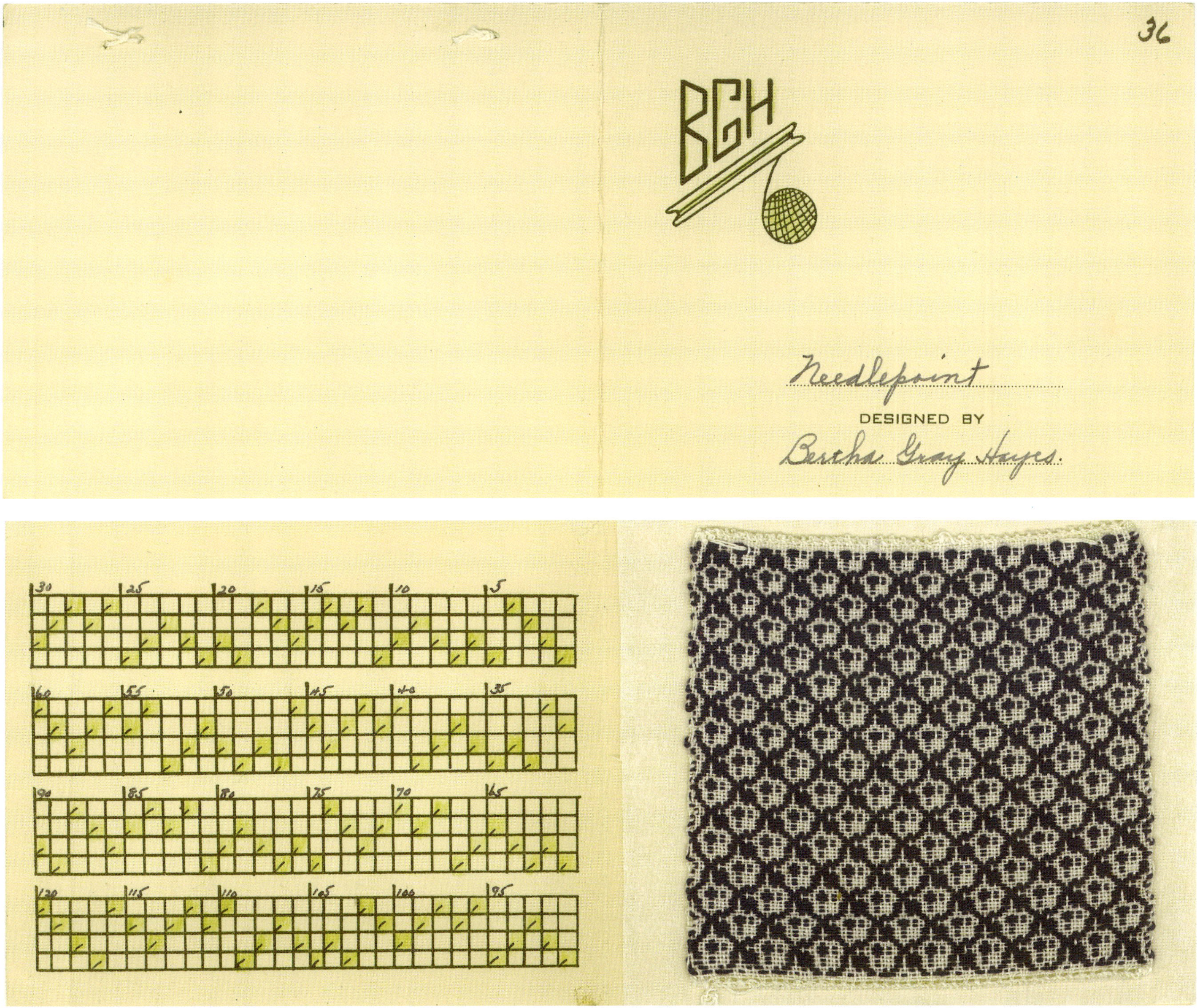

Figure 55.

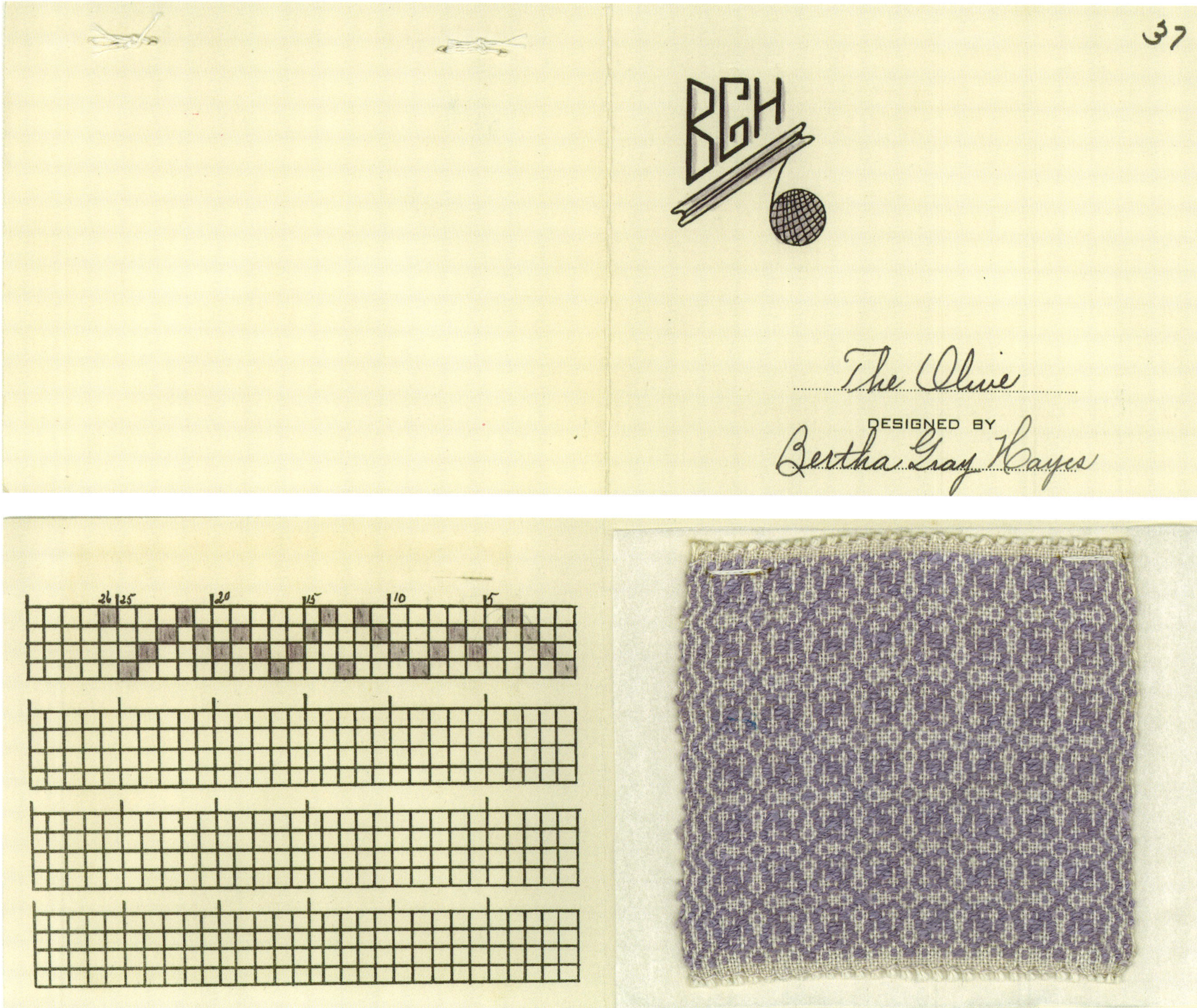

Figure 56.

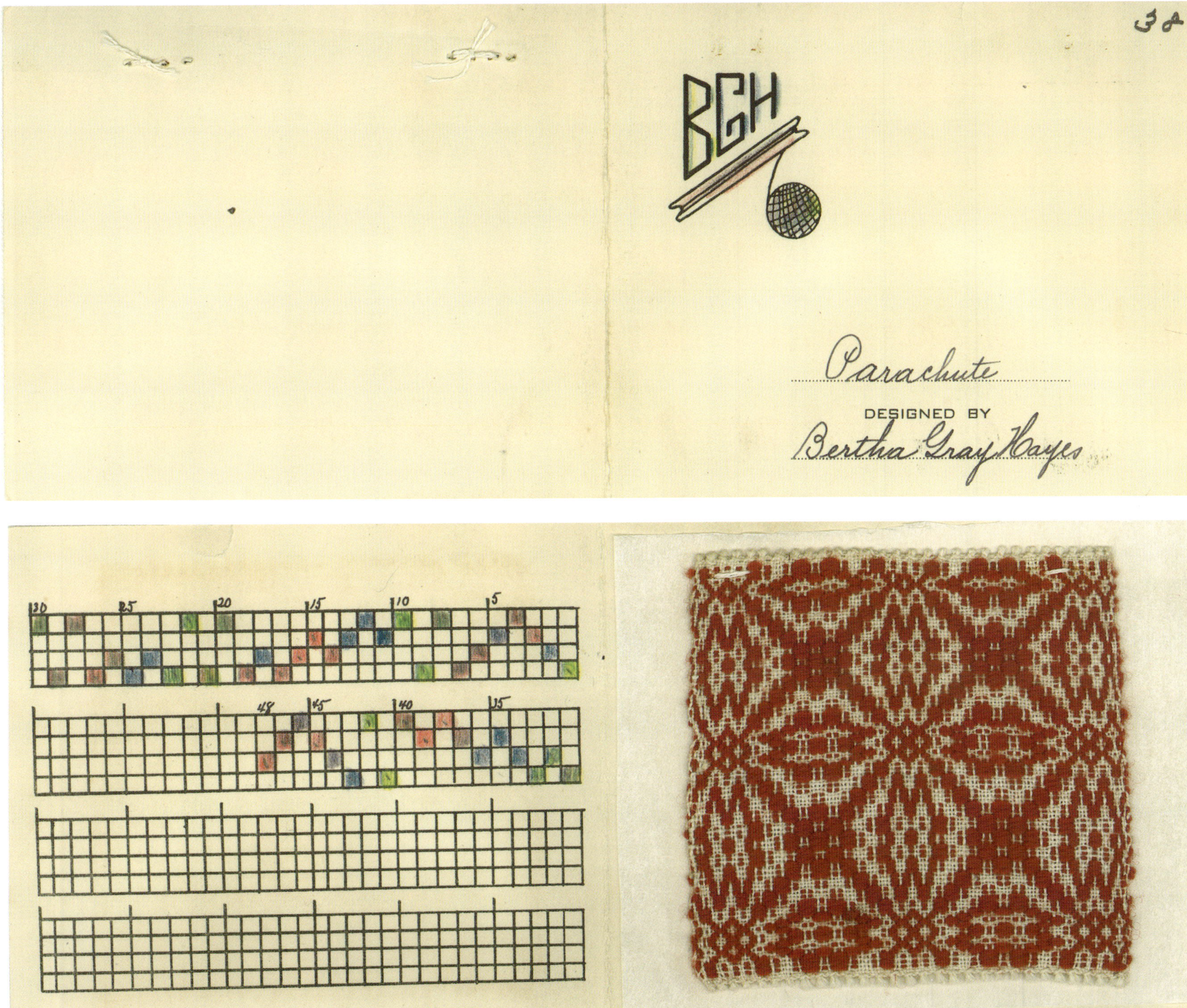
38
BGH
Parachute
DESIGNED BY
Bertha Gray Hayes
30
25
20
15
10
5
48
45
40
35

Figure 57.

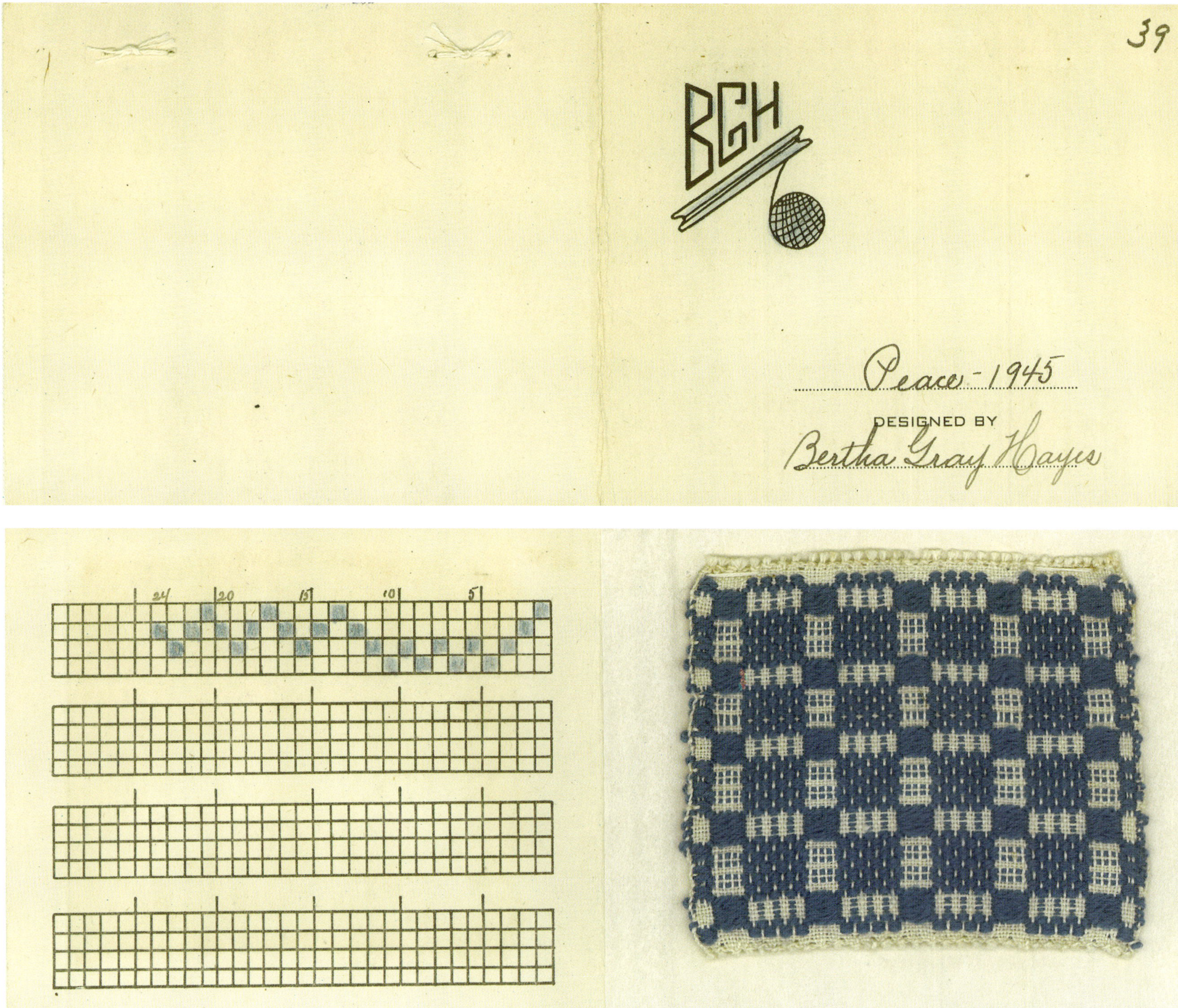

Figure 58.

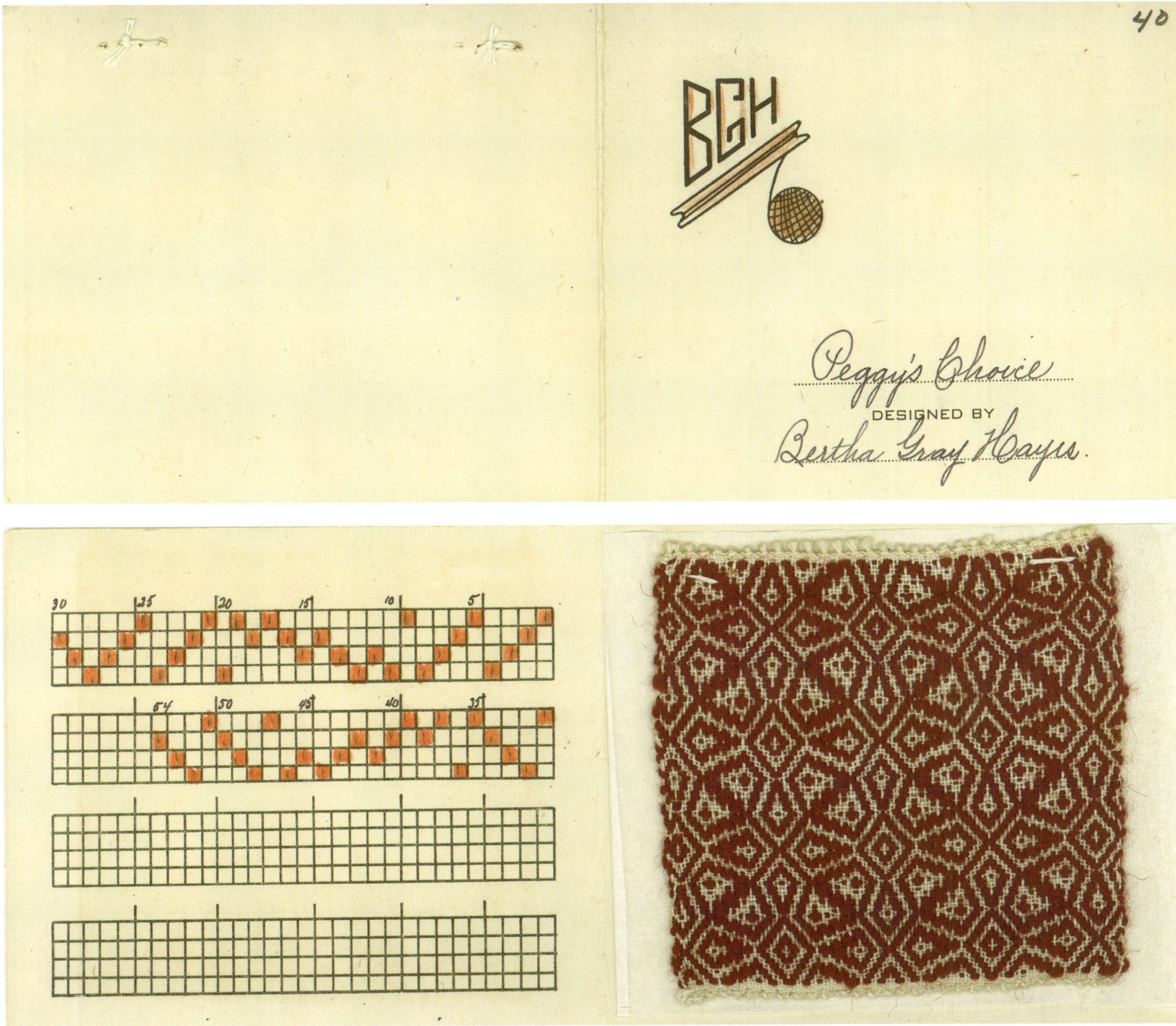
40
BGH
Peggy's Choice
DESIGNED BY
Bertha Gray Hayes.
30
25
20
15
10
5
54
50
45
40
35

Figure 59.

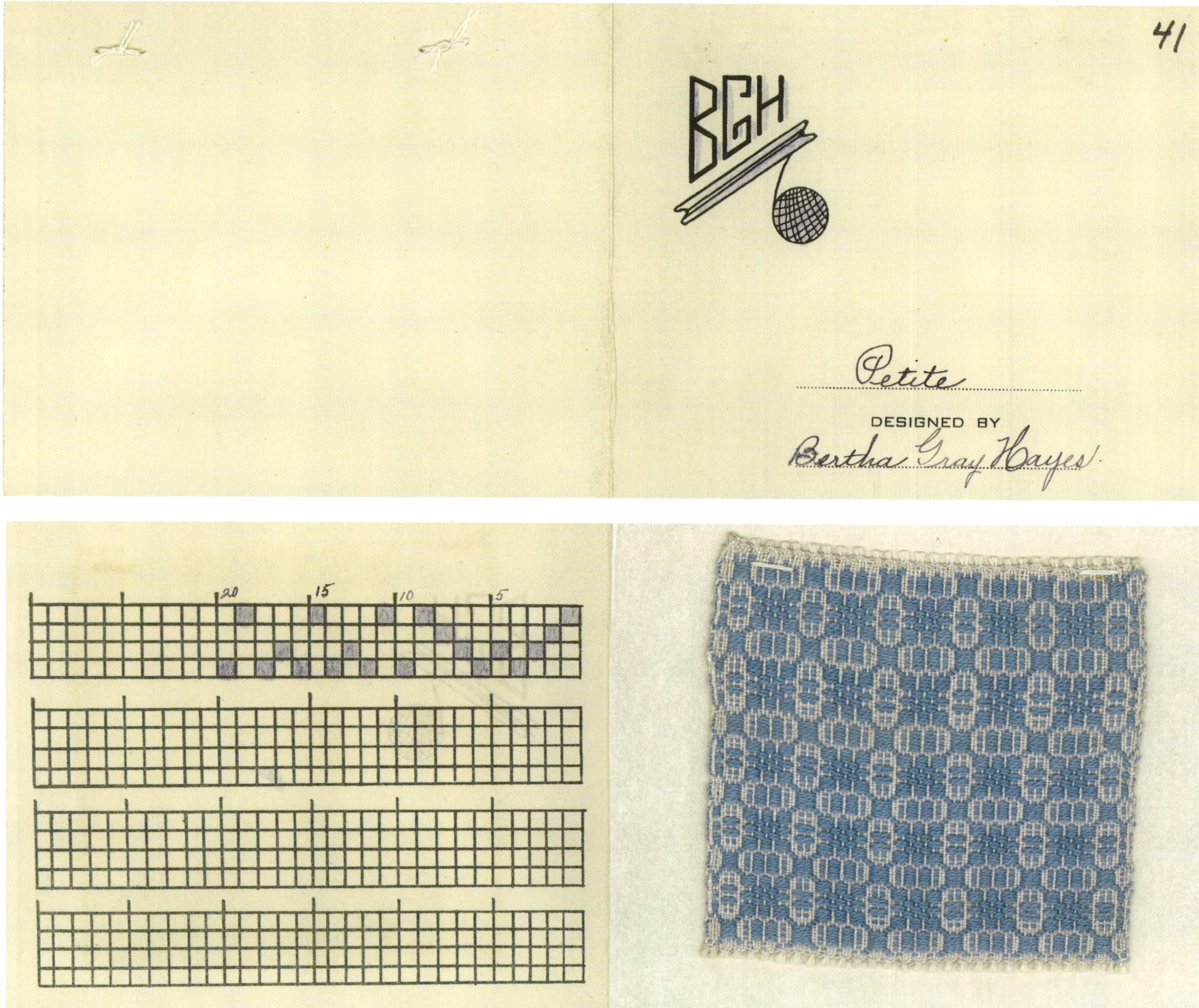

Figure 60.

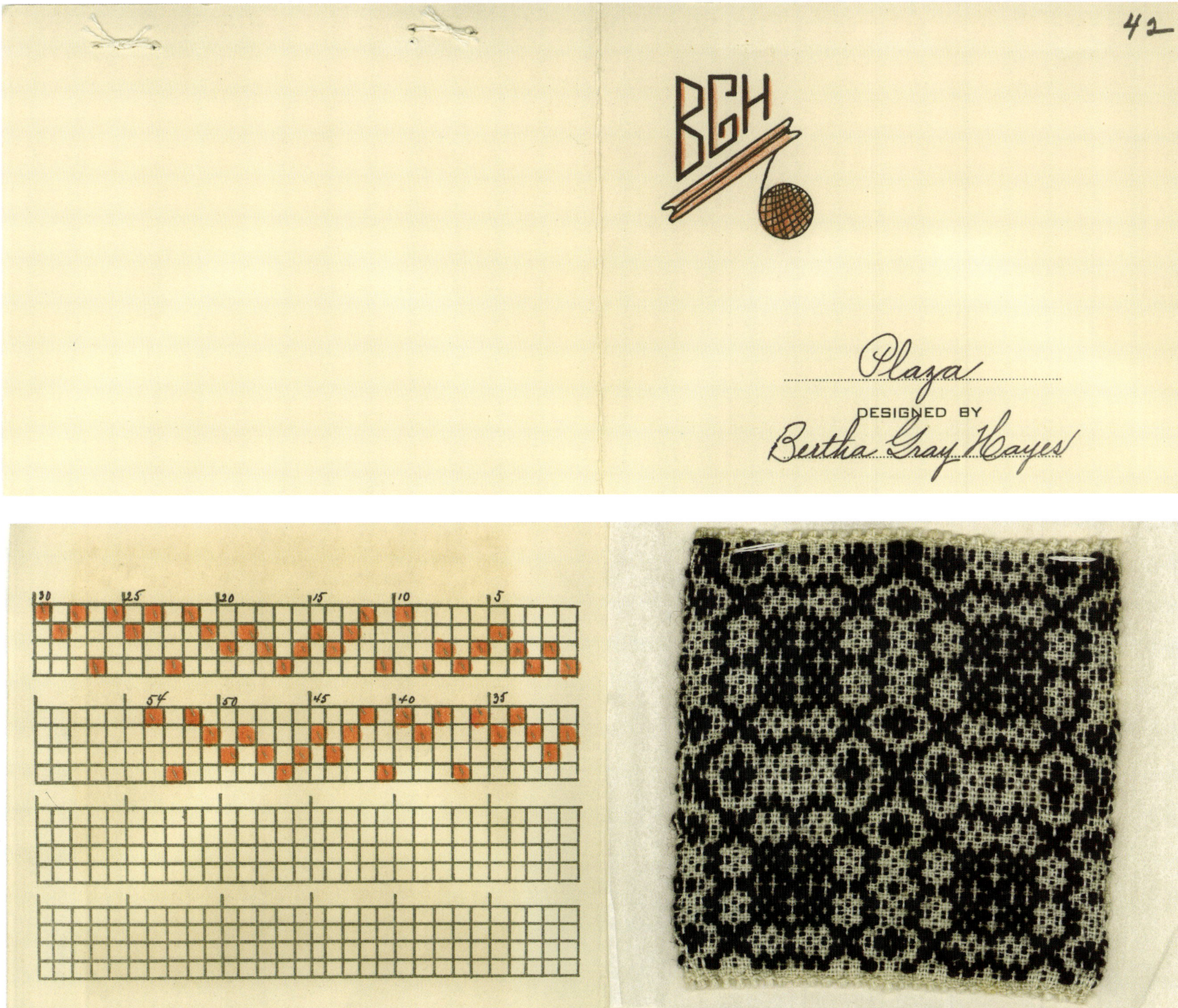
42
BGH
Plaza
DESIGNED BY
Bertha Gray Hayes
30
25
20
15
10
5
54
50
45
40
35

Figure 61.

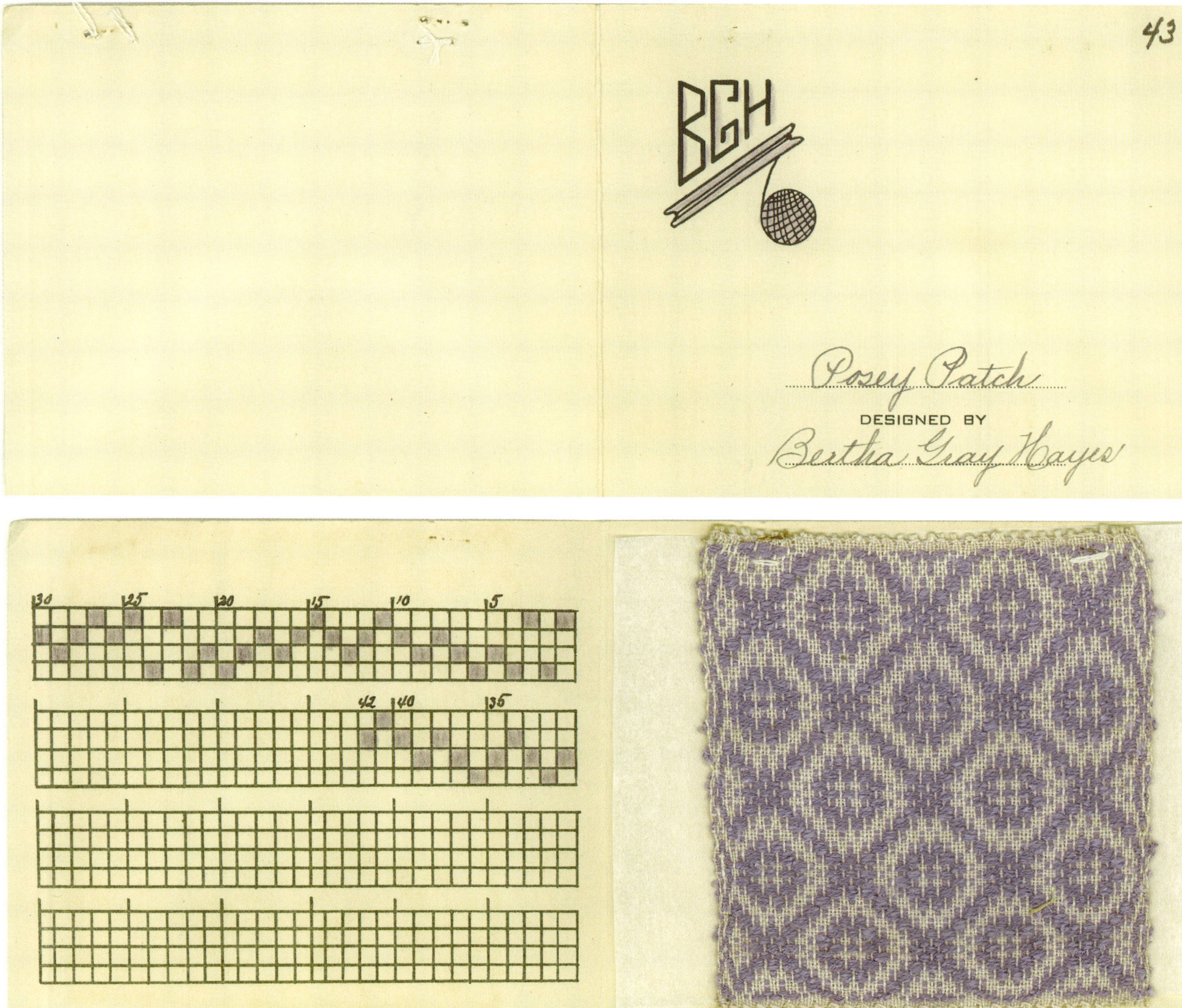
43
BGH
Posey Patch
DESIGNED BY
Bertha Gray Hayes
30 25 20 15 10 5
42 40 35

Figure 62.

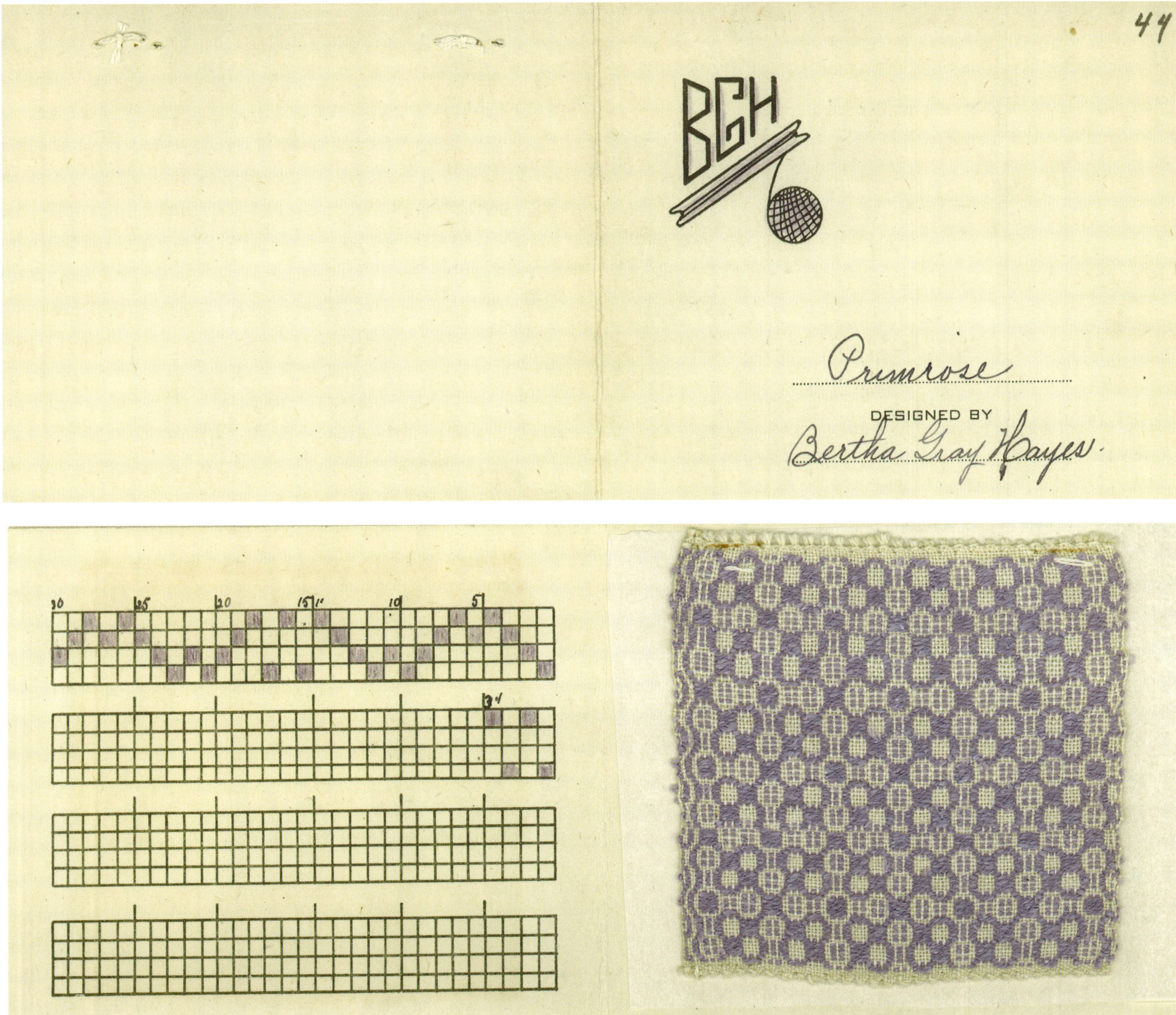

Figure 63.

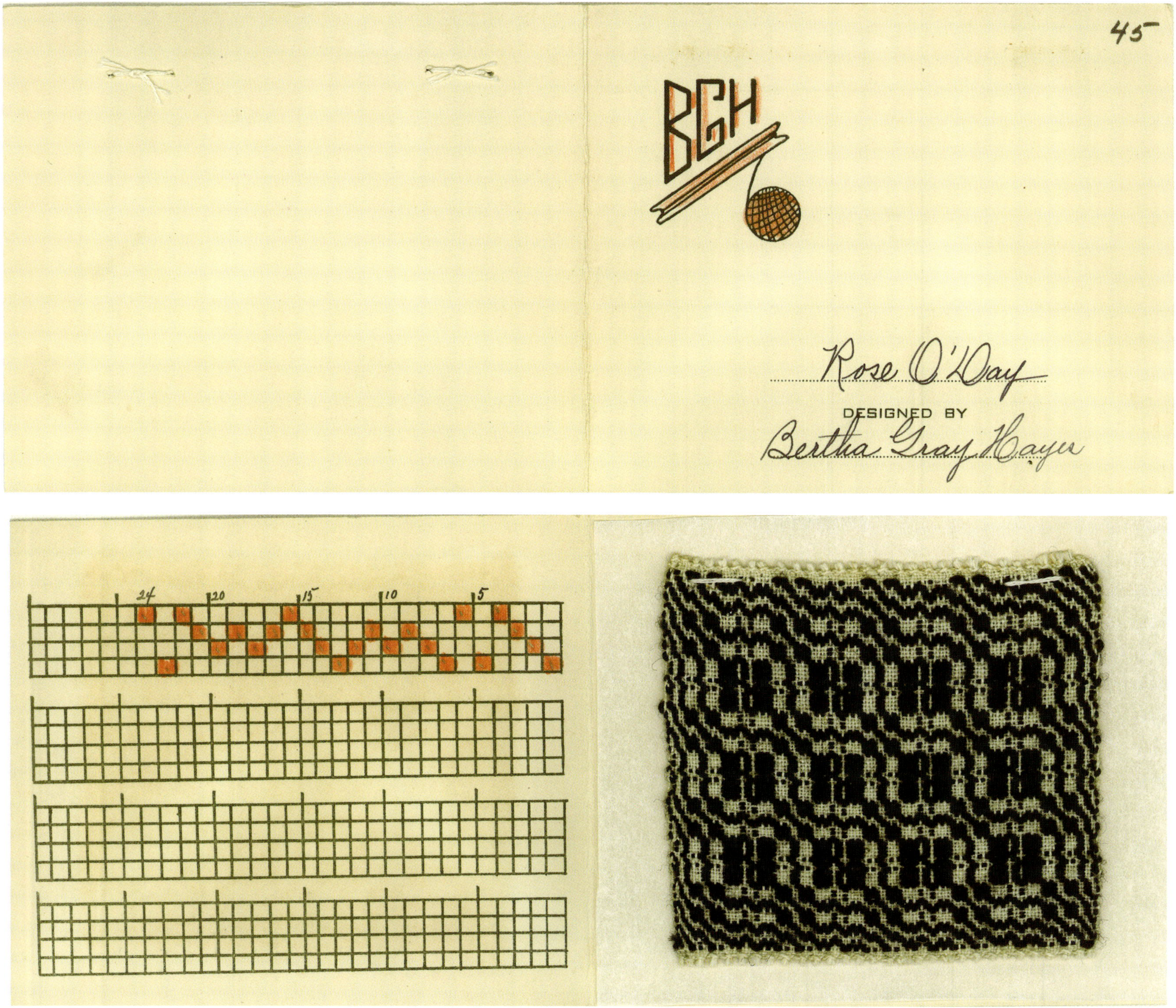

Figure 64.

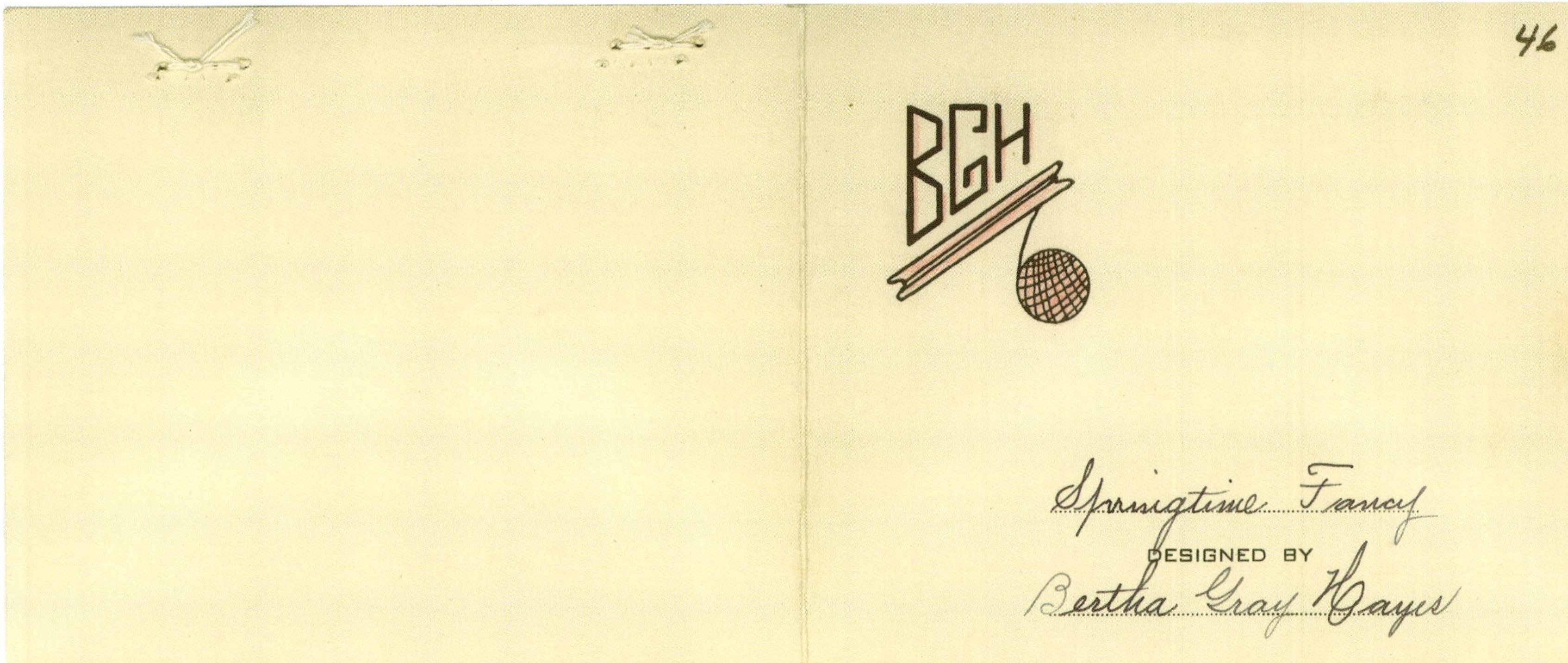
46
BGH
Springtime Fancy
DESIGNED BY
Bertha Gray Hayes

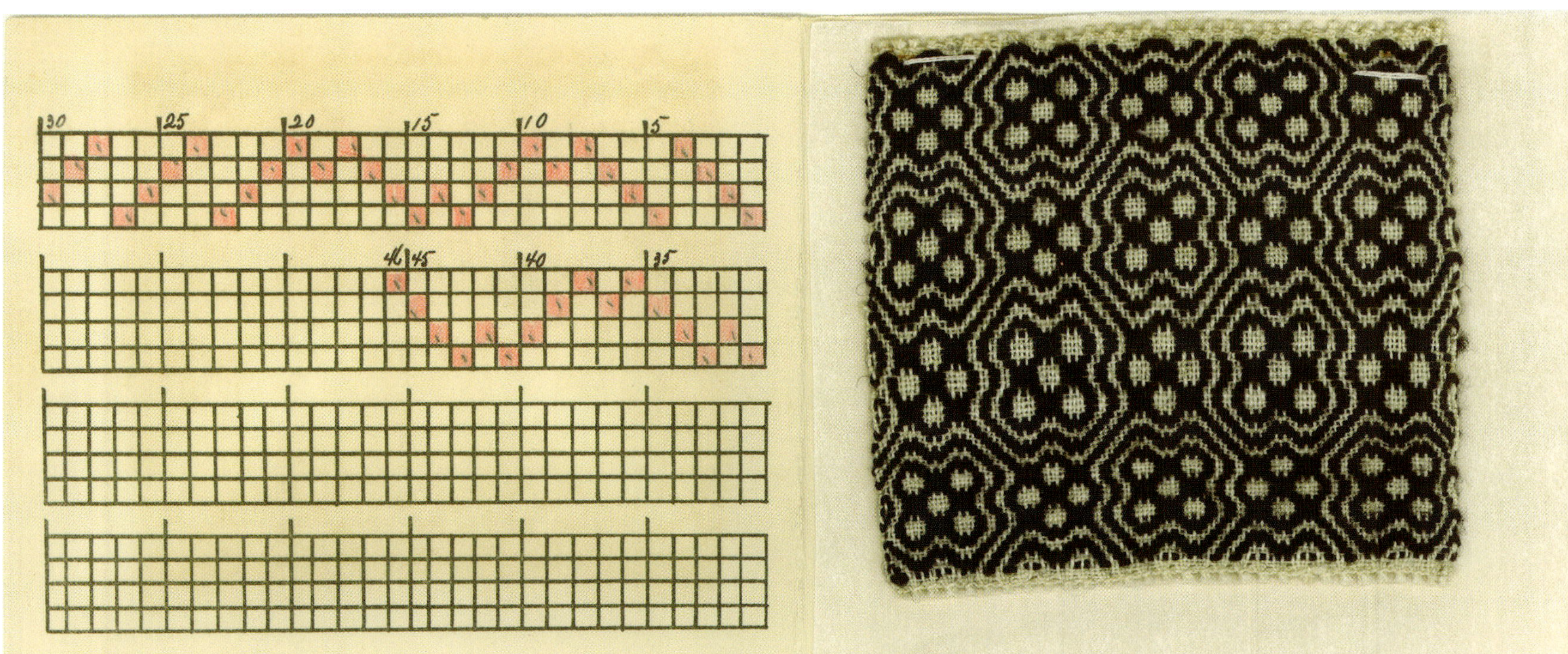
30
25
20
15
10
5
46
45
40
35

Figure 65.

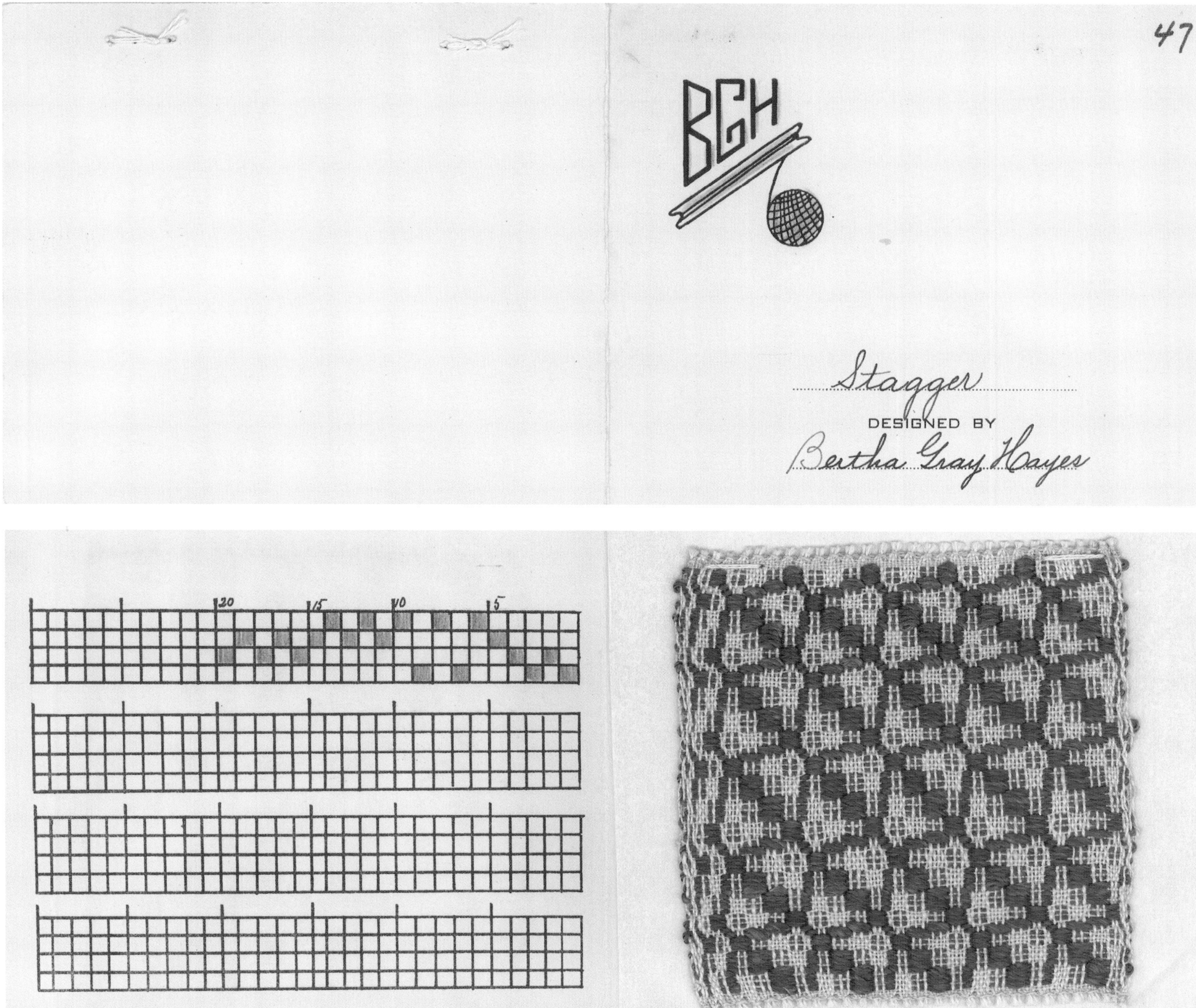

Figure 66.

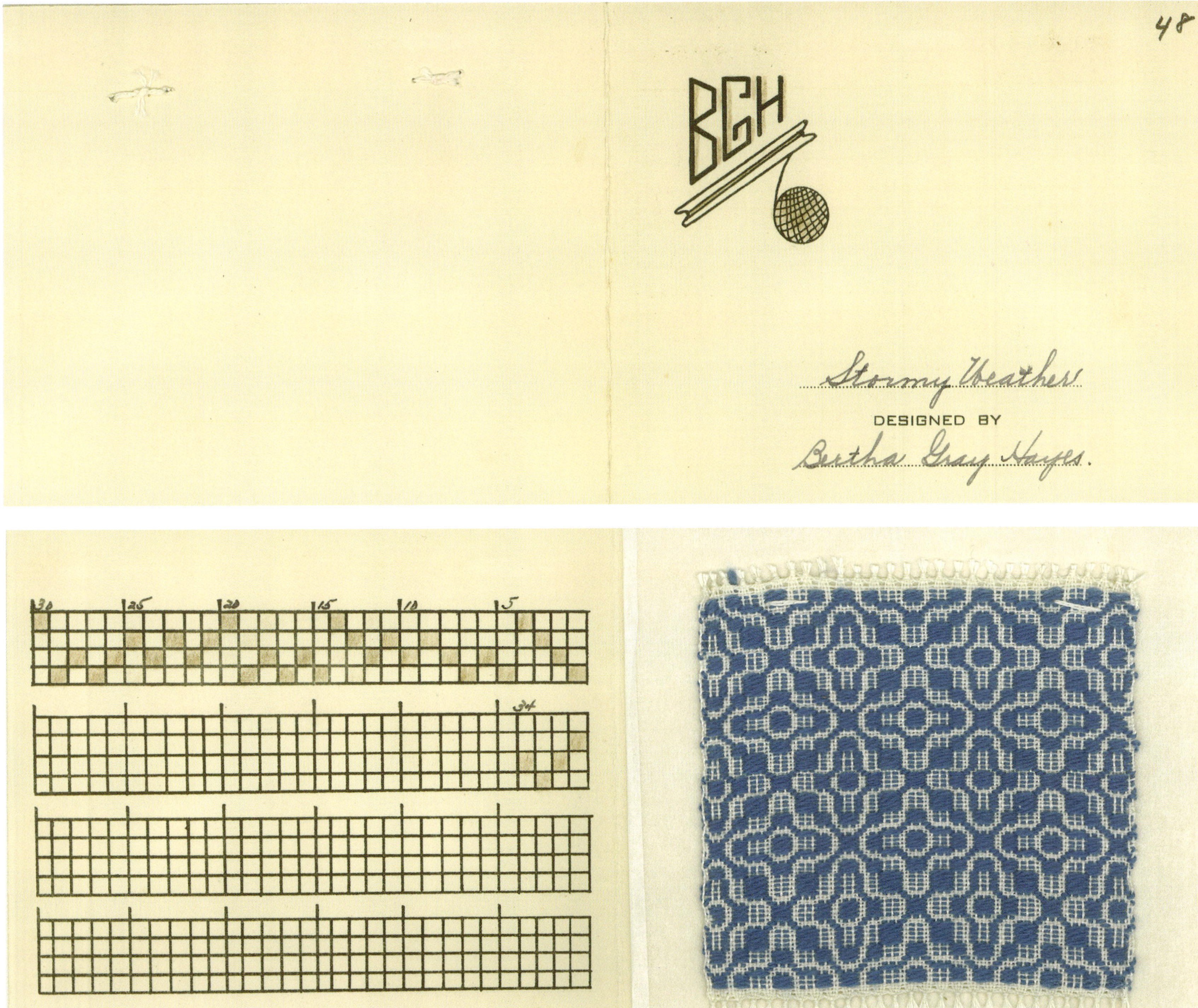
48
BGH
Stormy Weather
DESIGNED BY
Bertha Gray Hayes.
30
25
20
15
10
5
34

Figure 67.

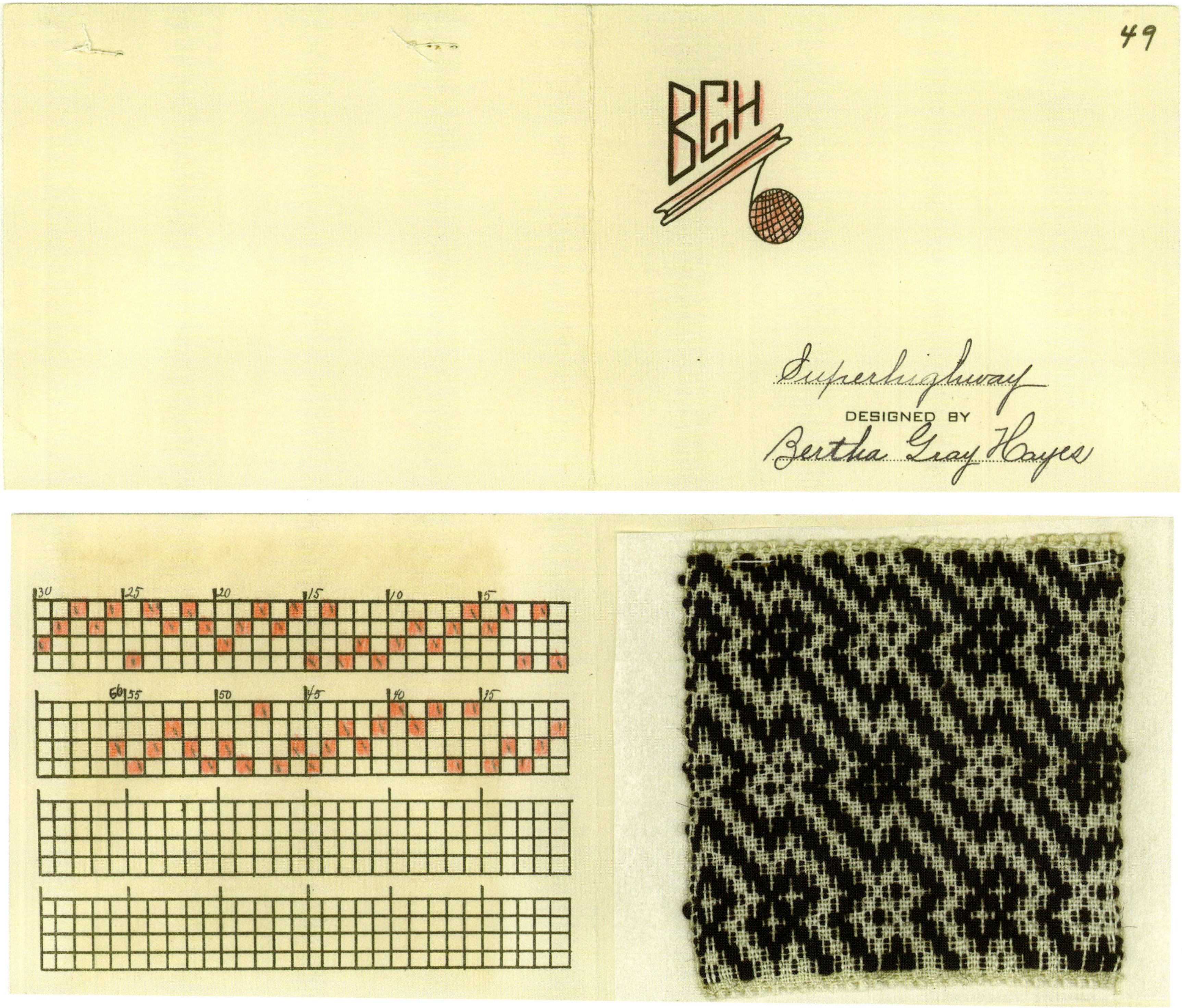

Figure 68.

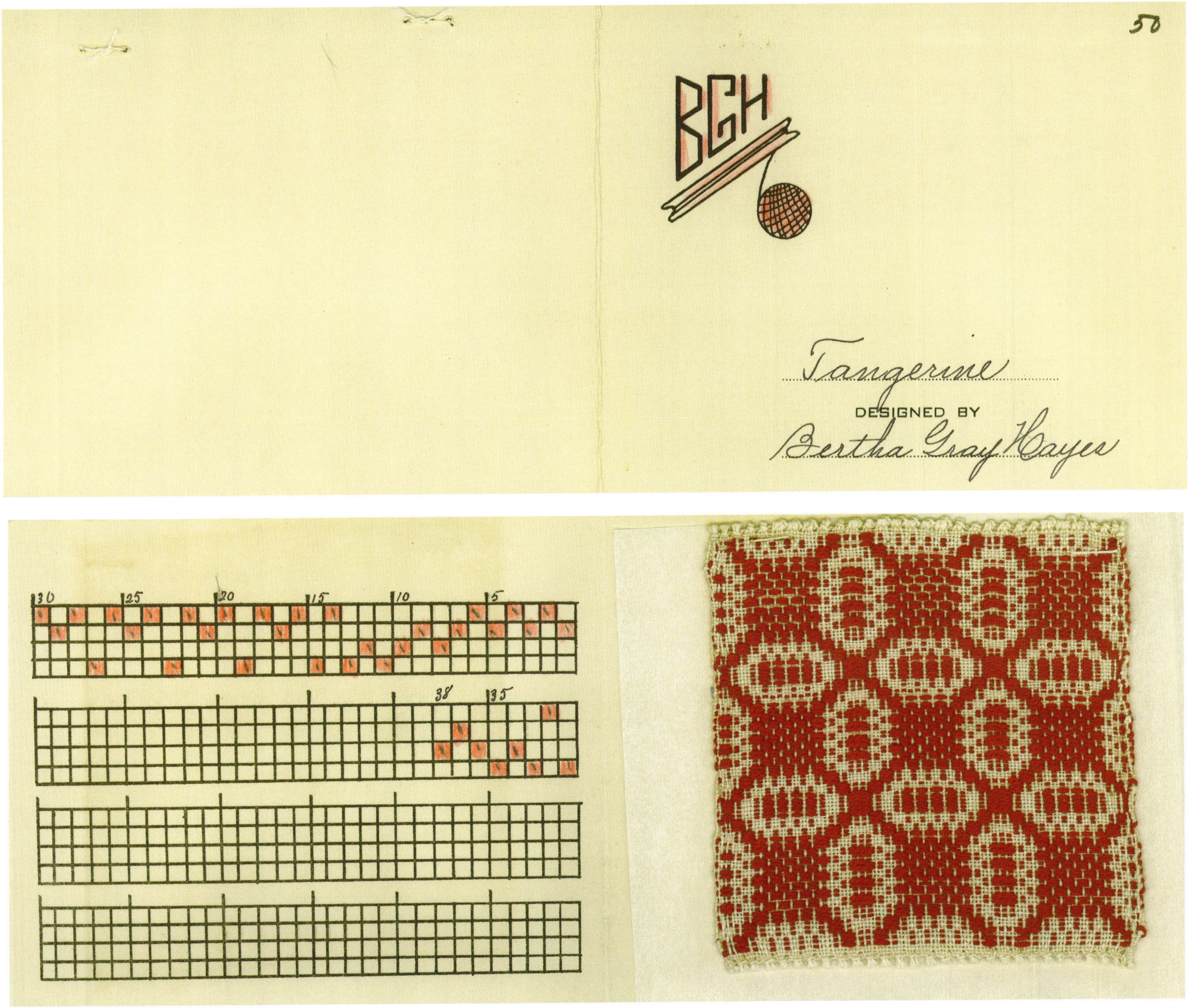
50
BGH
Tangerine
DESIGNED BY
Bertha Gray Hayes
30
25
20
15
10
5
38
35

Figure 69.

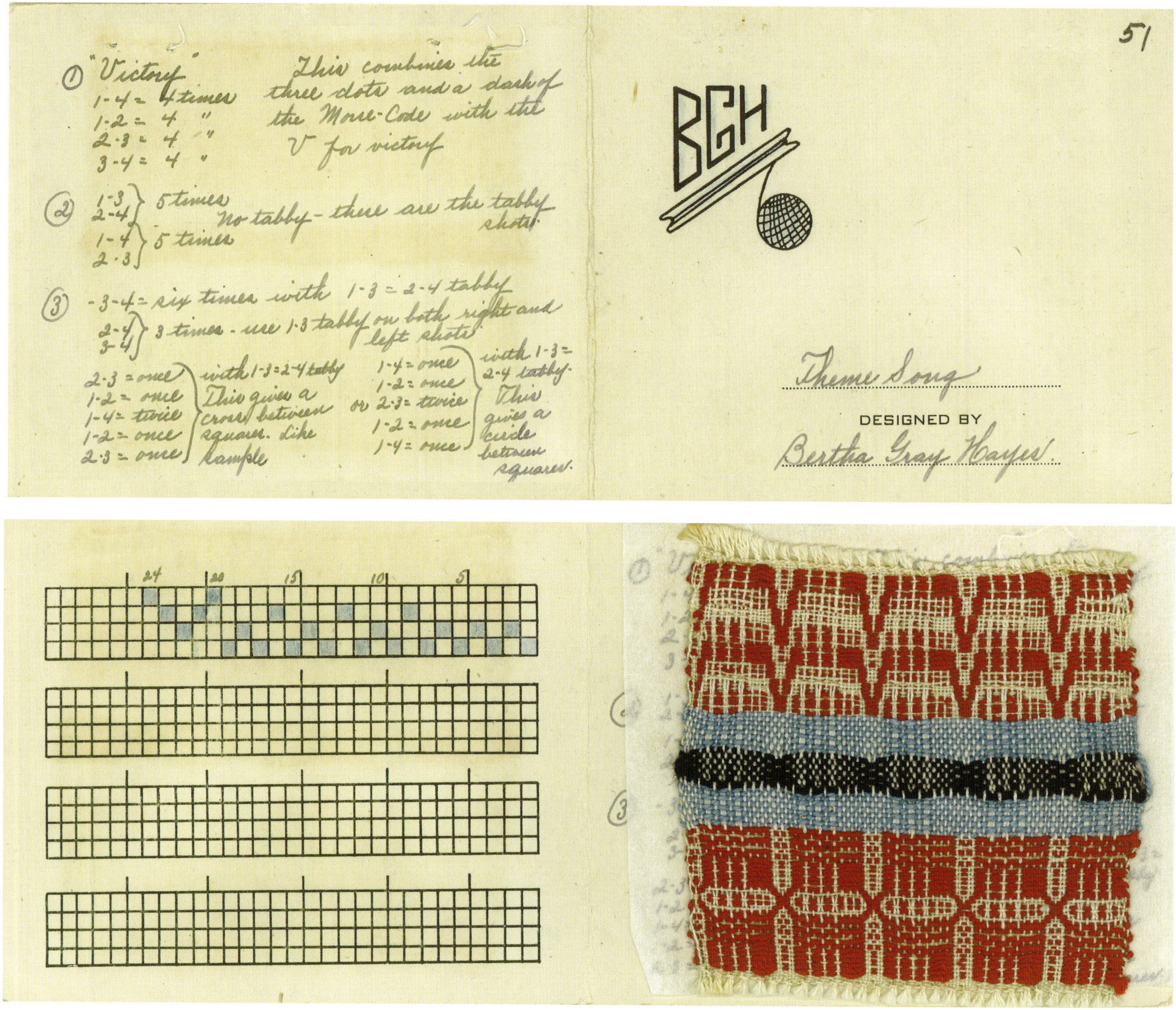

51
① "Victory"
1-4 = 4 times
1-2 = 4 "
2-3 = 4 "
3-4 = 4 "
This combines the three dots and a dash of the Morse-Code with the V for victory
② 1-3 } 2-4 } 5 times
1-4 } 2-3 } 5 times
No tabby - these are the tabby shots.
③ 3-4 = six times with 1-3 = 2-4 tabby
2-4 } 3-4 } 3 times - use 1-3 tabby on both right and left shots
2-3 = once
1-2 = once
1-4 = twice
1-2 = once
2-3 = once
with 1-3 = 2-4 tabby This gives a cross between squares. Like sample
or
1-4 = once
1-2 = once
2-3 = twice
1-2 = once
1-4 = once
with 1-3 = 2-4 tabby. This gives a circle between squares.
BGH
Theme Song
DESIGNED BY
Bertha Gray Hayes.
24 20 15 10 5

Figure 70.

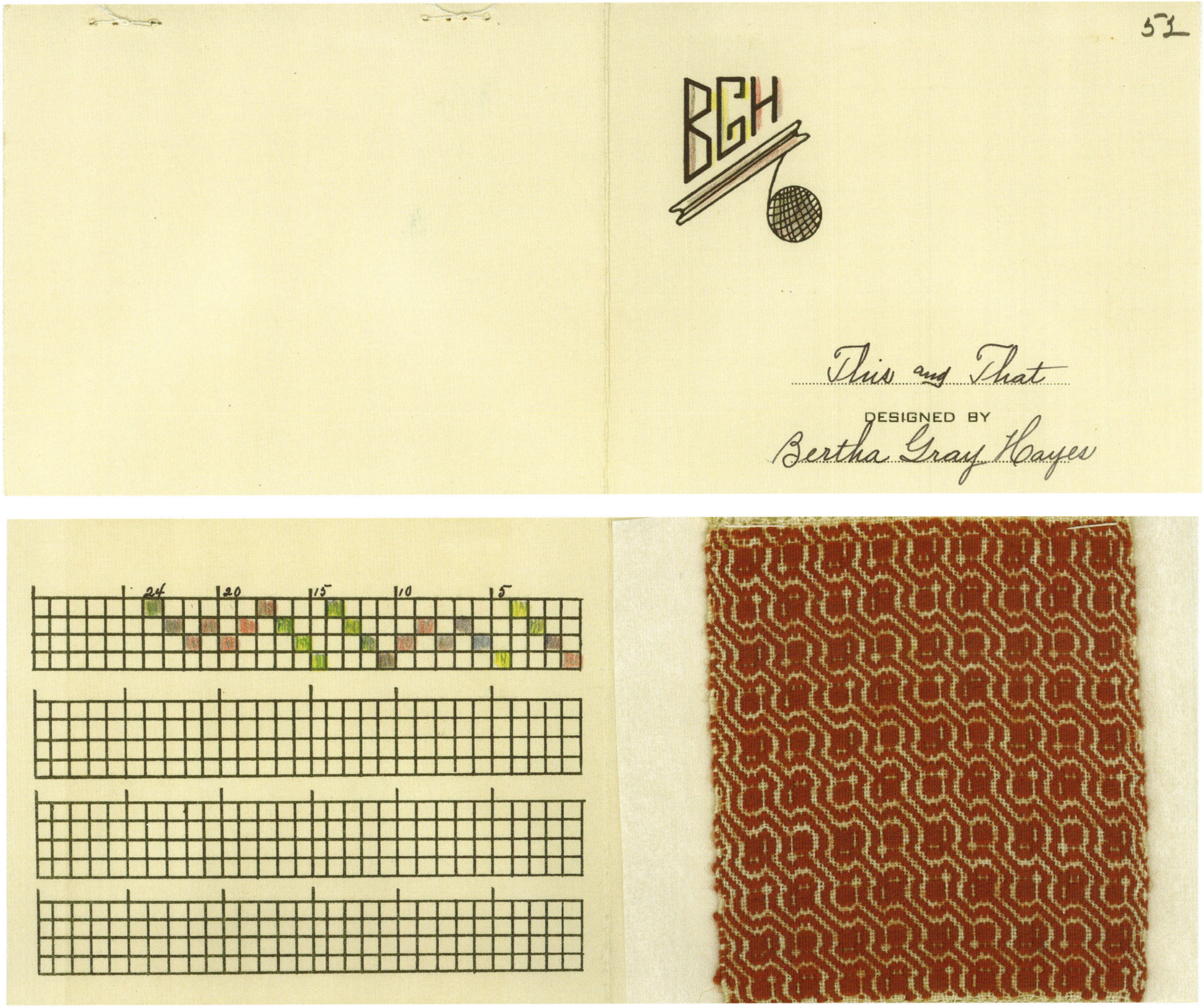
51
BGH
This and That
DESIGNED BY
Bertha Gray Hayes
24
20
15
10
5

Figure 71.

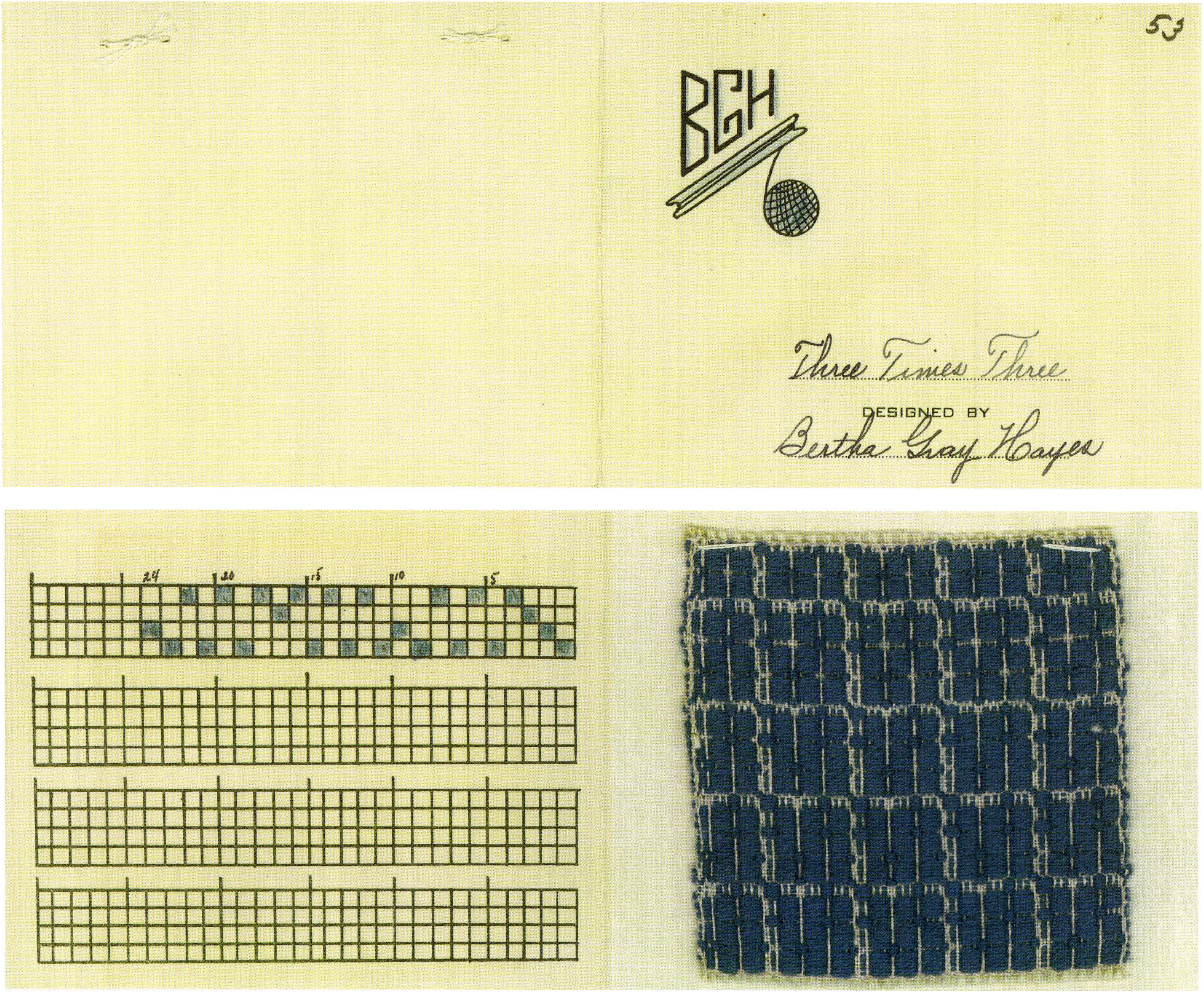
53
BGH
Three Times Three
DESIGNED BY
Bertha Gray Hayes
24
20
15
10
5

Figure 72.

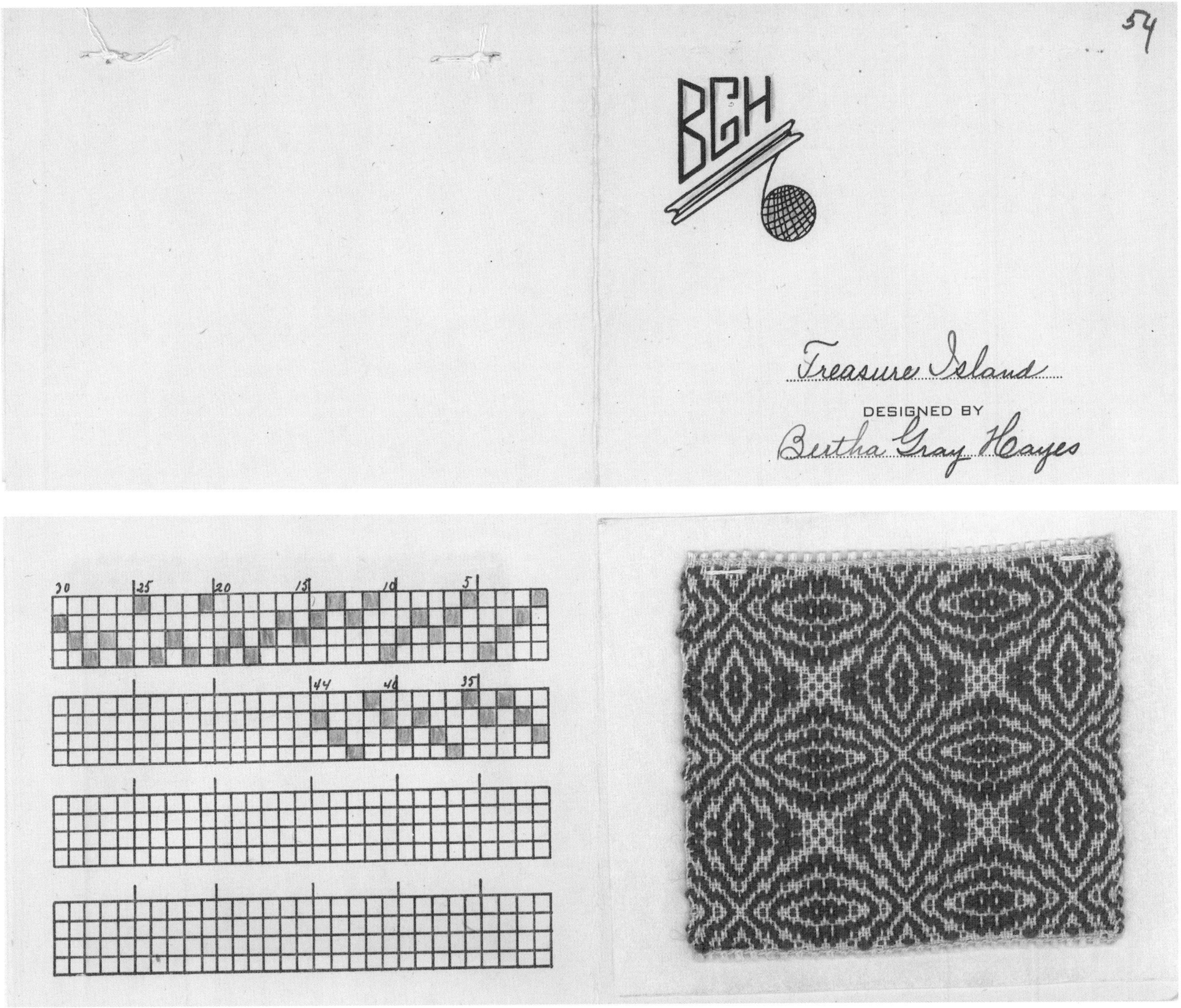
54
BGH
Treasure Island
DESIGNED BY
Bertha Gray Hayes
30
25
20
15
10
5
44
40
35

Figure 73.

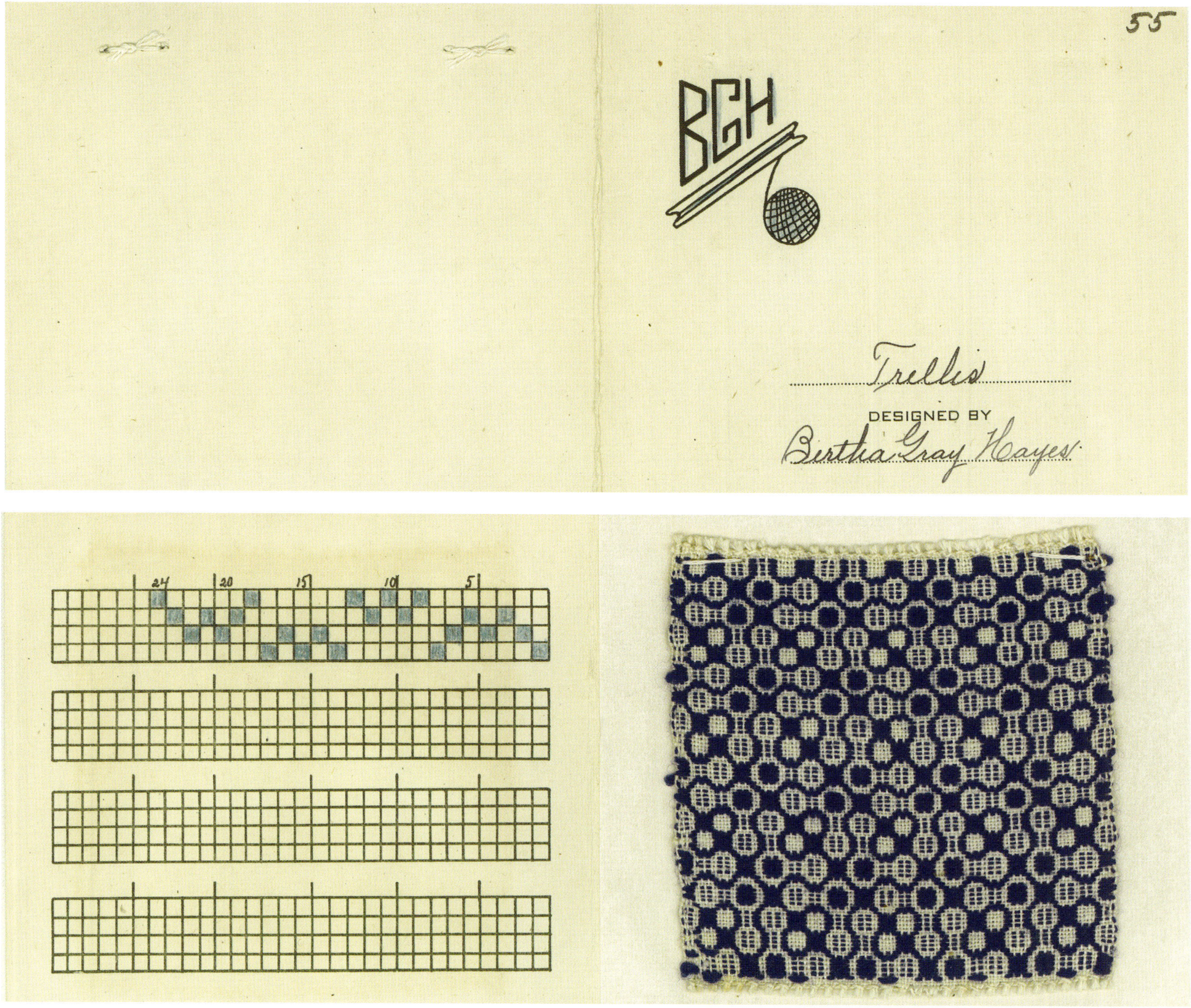

Figure 74.

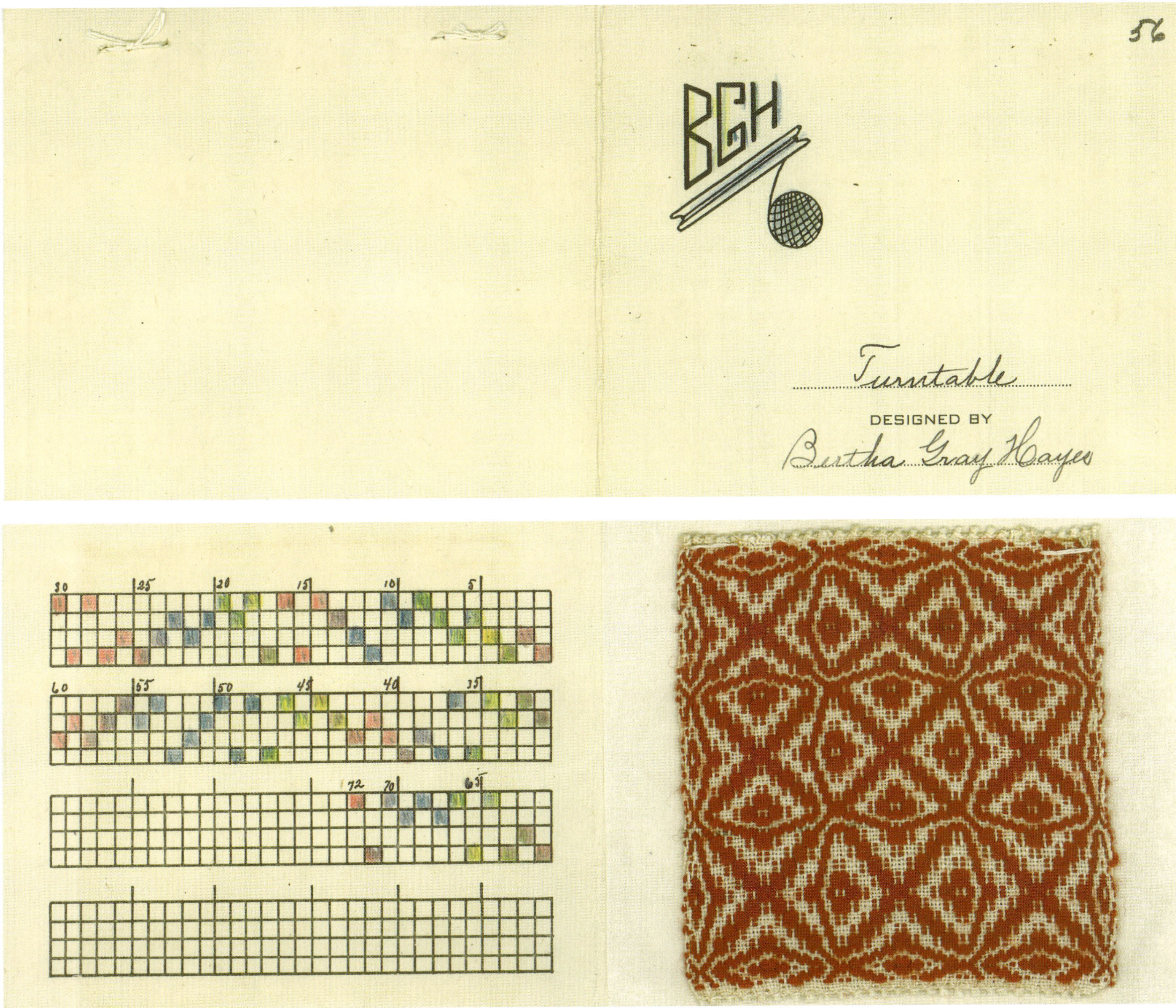

Figure 75.

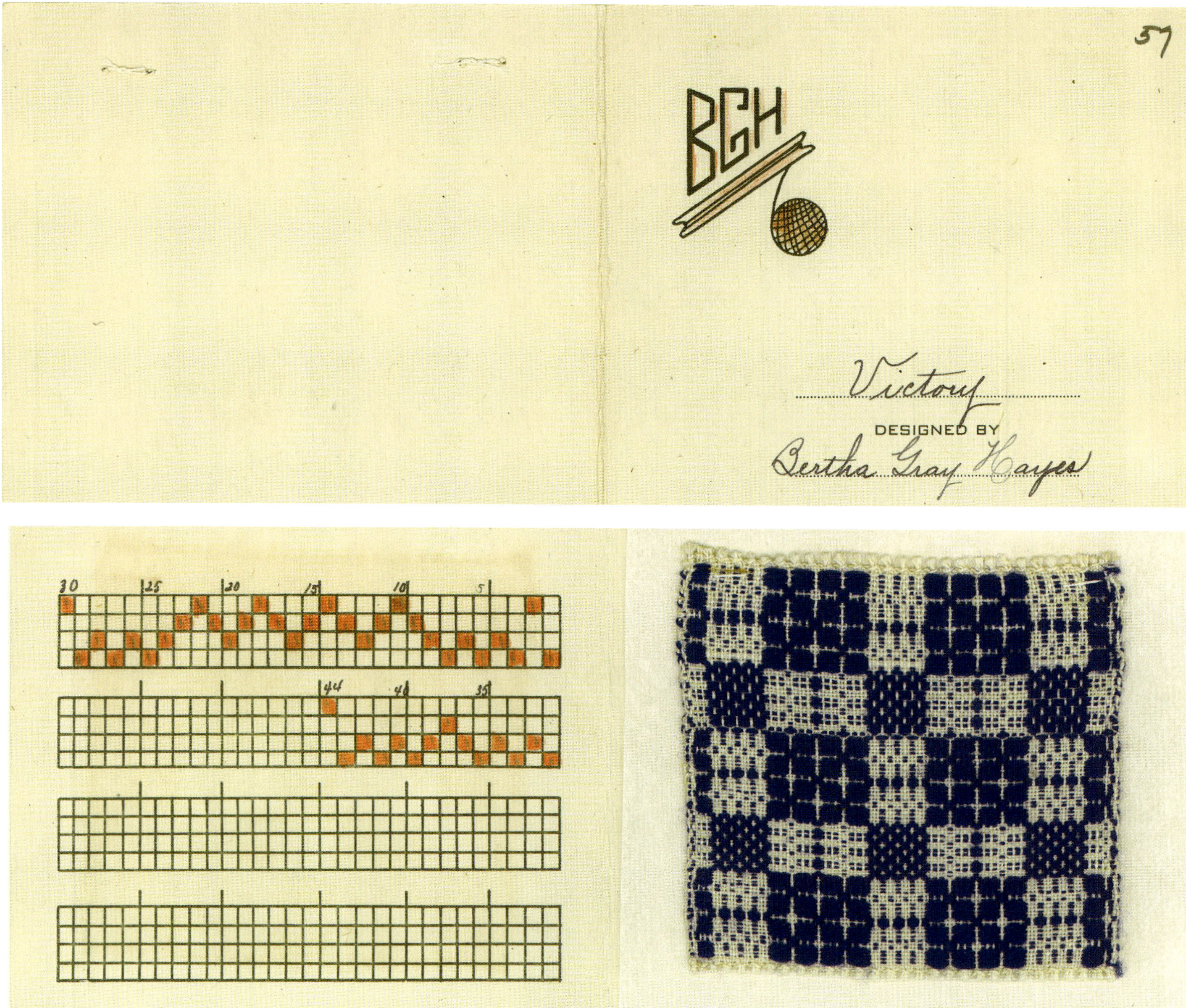
57
BGH
Victory
DESIGNED BY
Bertha Gray Hayes
30
25
20
15
10
5
44
40
35

Figure 76.

58
BGH
Wibraska
DESIGNED BY
Bertha Gray Hayes

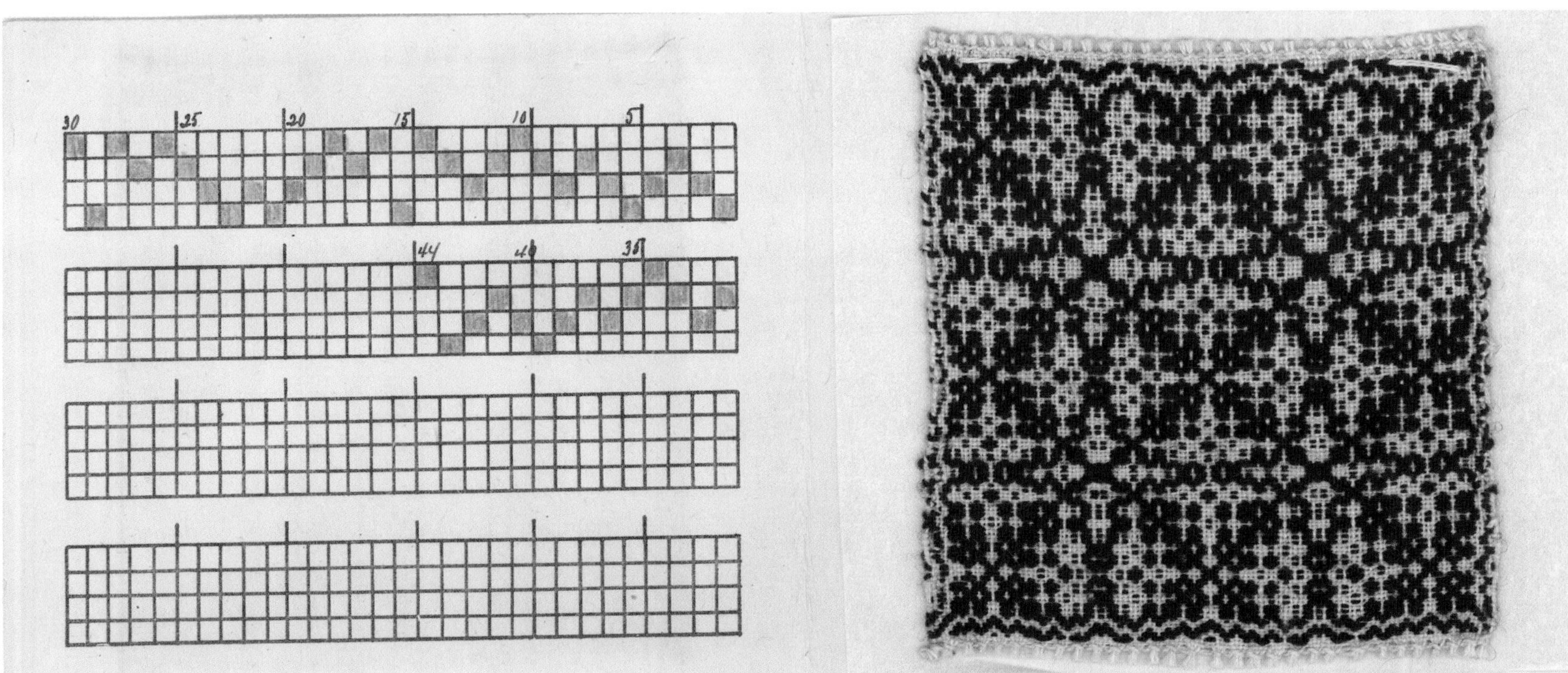
30
25
20
15
10
5
44
40

Figure 77.

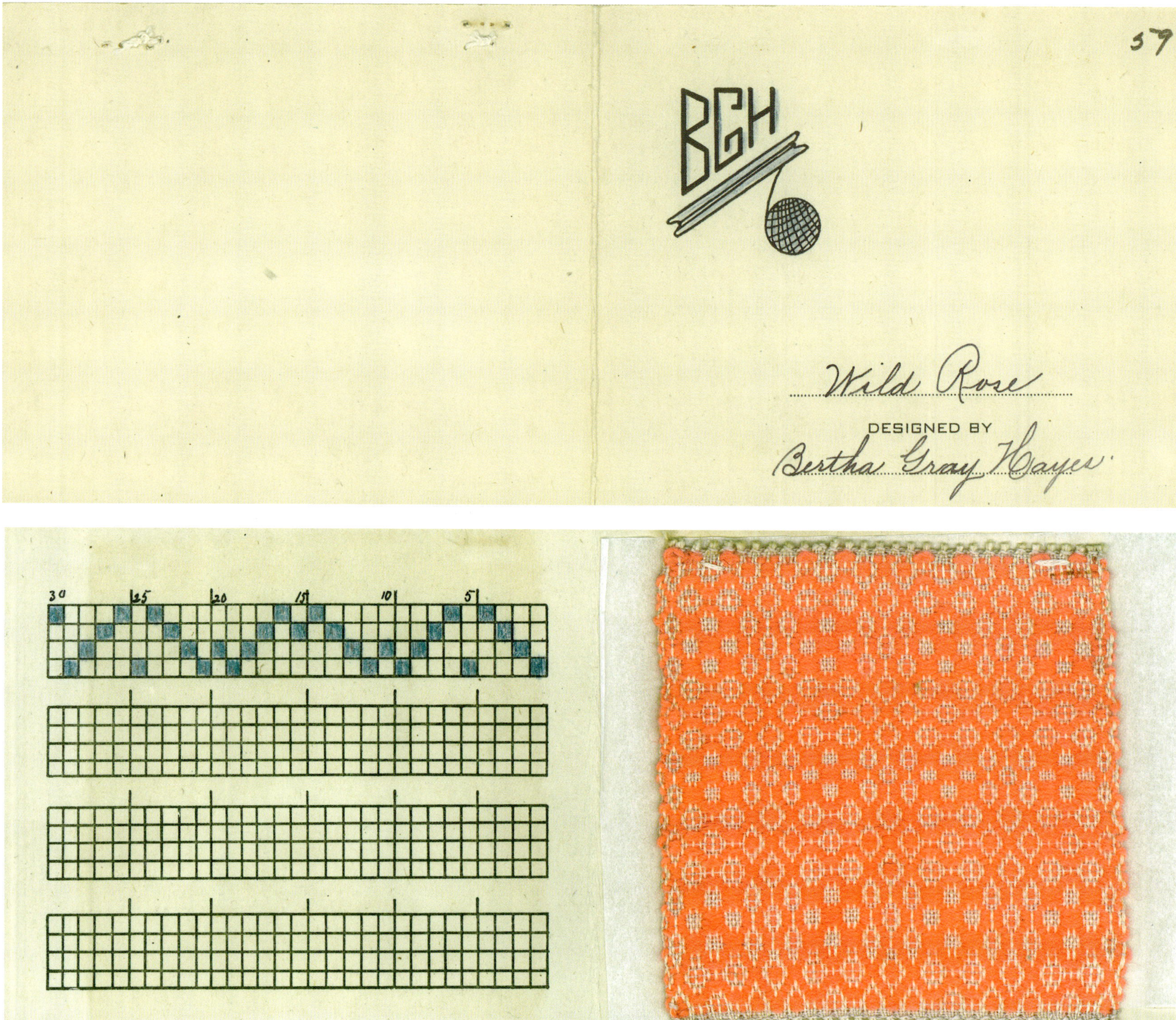

Figure 78.

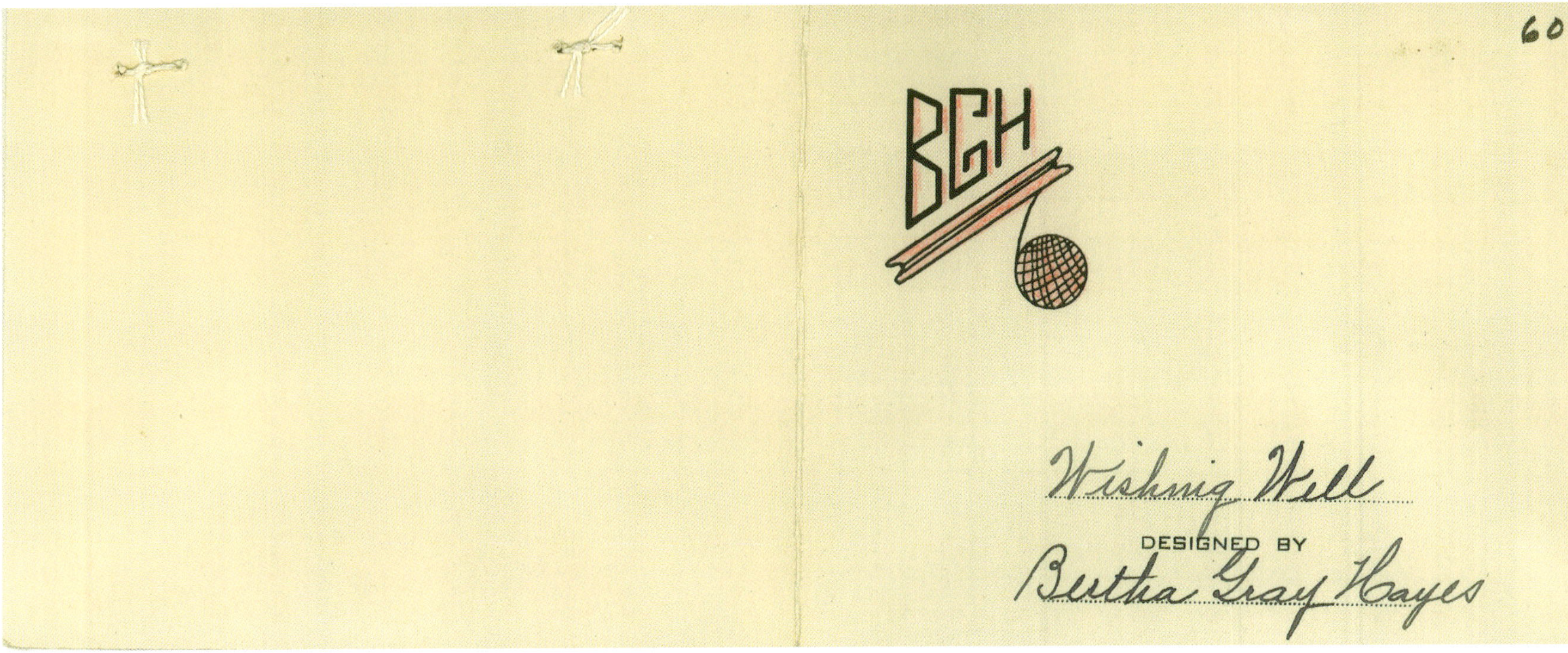
60
BGH
Wishing Well
DESIGNED BY
Bertha Gray Hayes

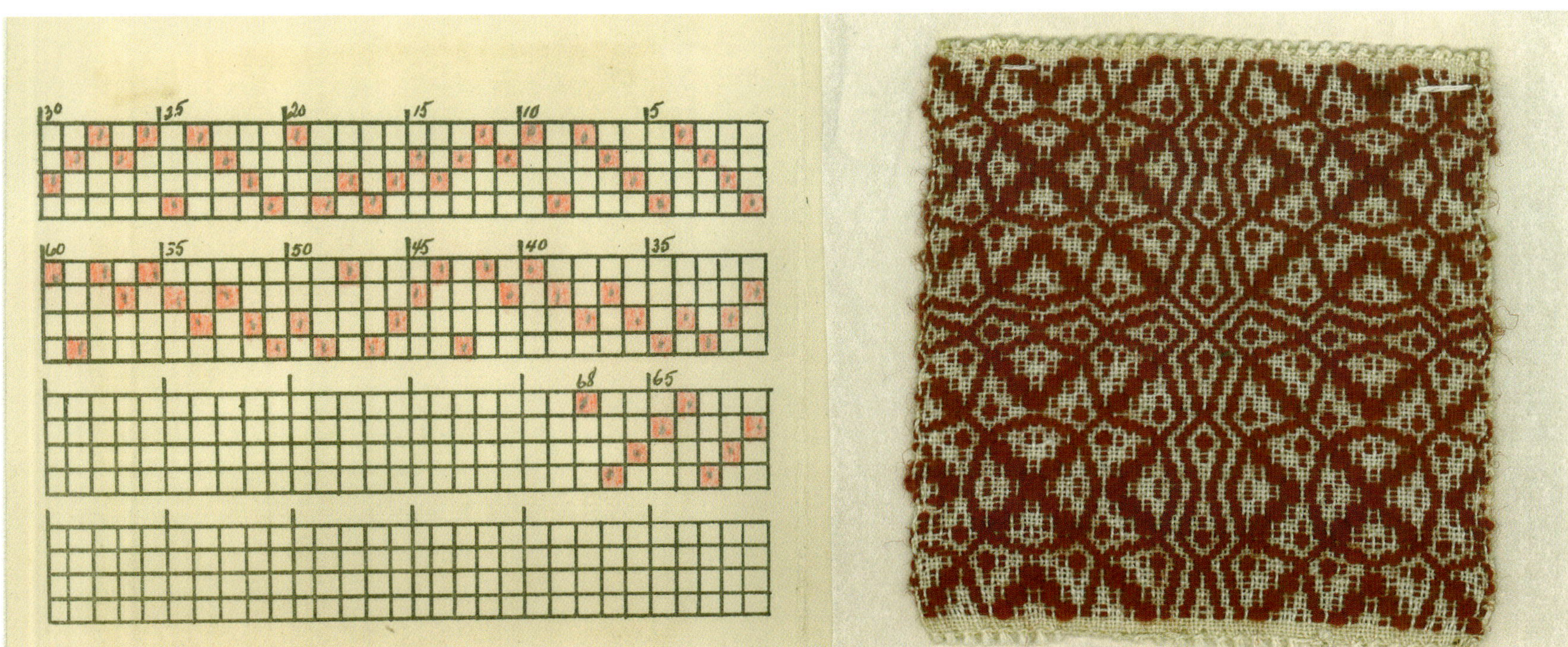
30
25
20
15
10
5
60
55
50
45
40
35
68
65

Figure 79.

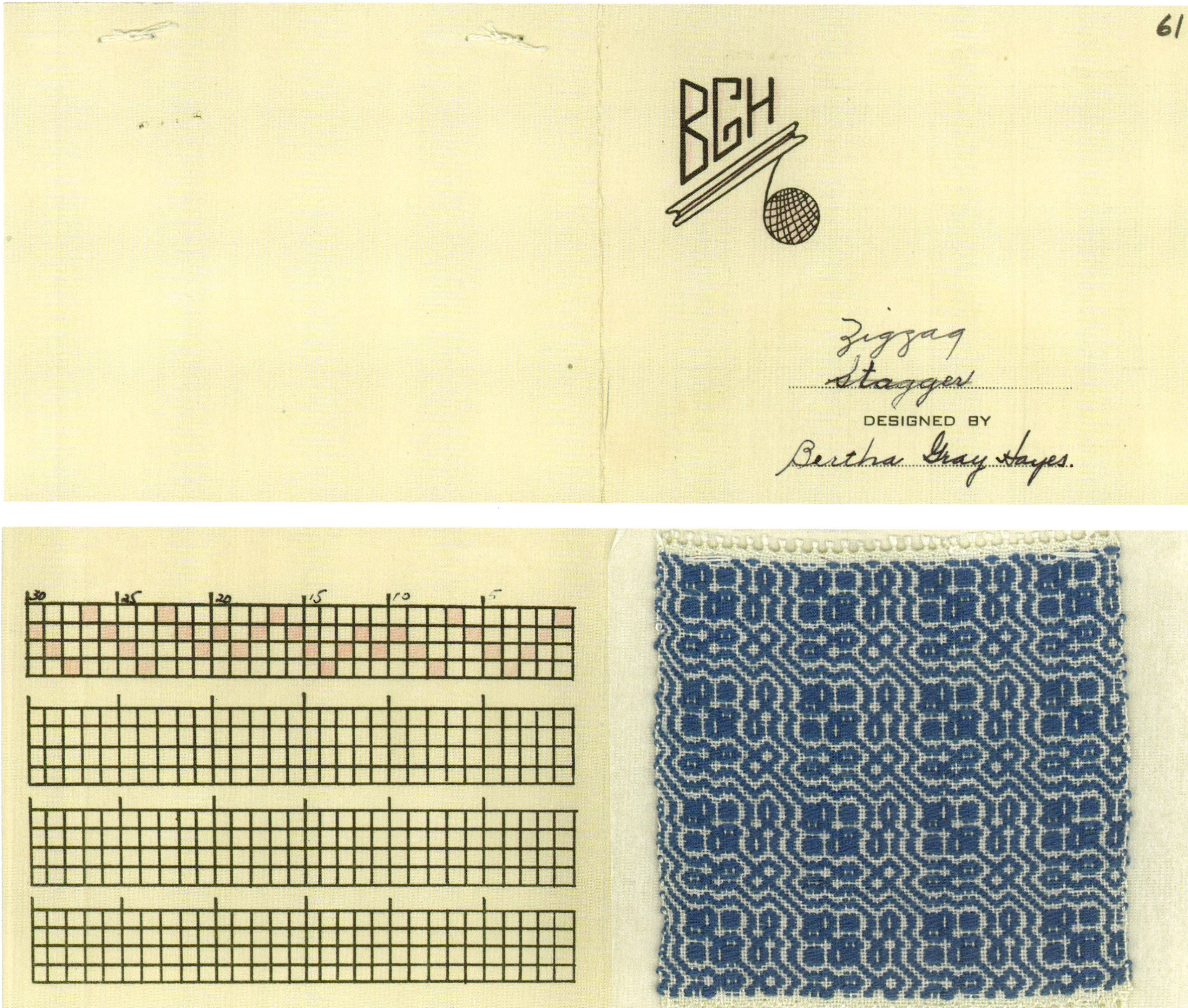
61
BGH
Zigzag
Stagger
DESIGNED BY
Bertha Gray Hayes.
30
25
20
15
10
5

Figure 80.

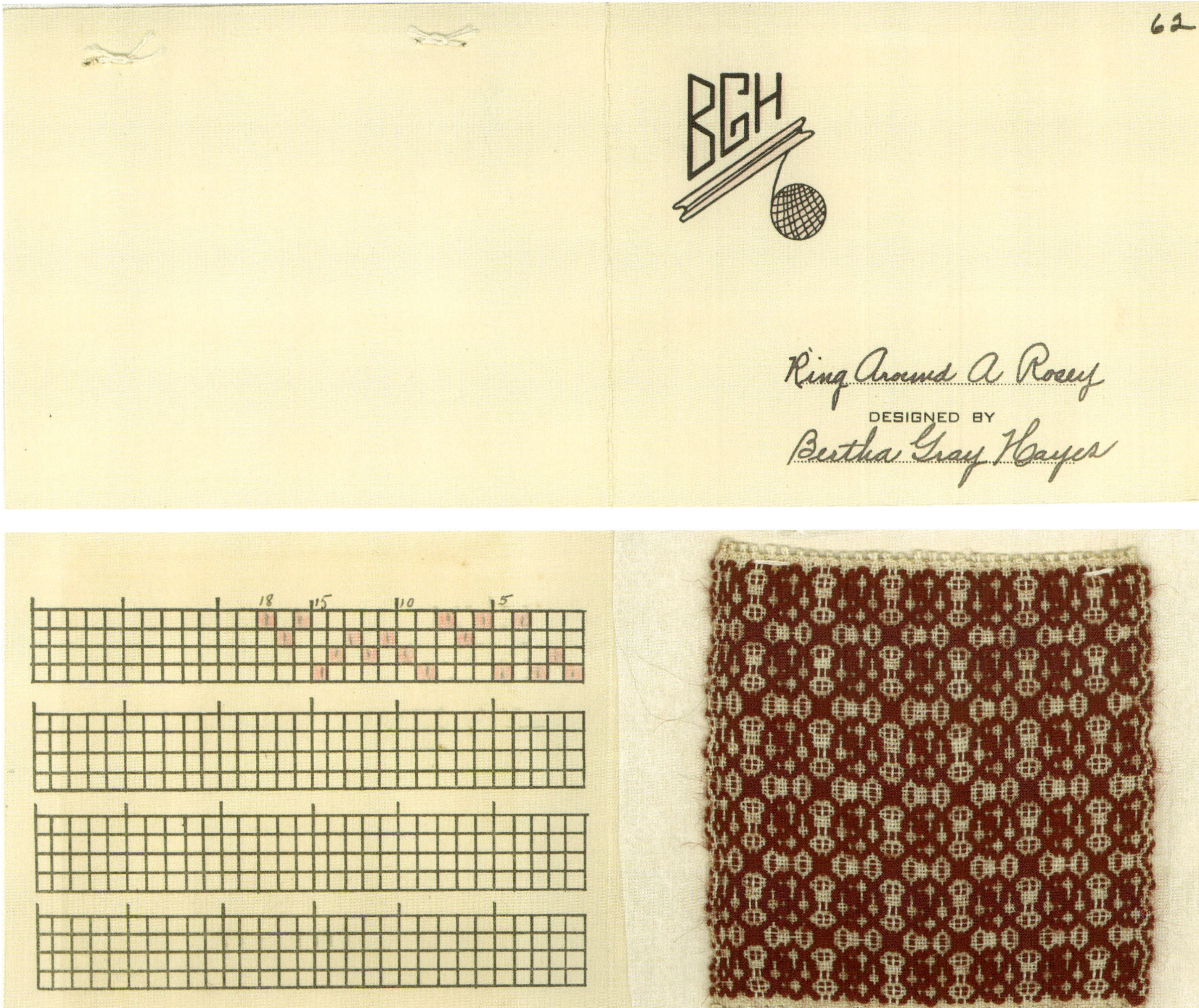
62
BGH
Ring Around A Rosey
DESIGNED BY
Bertha Gray Hayes
18
15
10
5

Figure 81.

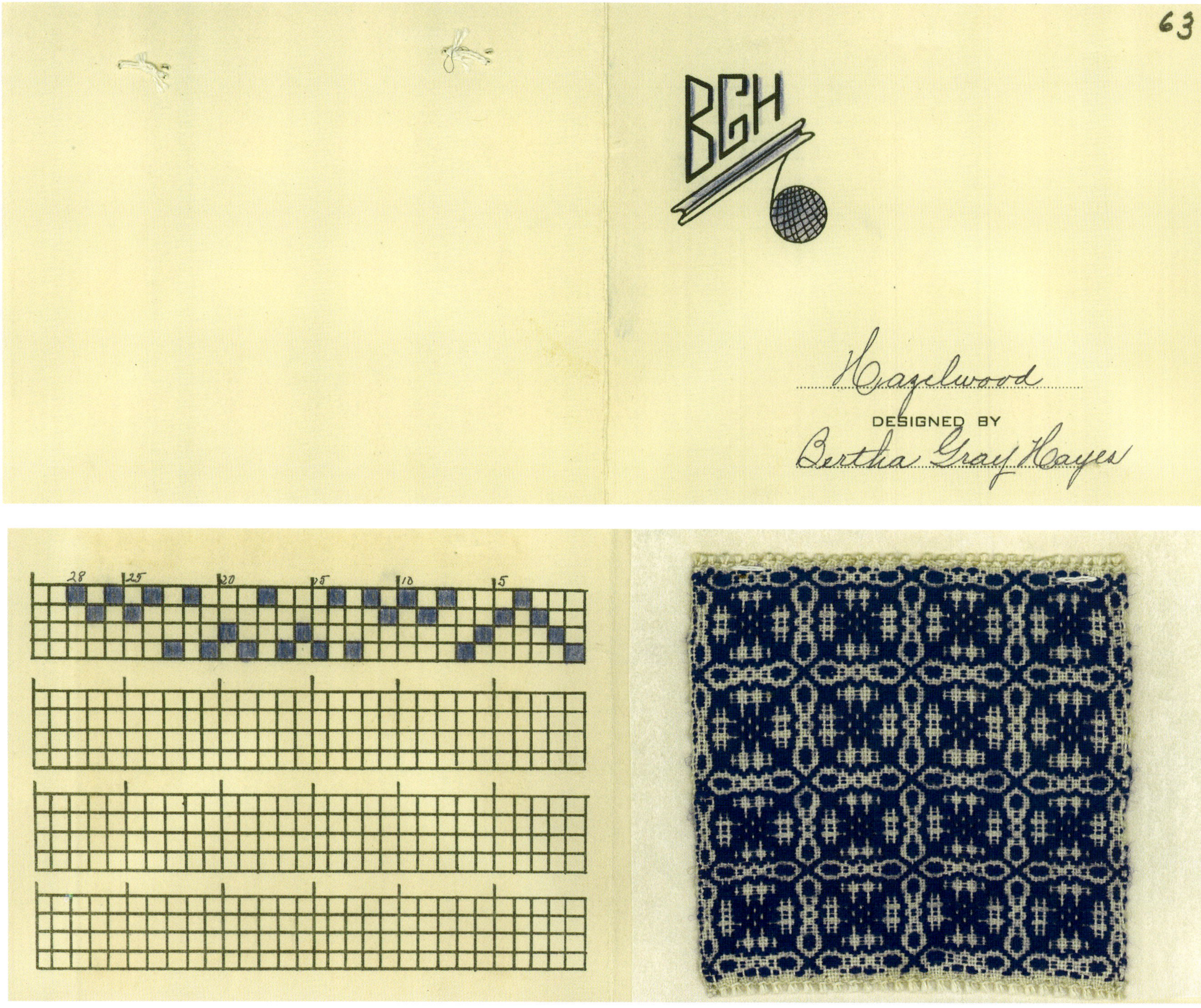
63
BGH
Hazelwood
DESIGNED BY
Bertha Gray Hayes
28
25
20
15
10
5

Figure 82.

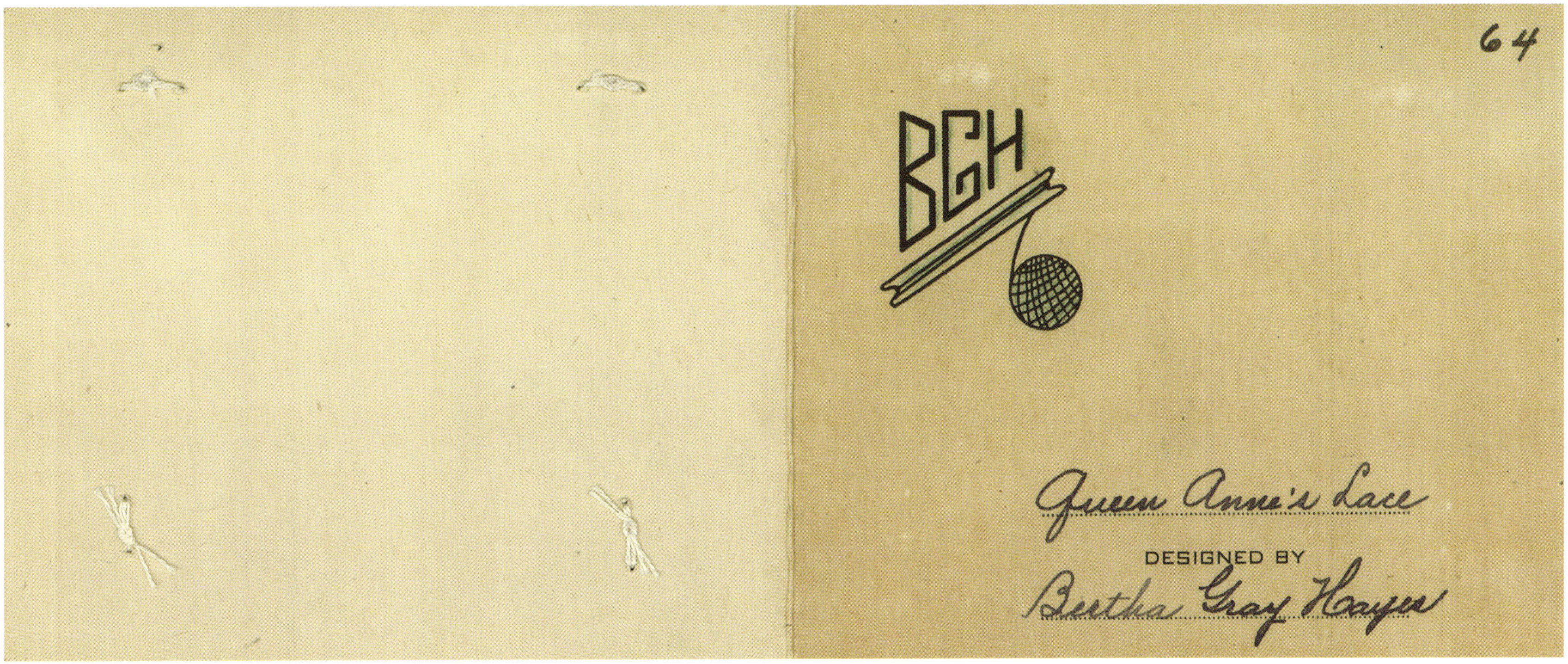

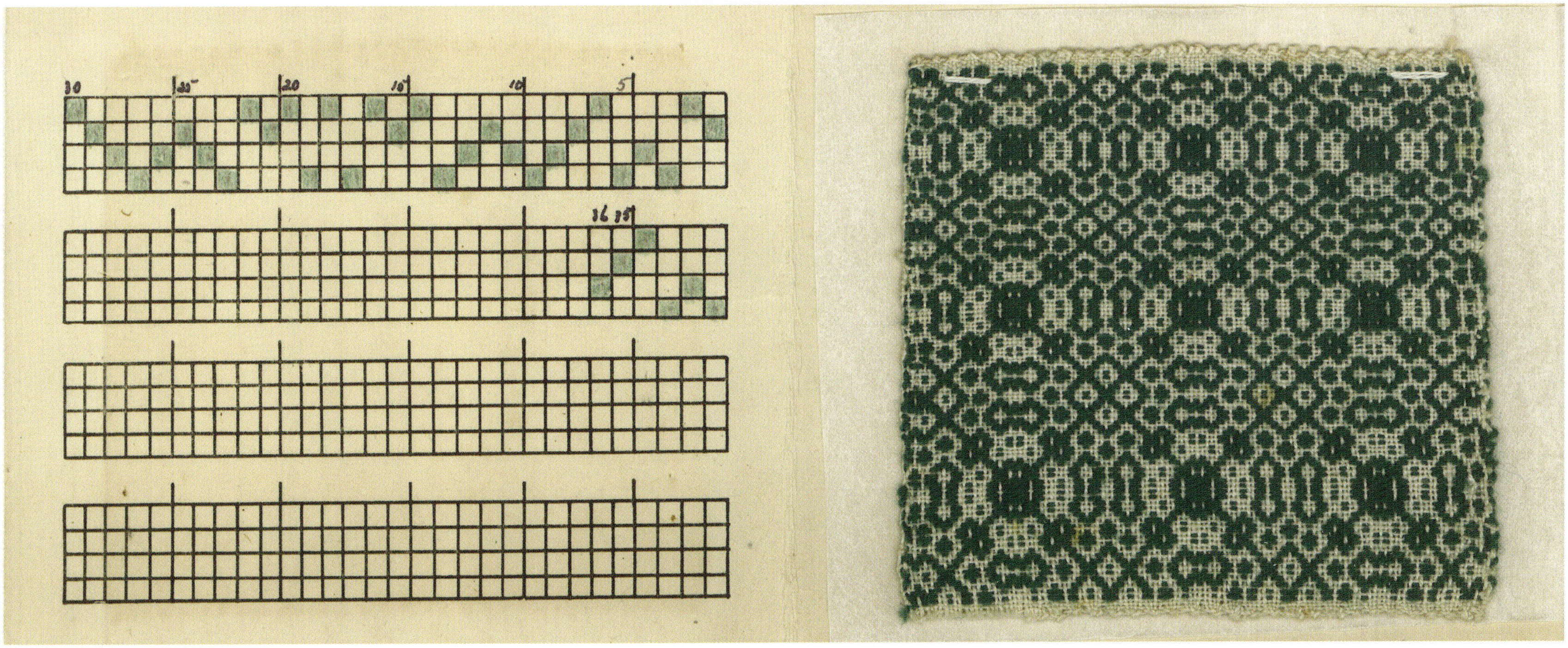

Figure 83.

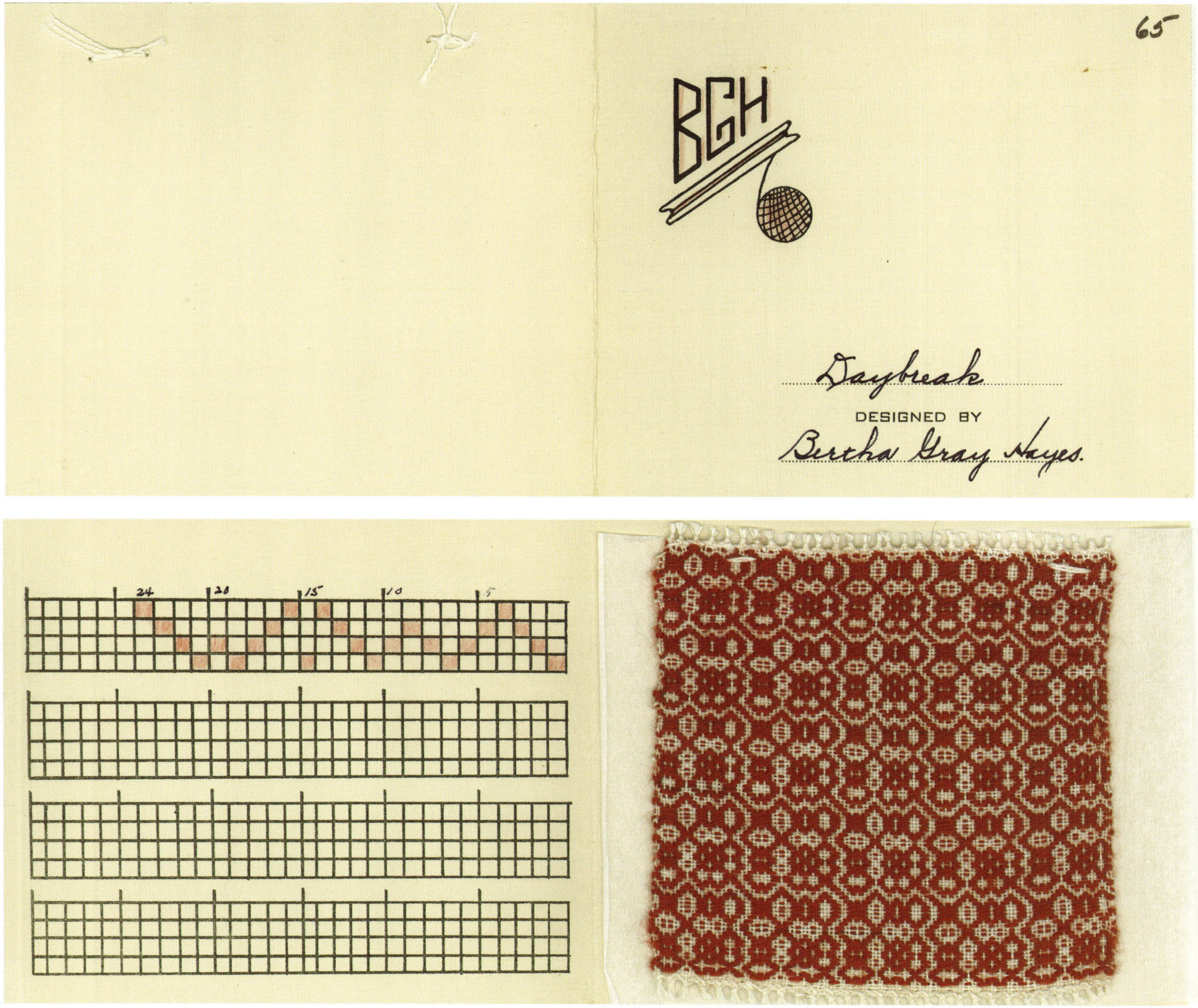

Figure 84.

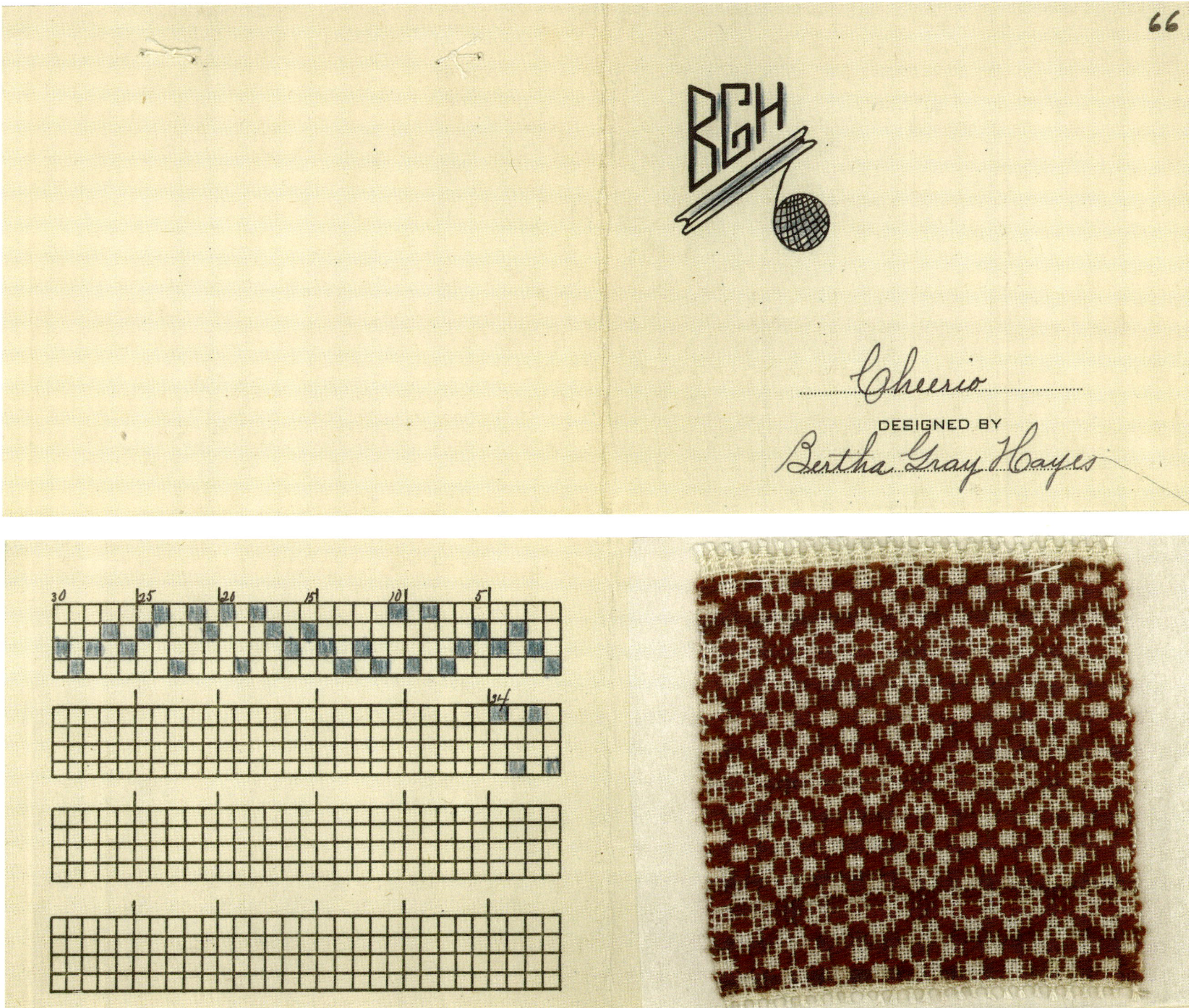
66
BGH
Cheerio
DESIGNED BY
Bertha Gray Hayes
30
25
20
15
10
5
34

Figure 85.

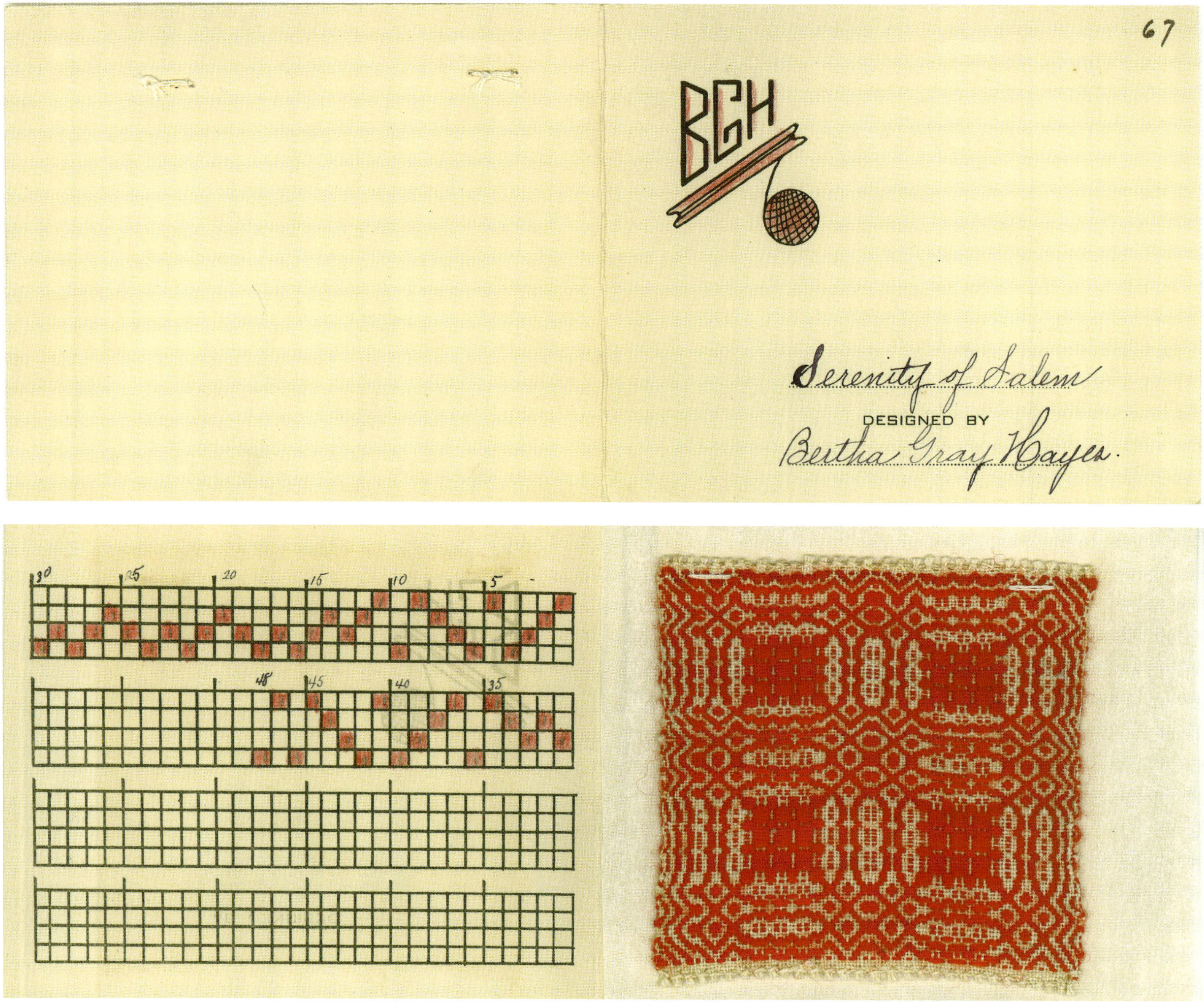
67
BGH
Serenity of Salem
DESIGNED BY
Bertha Gray Hayes.
30
25
20
15
10
5
48
45
40
35

Figure 86.

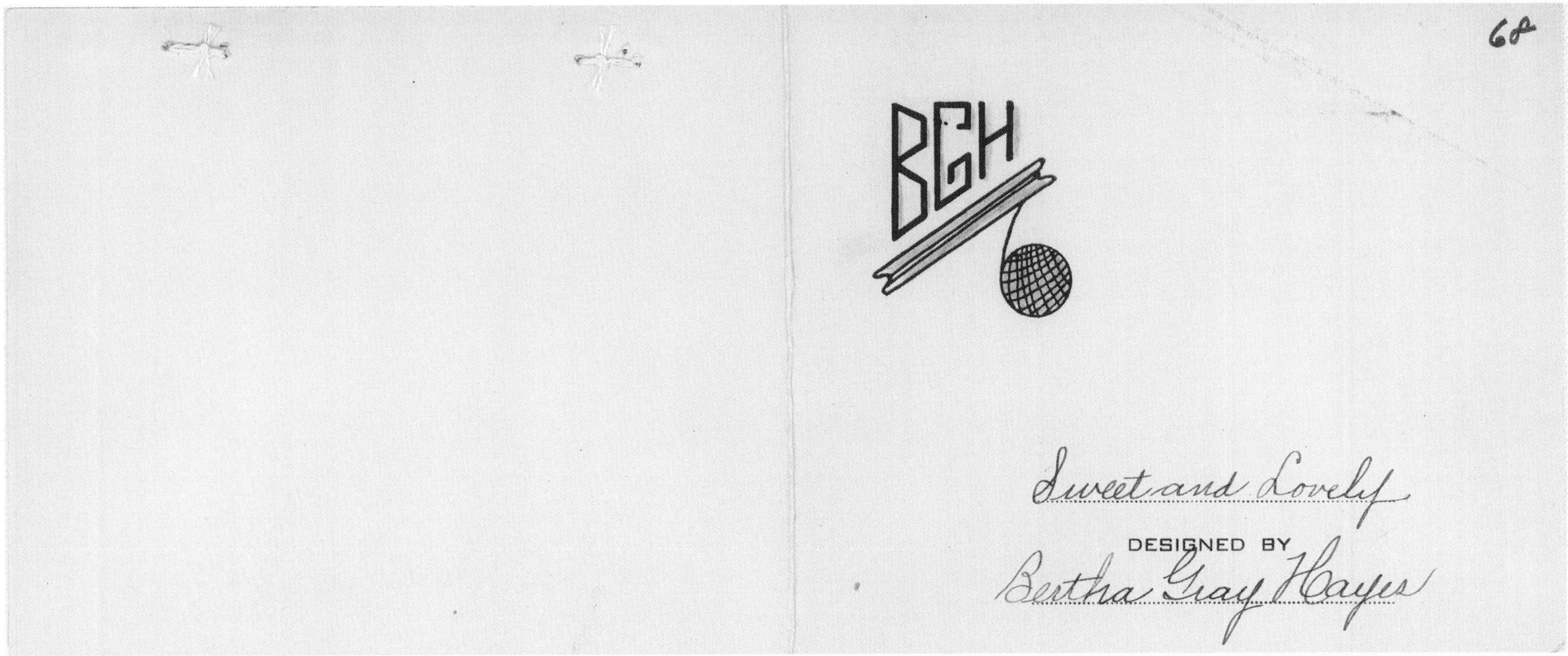
68
BGH
Sweet and Lovely
DESIGNED BY
Bertha Gray Hayes

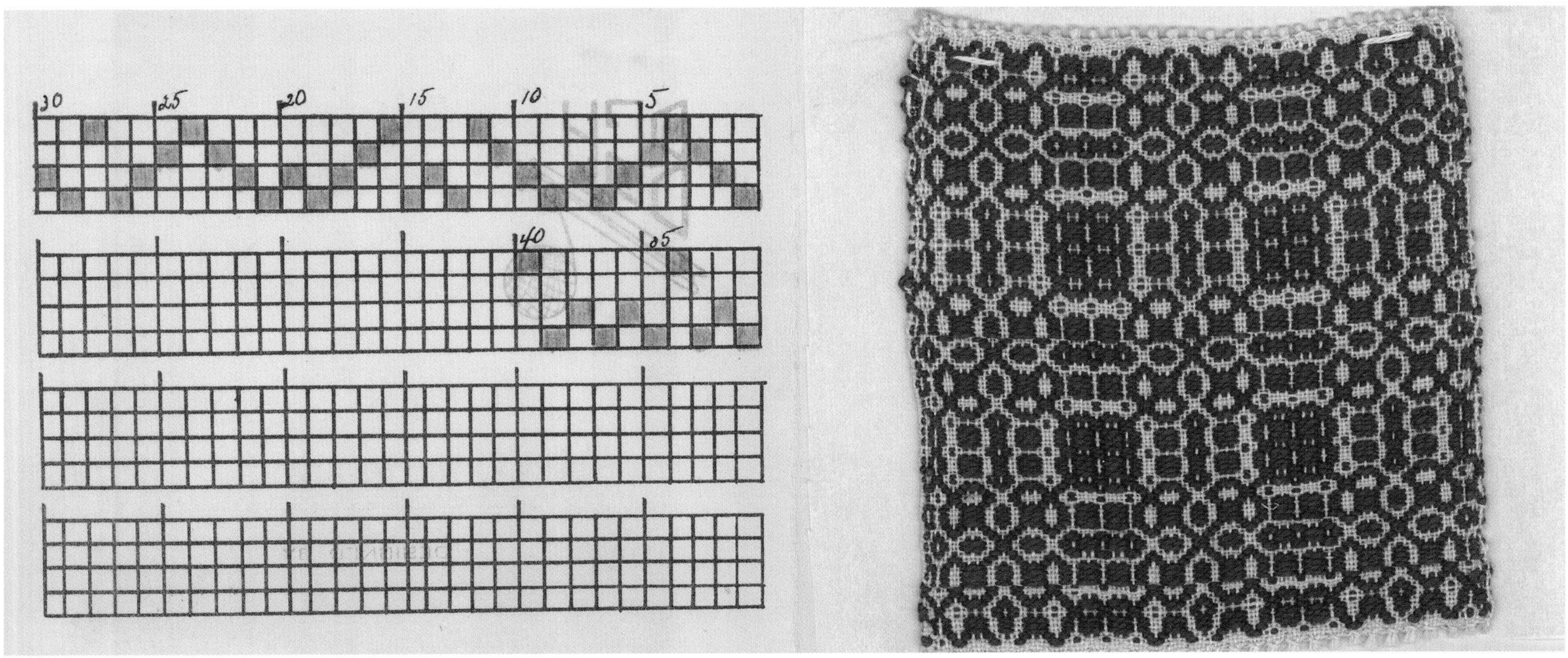
30
25
20
15
10
5
40
35

Figure 87.

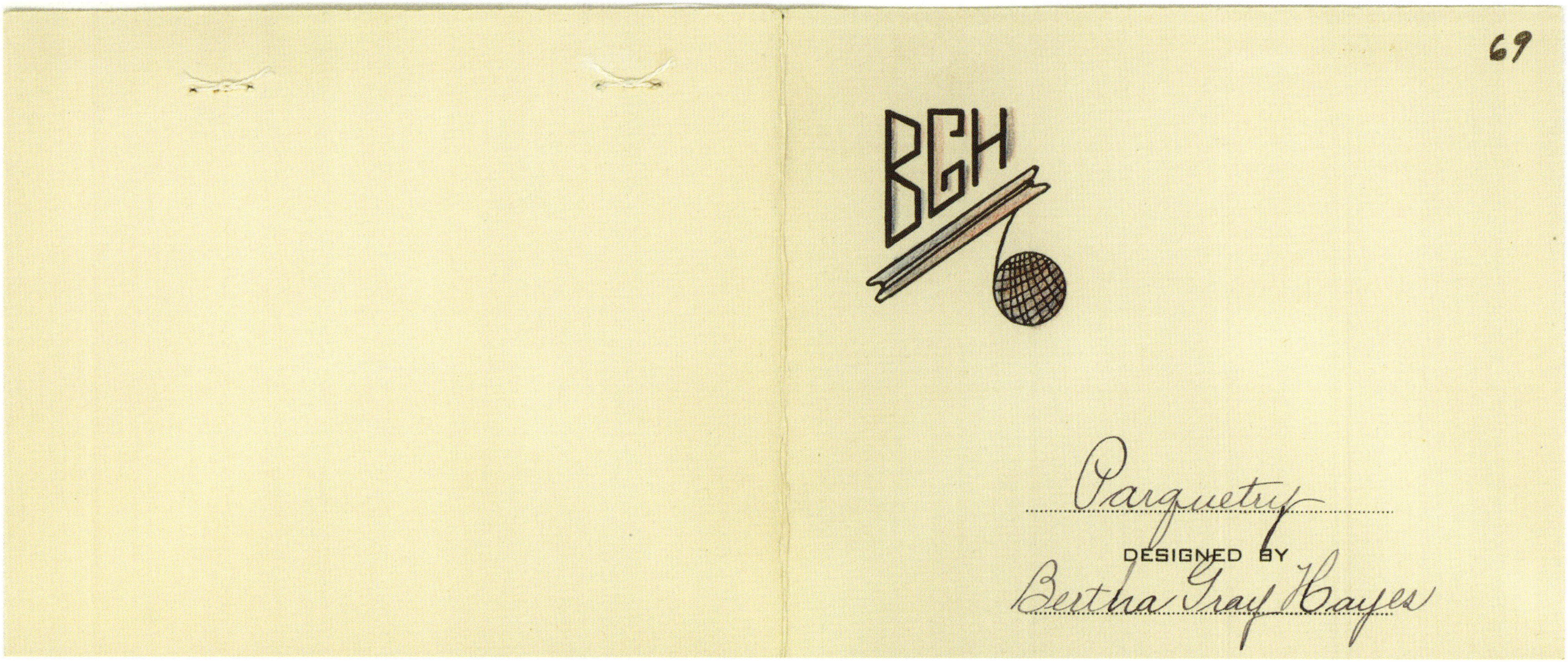

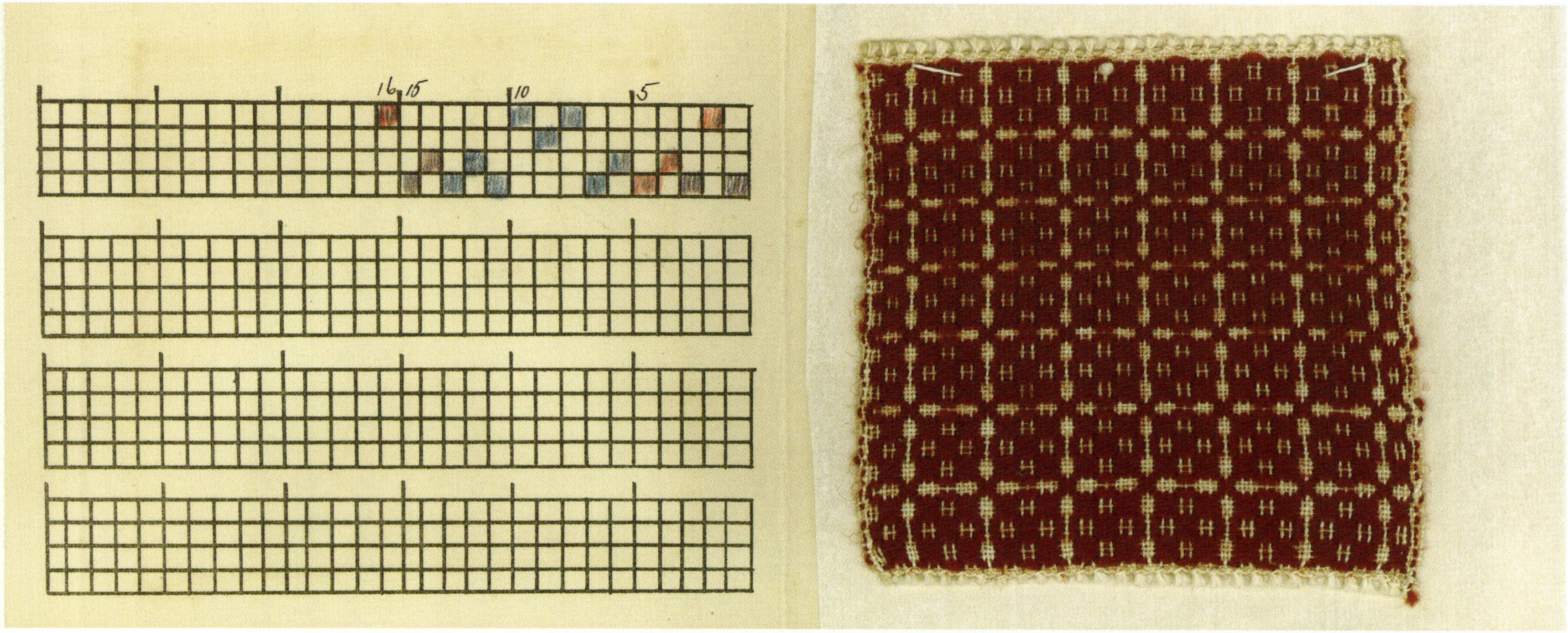

Figure 88.

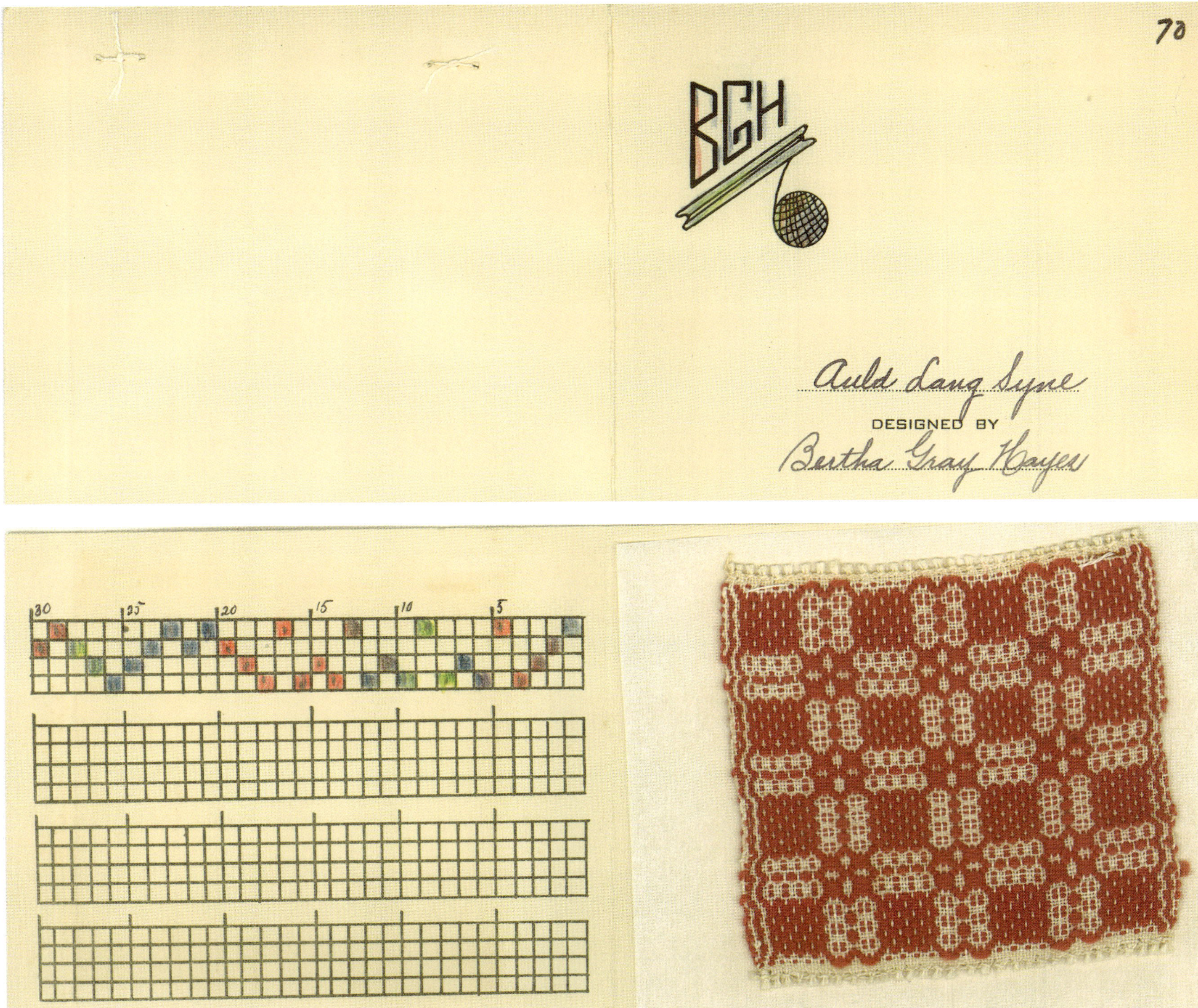
70
BGH
Auld Lang Syne
DESIGNED BY
Bertha Gray Hayes
30
25
20
15
10
5

Figure 89.

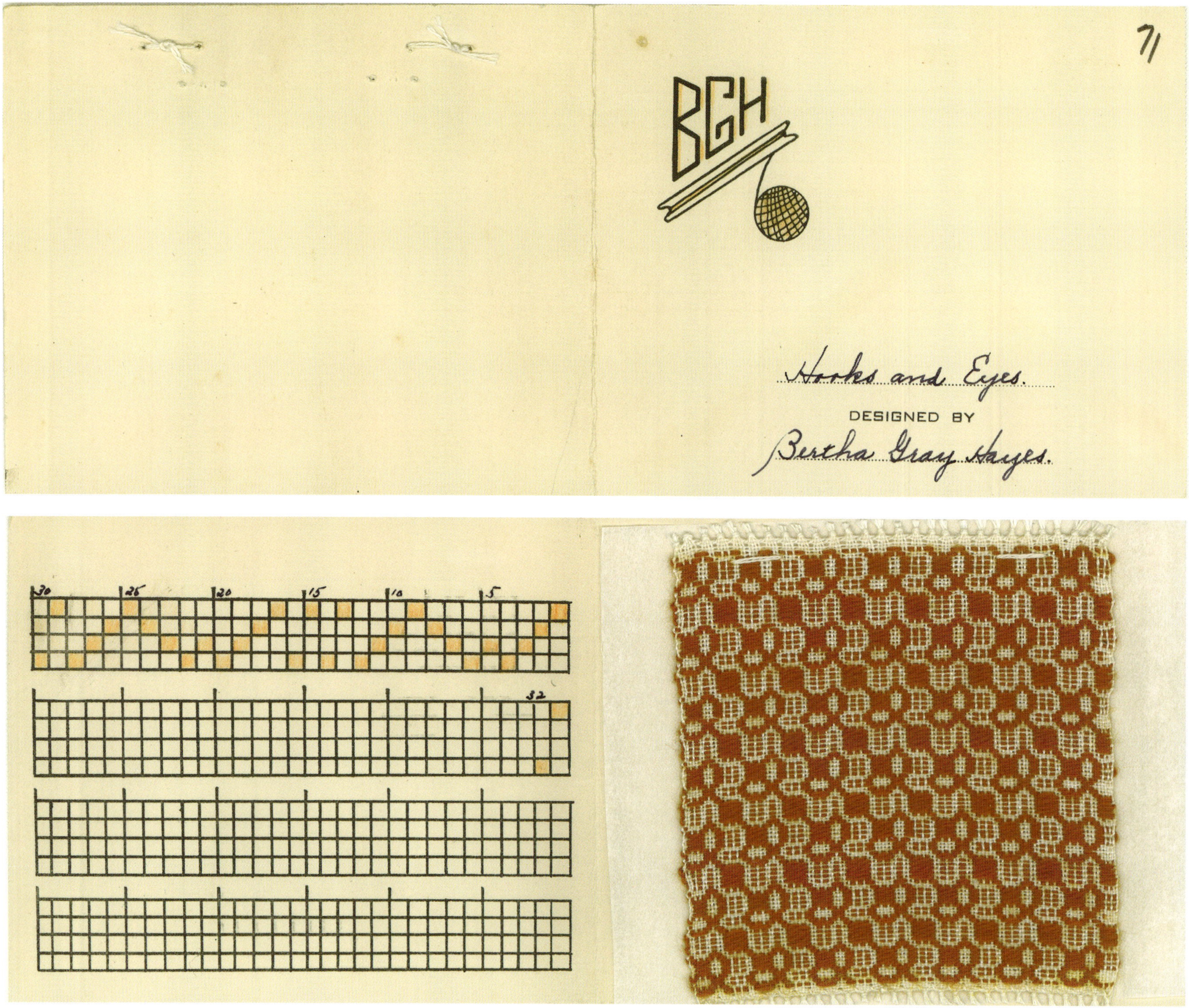
71
BGH
Hooks and Eyes.
DESIGNED BY
Bertha Gray Hayes.
30
25
20
15
10
5
32

Figure 90.

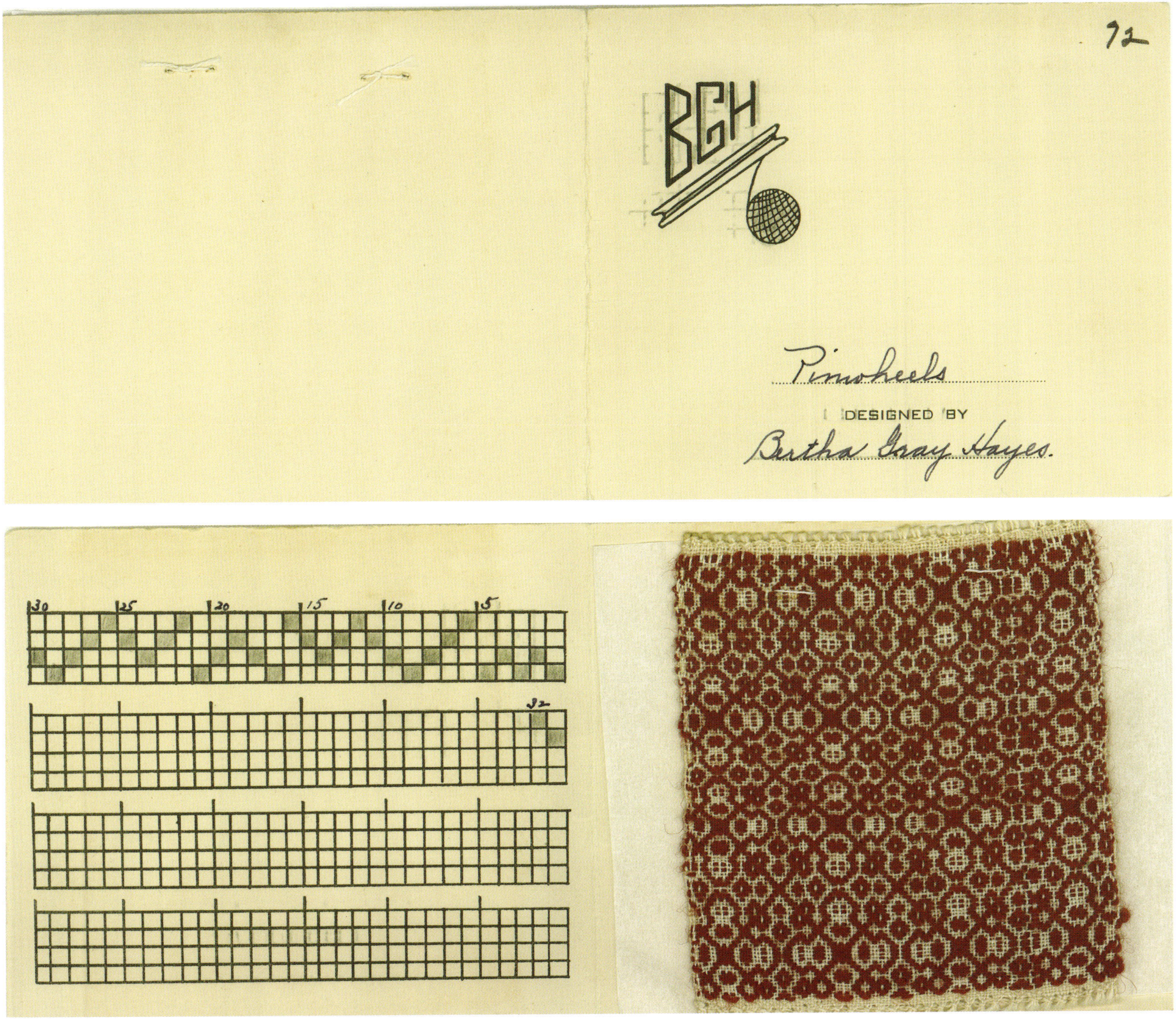
92
BGH
Pinwheels
DESIGNED BY
Bertha Gray Hayes.
30
25
20
15
10
5
32

Figure 91.

Computer-generated Drawdowns of the First 72 Designs

With the reader in mind, the drawdowns were created at a consistent 24 epi and are therefore at a slightly larger scale than Miss Hayes' woven samples (30 epi.) The tie-up is rising shed.

Figure 92. *Flower of Cromaine* **(Design 1).**

Figure 93. *Waldenweave* (Design 2).

Figure 94. *Waldenweave - enlarged* **(Design 3).**

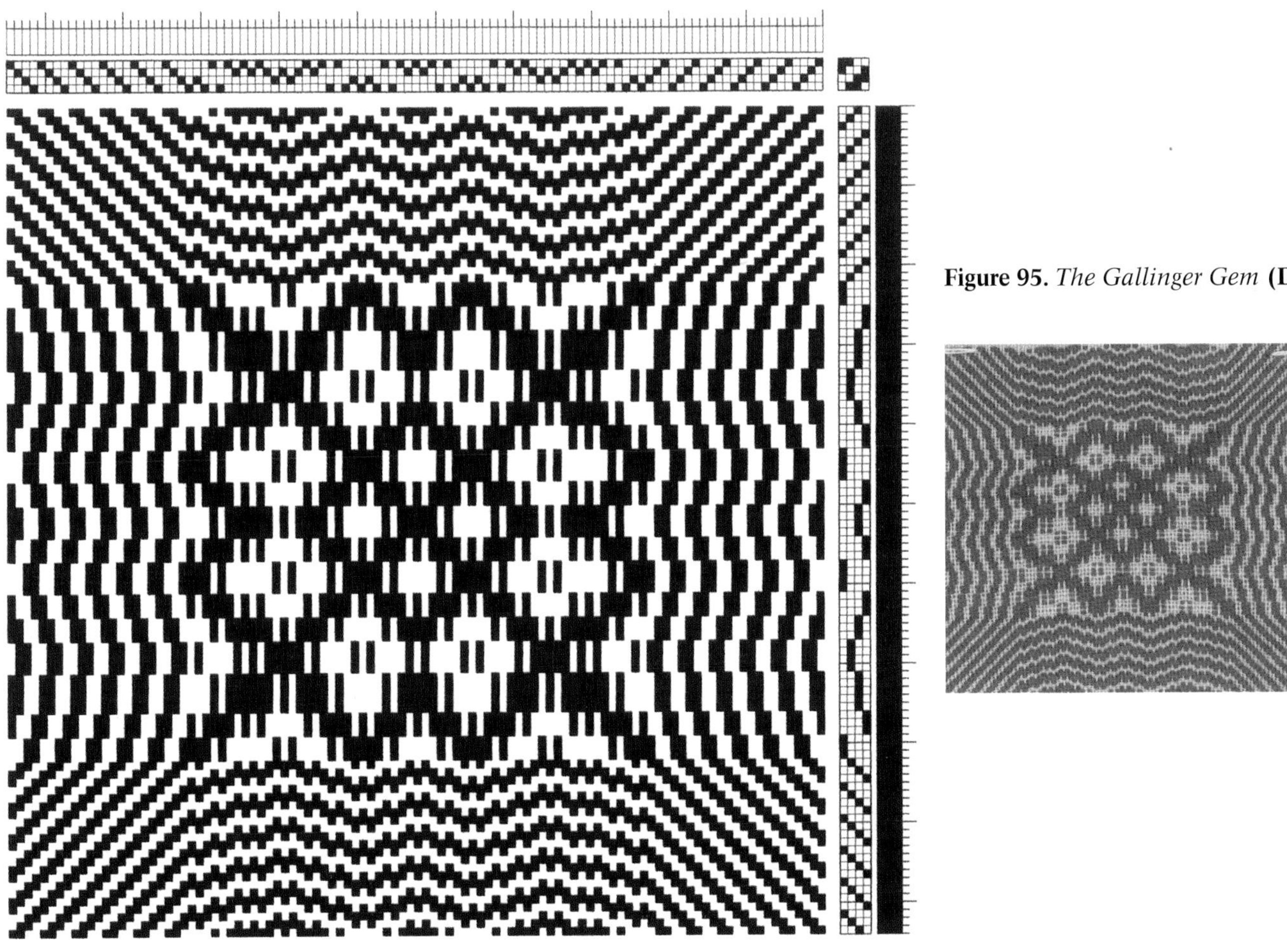

Figure 95. *The Gallinger Gem* (Design 4).

Figure 96. *The Gallinger Gem - miniature* **(Design 5).**

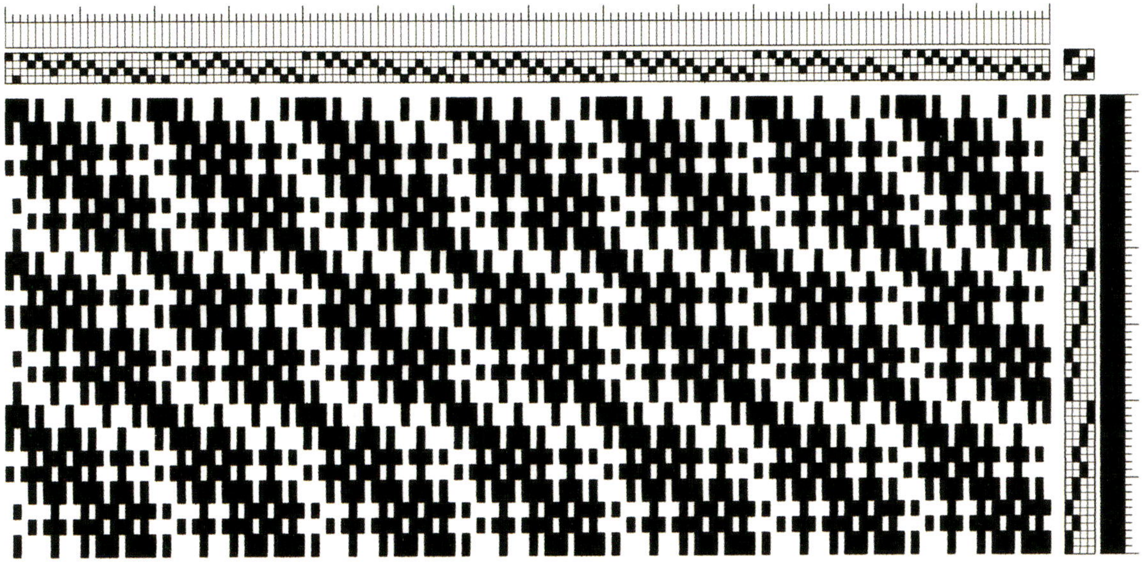

Figure 97. *Meigs Mountain* **(Design 6).** Reduced to 96%.

Figure 98*. *Remembrance* **(Design 7).** Reduced to 96%.

Figure 99. *Stars of Victory* **(Design 8).** Reduced to 88%.

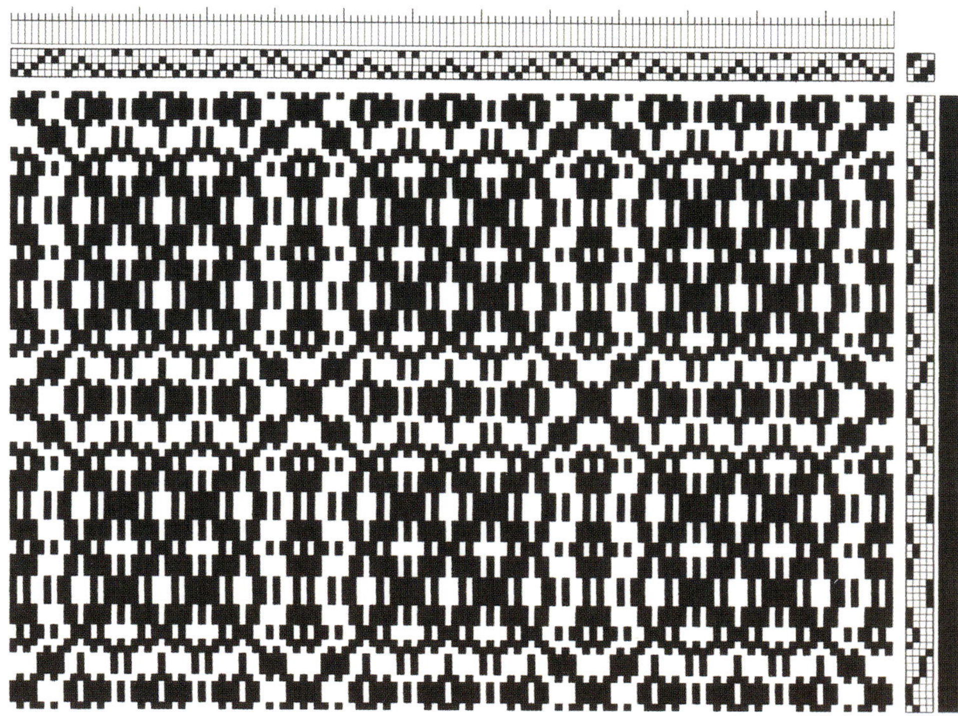

Figure 100. *The Yankee* **(Design 9).** Reduced to 88%.

Figure 101. *Hoosier Tallyho* **(Design 10).**

Figure 102. *Bagatelle* (Design 11). Reduced to 91%.

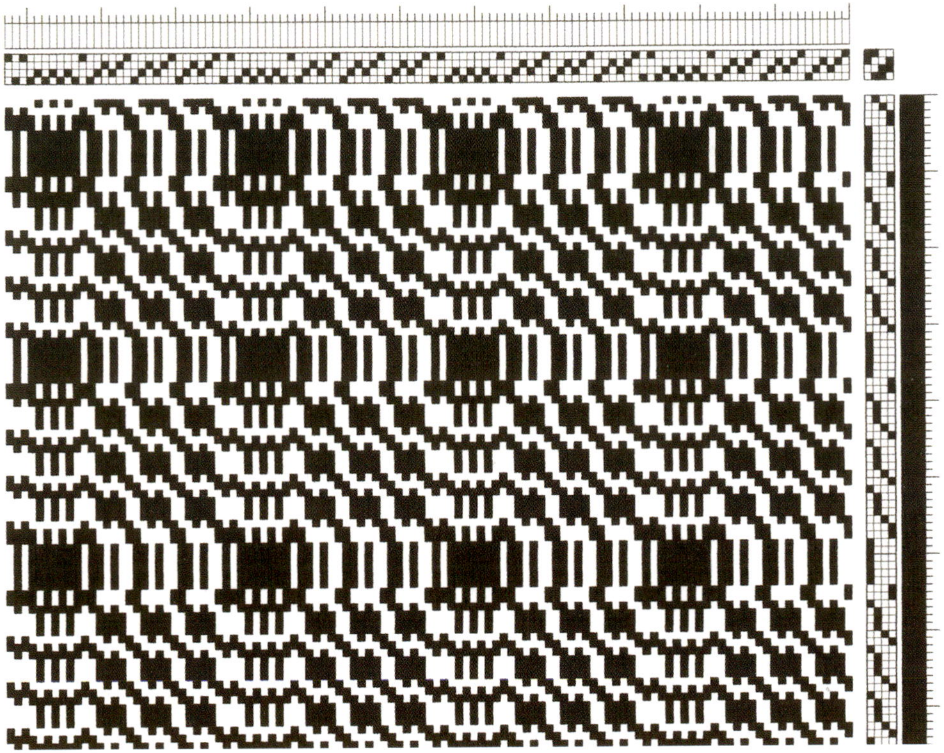

Figure 103. *Balaliaka* **(Design 12).** Reduced to 96%.

Figure 104. *Blossom* **(Design 13).** Reduced to 96%.

Figure 105. *Bomber Flight* (Design 14).

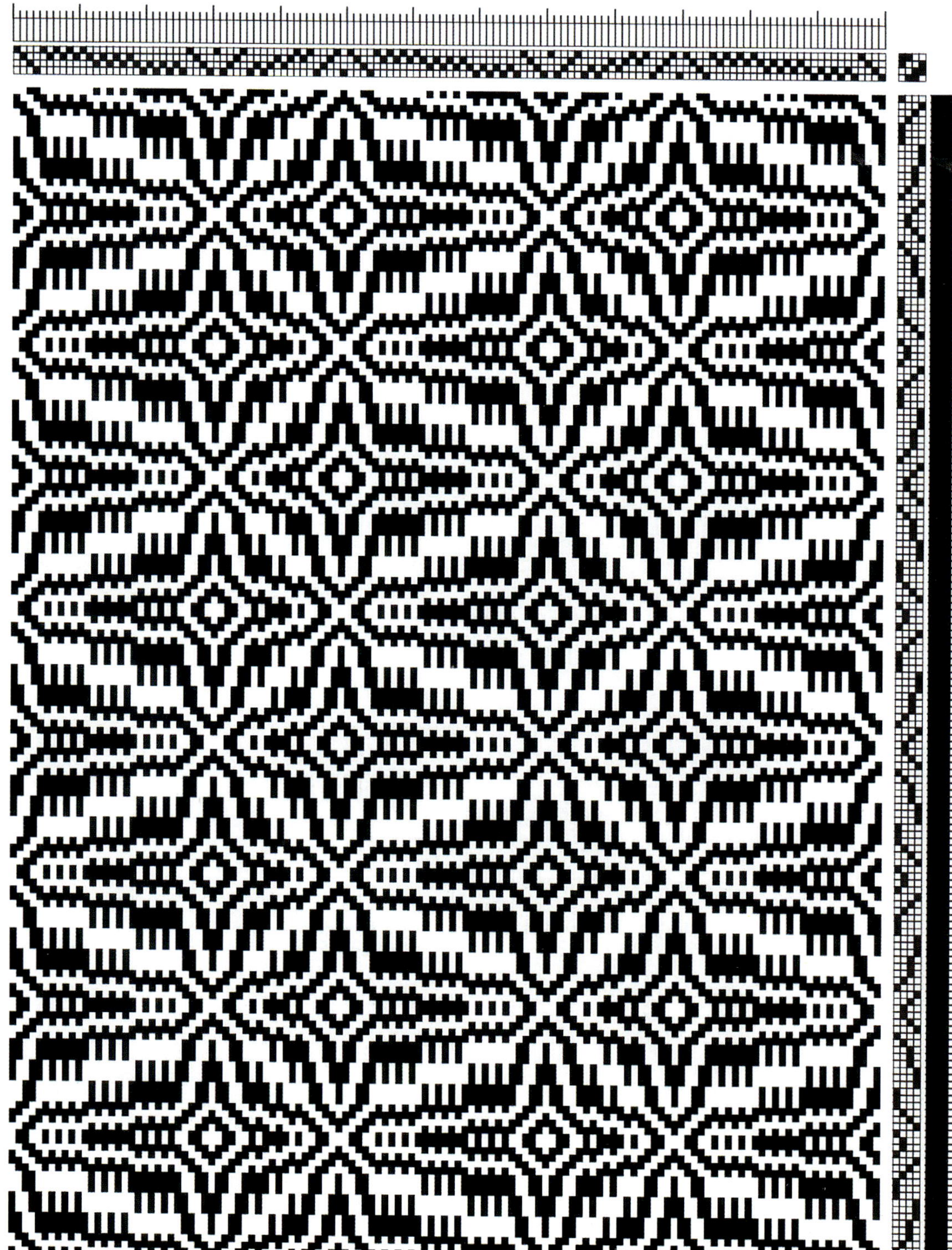

Figure 106. *Butterfly* (Design 15).

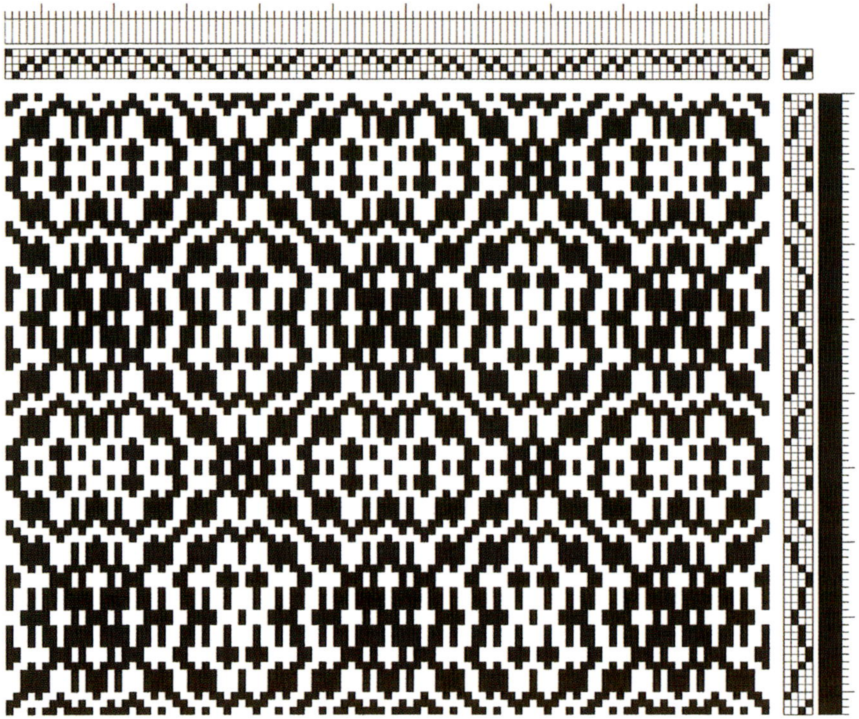

Figure 107. *Cameo* **(Design 16).** Reduced to 94%.

Figure 108. *Chintz* **(Design 17).** Reduced to 94%.

Figure 109. *Cornerstones* **(Design 18).** Reduced to 96%.

Figure 110. *Cretonne* **(Design 19).** Reduced to 96%.

Figure 111. *Delight* **(Design 20).** Reduced to 89%.

Figure 112. *Domino* **(Design 21).** Reduced to 89%.

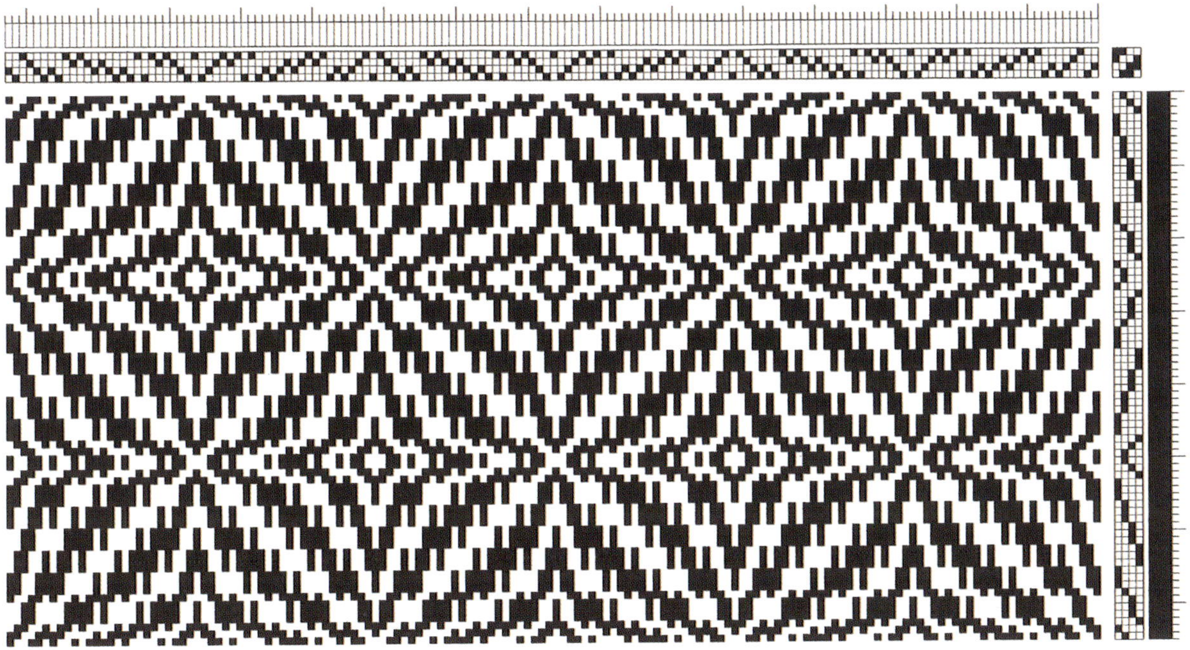

Figure 113. *Estrellita* **(Design 22).** Reduced to 92%.

Figure 114. *Fantasia* **(Design 23).** Reduced to 92%.

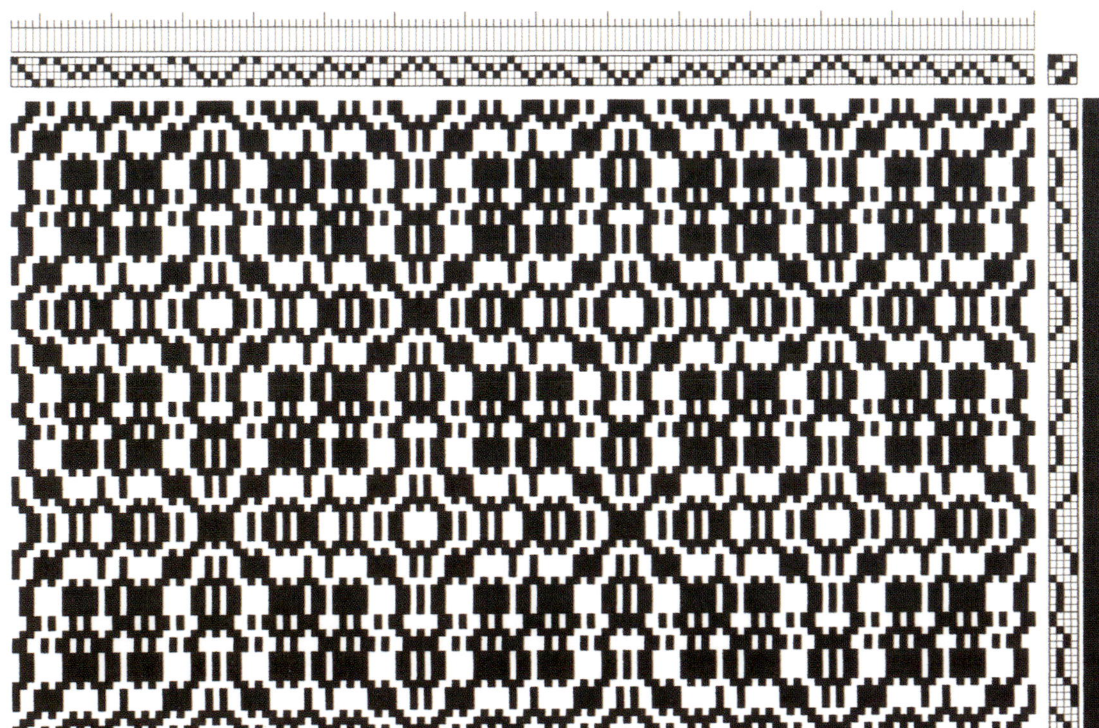

Figure 115. *Fascination* **(Design 24).**

Figure 116. *Ferns and Flowers* (Design 25).

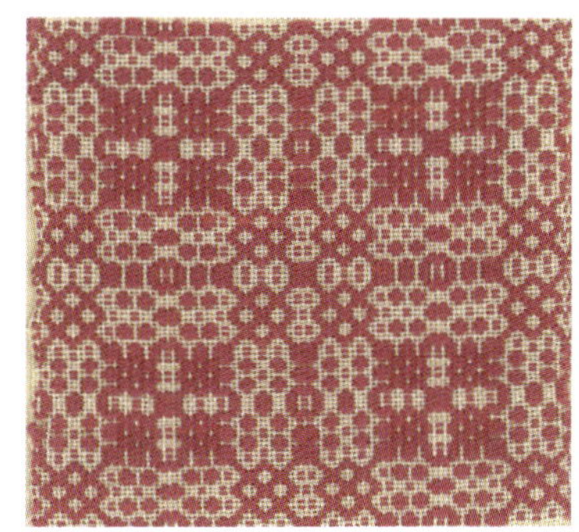

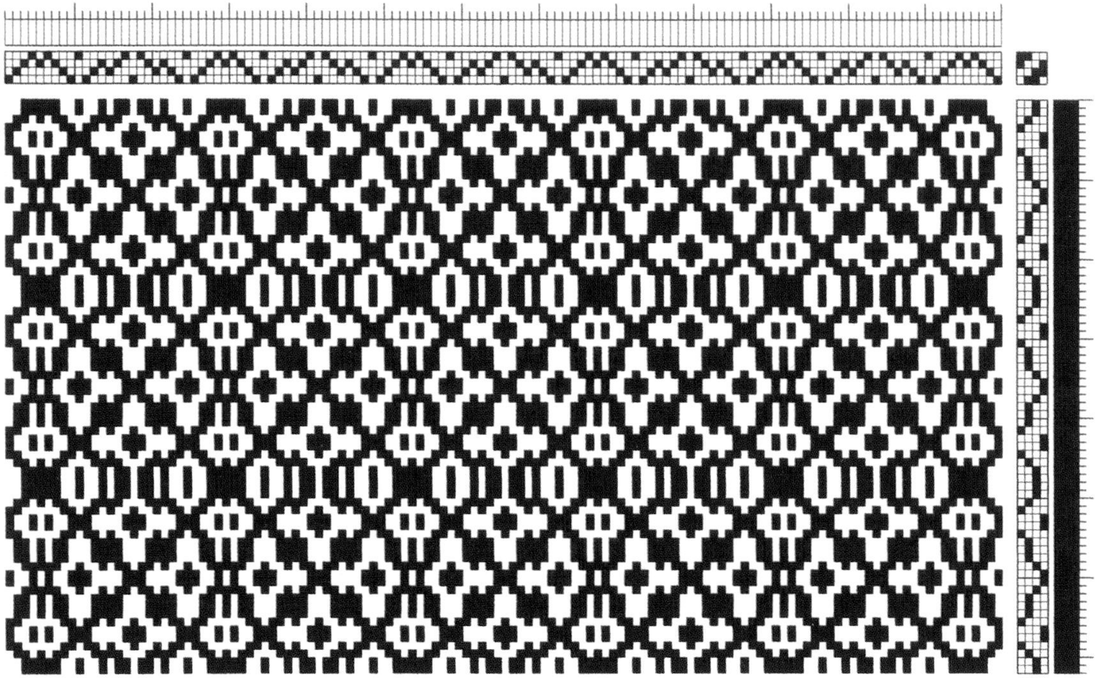

Figure 117. *Filigree* (Design 26).

Figure 118. *Flagstones* (Design 27).

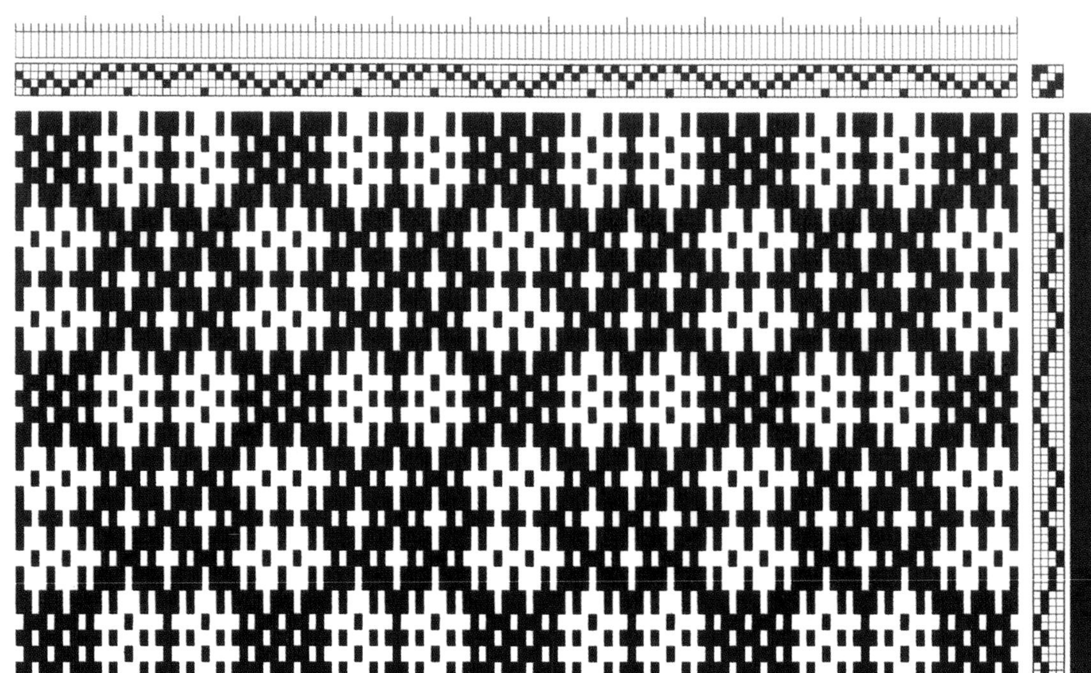

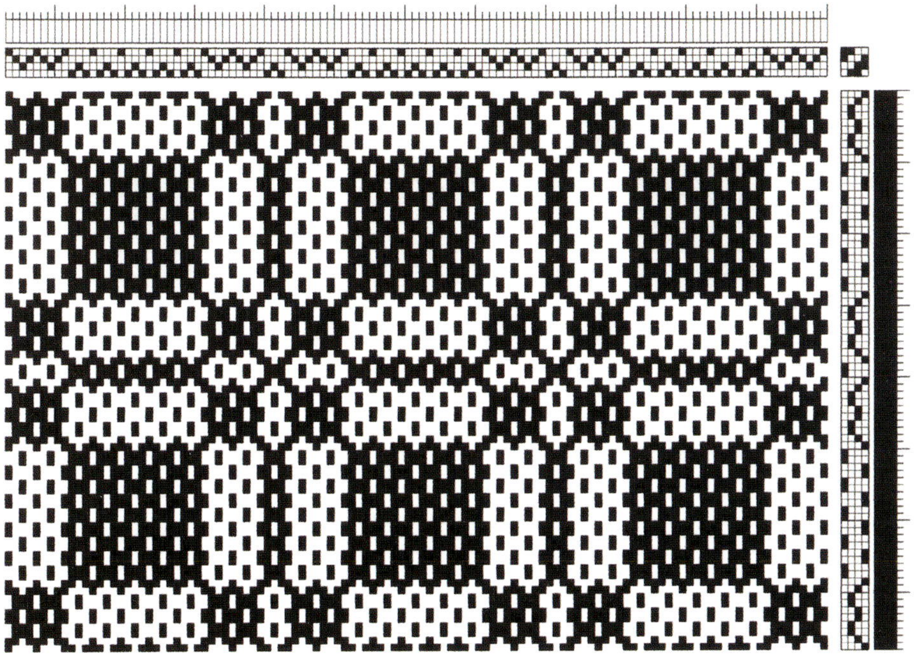

Figure 119. *Foursquare* **(Design 28).** Reduced to 90%.

Figure 120. *Gone with the Wind* **(Design 29).** Reduced to 90%.

Figure 121. *Honiton* **(Design 30).** Reduced to 95%.

Figure 122. *Jitterbug* **(Design 31).** Reduced to 85%.

Figure 123. *Lambeth Walk* **(Design 32).**

Figure 124. *Labyrinth* (Design 33).

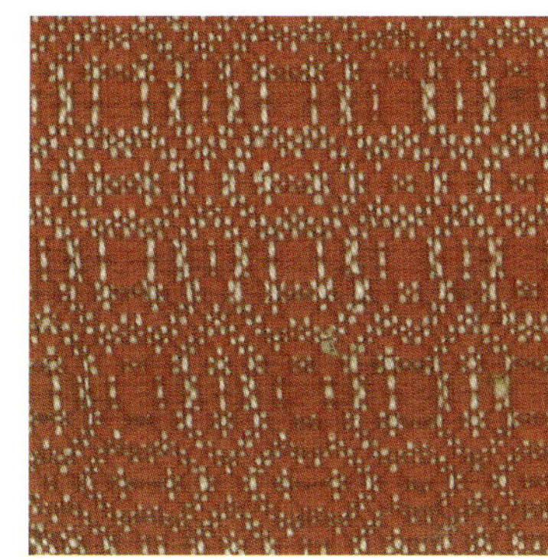

Figure 125. *Linoleum* (Design 34).

Figure 126. *Mosaic* **(Design 35).** Reduced to 98%.

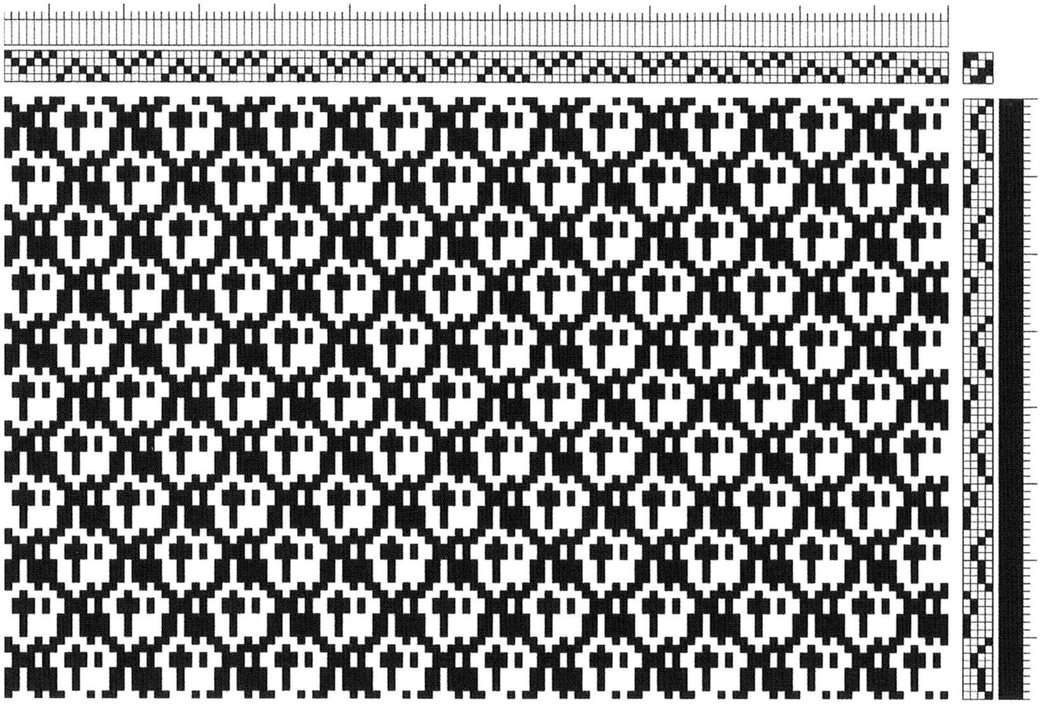

Figure 127. *Needlepoint* **(Design 36).** Reduced to 97%.

Figure 128. *The Olive* **(Design 37).** Reduced to 97%.

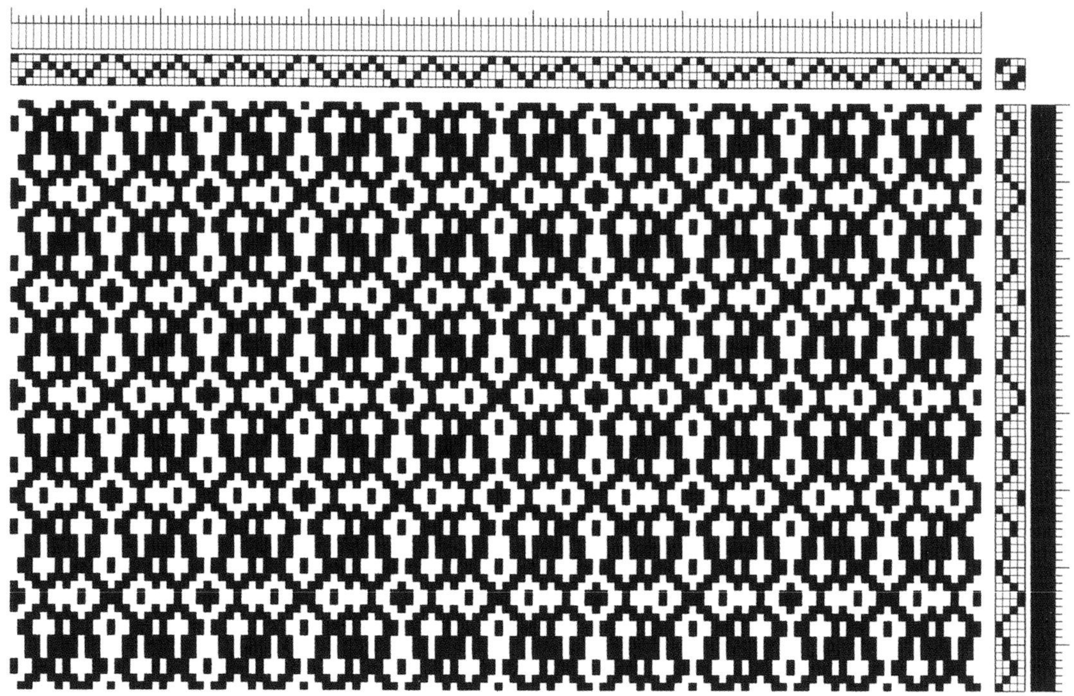

Figure 129. *Parachute* **(Design 38).** Reduced to 87%.

Figure 130. *Peace-1945* **(Design 39).**

Figure 131. *Peggy's Choice* (Design 40).

Figure 132. *Petite* **(Design 41).**

Figure 133. *Plaza* **(Design 42).** Reduced to 97%.

Figure 134. *Posey Patch* **(Design 43).** Reduced to 86%.

Figure 135. *Primrose* **(Design 44).** Reduced to 86%.

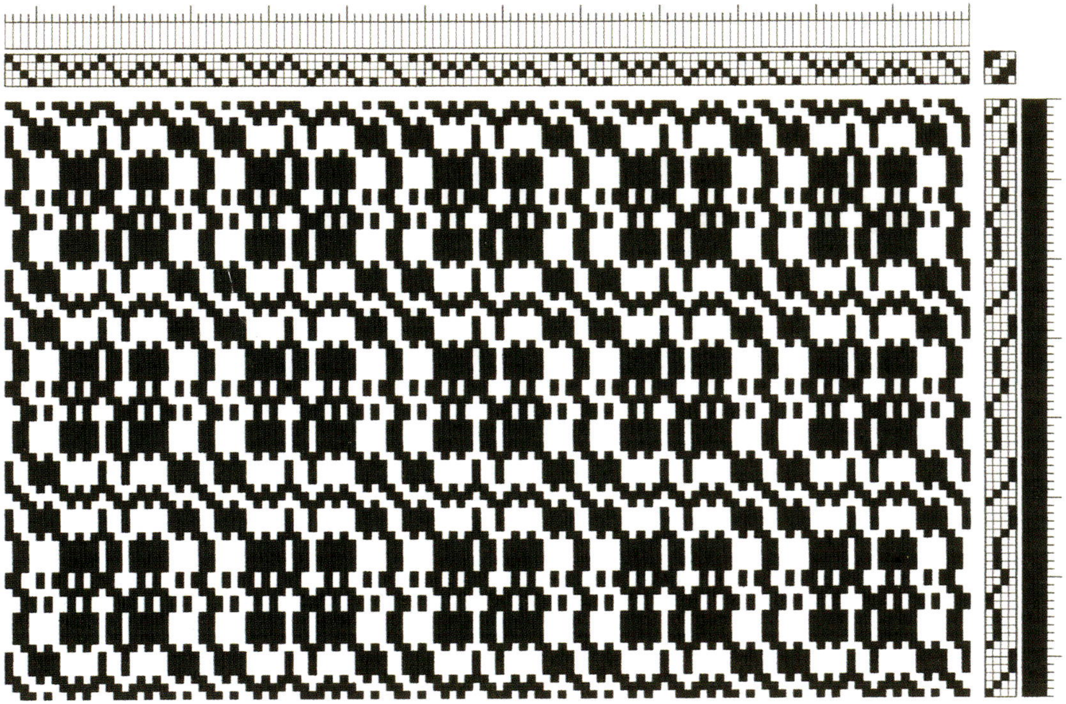

Figure 136. *Rose O'Day* (Design 45).

Figure 137. *Springtime Fancy* (Design 46).

Figure 138. *Stagger* (Design 47).

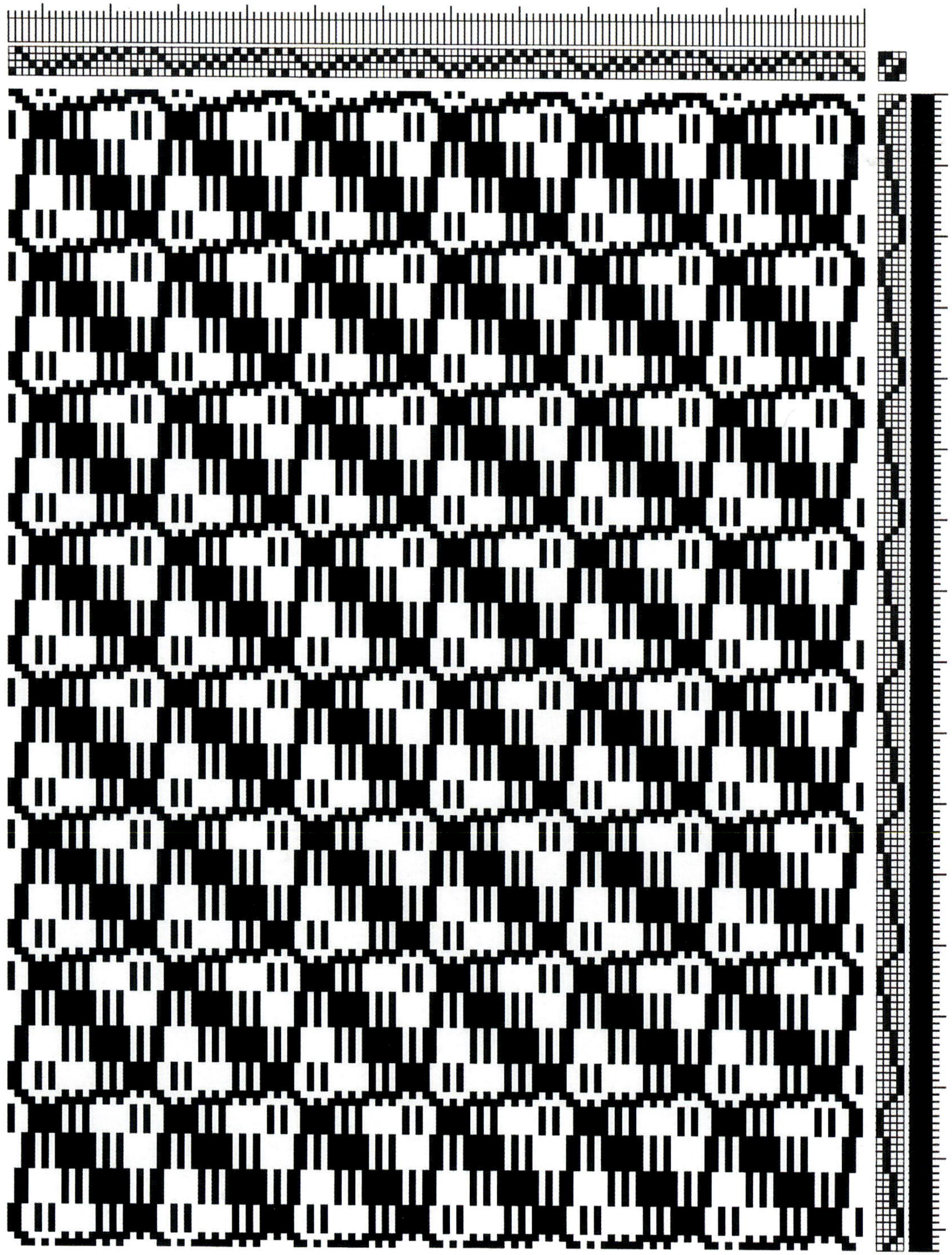

Figure 139. *Stormy Weather* (Design 48).

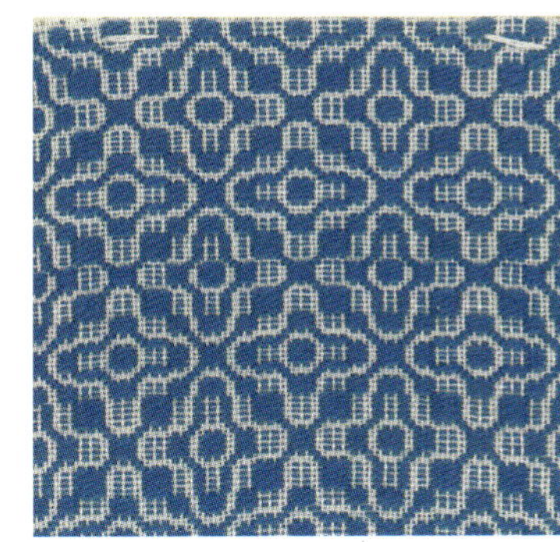

Figure 140. *Superhighway* **(Design 49).** Reduced to 94%.

Figure 141. *Tangerine* **(Design 50).**

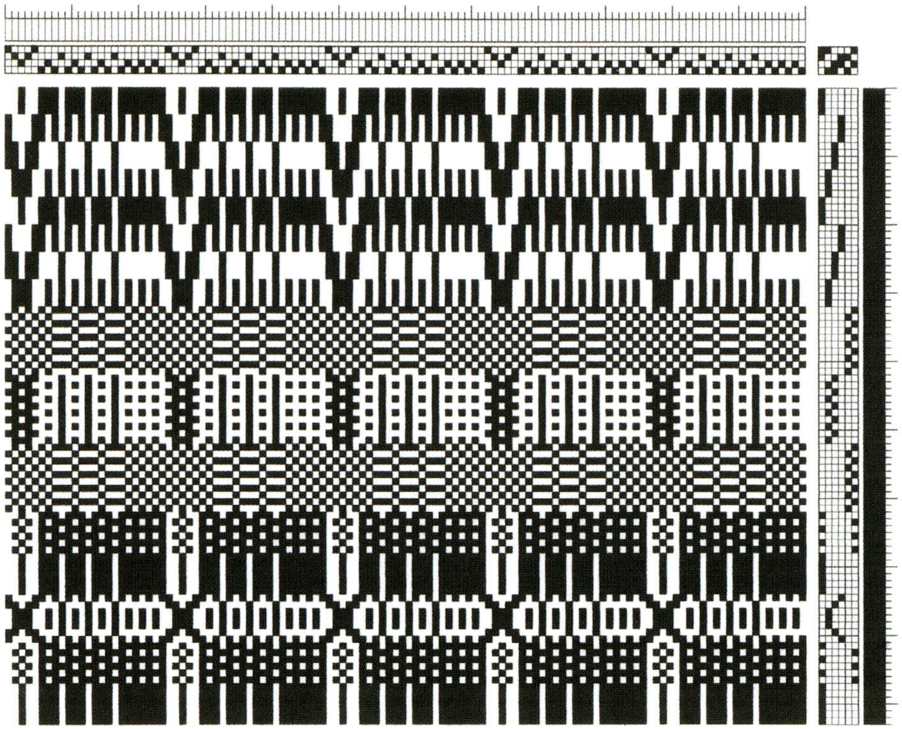

Figure 142. *Theme Song* **(Design 51).** Reduced to 86%.

Figure 143. *This and That* **(Design 52).** Reduced to 86%.

Figure 144. *Three Times Three* **(Design 53).**

Figure 145. *Treasure Island* **(Design 54).** Reduced to 87%.

Figure 146. *Trellis* **(Design 55).** Reduced to 87%.

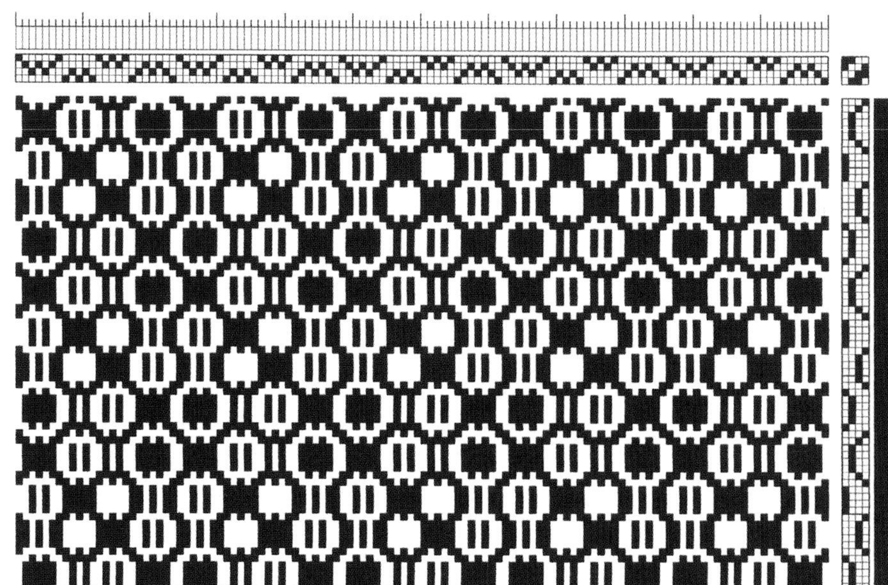

Figure 147. *Turntable* (Design 56).

Figure 148. *Victory* (Design 57).

Figure 149. *Wibraska* **(Design 58).** Reduced to 94%.

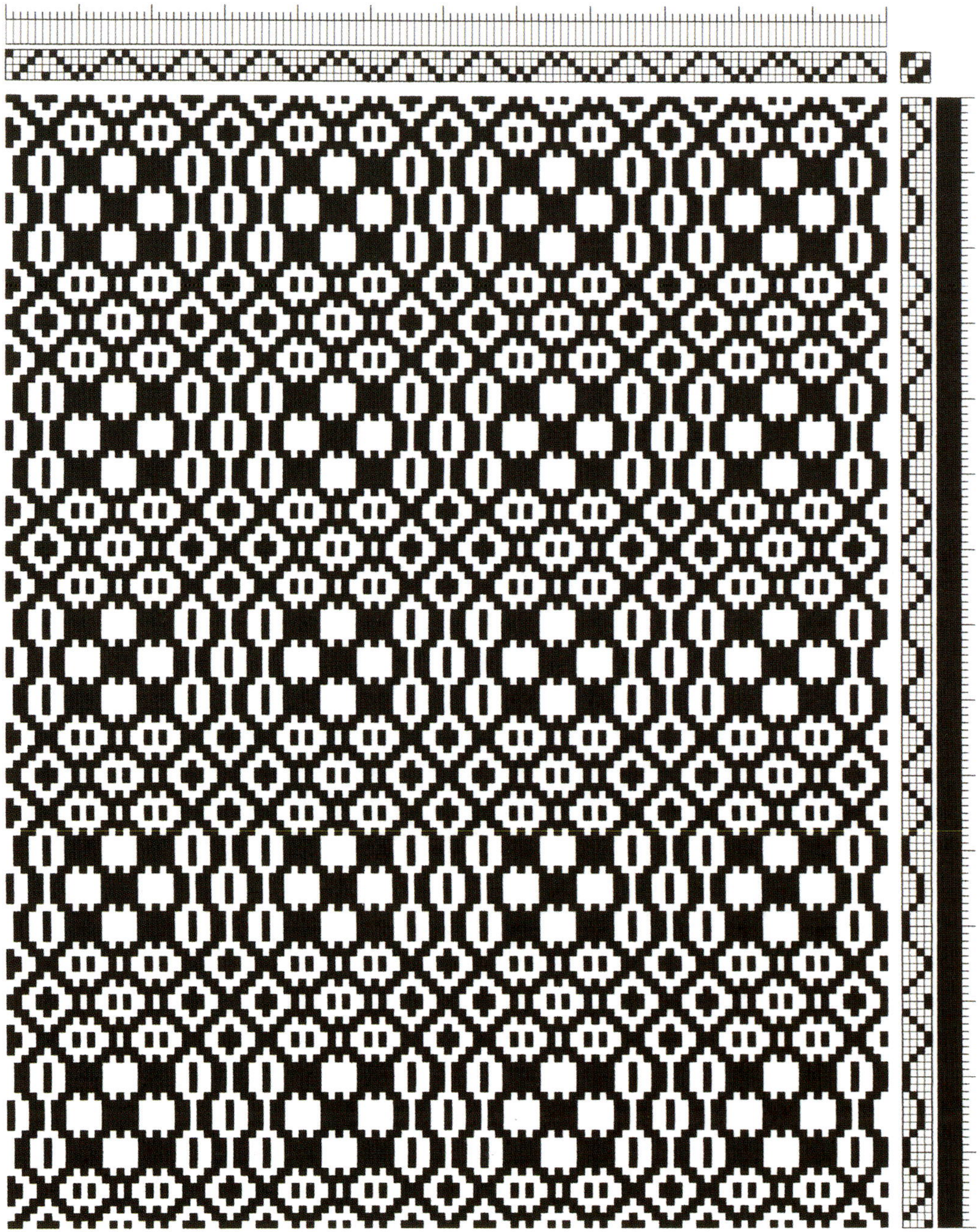

Figure 150. *Wild Rose* **(Design 59)**.

Figure 151. *Wishing Well* (Design 60).

Figure 152. *Zigzag* (Design 61).

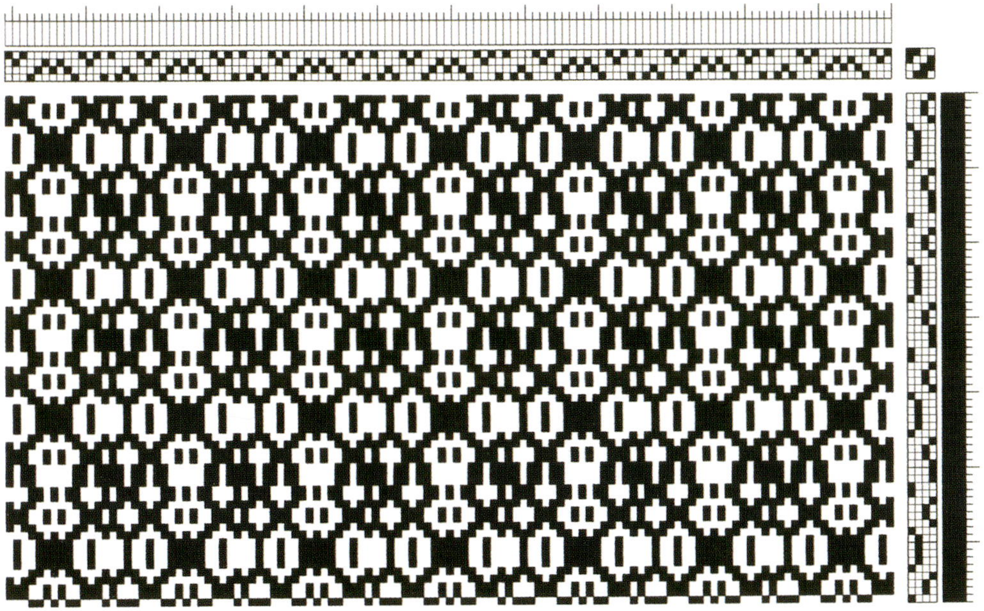

Figure 153. *Ring Around A Rosey* **(Design 62).** Reduced to 94%.

Figure 154. *Hazelwood* **(Design 63).** Reduced to 94%.

Figure 155. *Queen Anne's Lace* (Design 64).

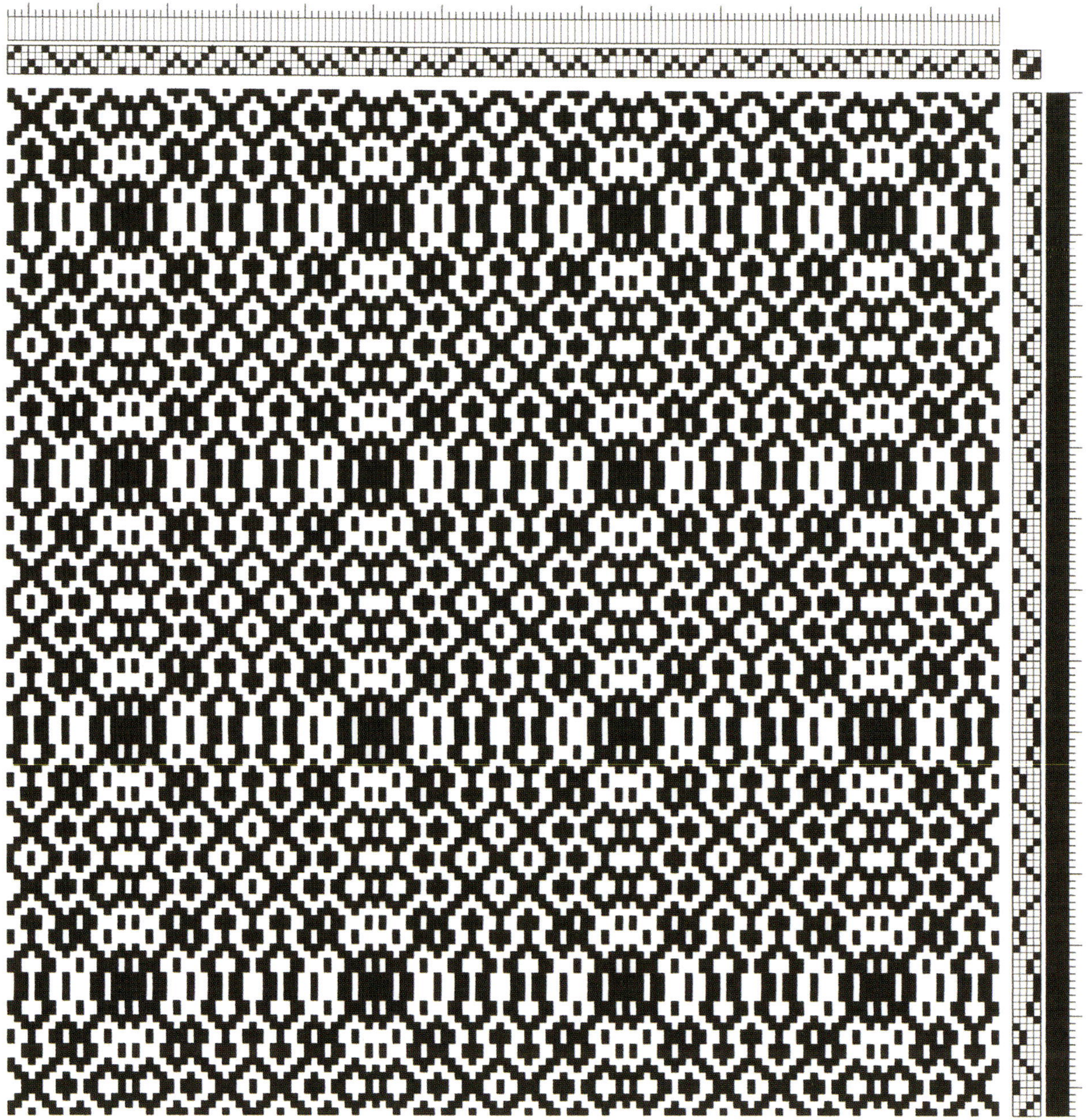

Figure 156. *Daybreak* **(Design 65).** Reduced to 98%.

Figure 157. *Cheerio* **(Design 66).** Reduced to 98%.

Figure 158. *Serenity of Salem* **(Design 67).**

Figure 159. *Sweet and Lovely* **(Design 68).** Reduced to 93%.

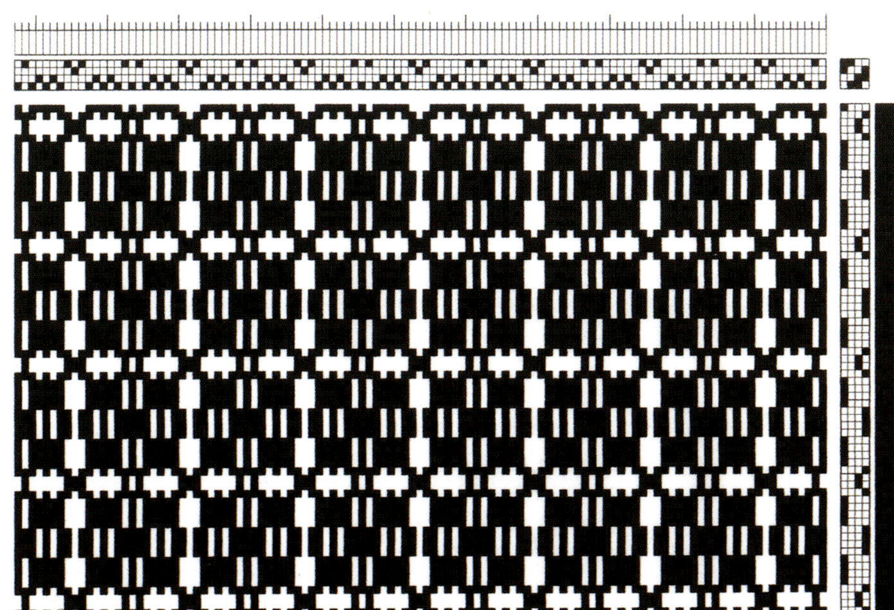

Figure 160. *Parquetry* **(Design 69).** Reduced to 93%.

Figure 161. *Auld Lang Syne* (Design 70).

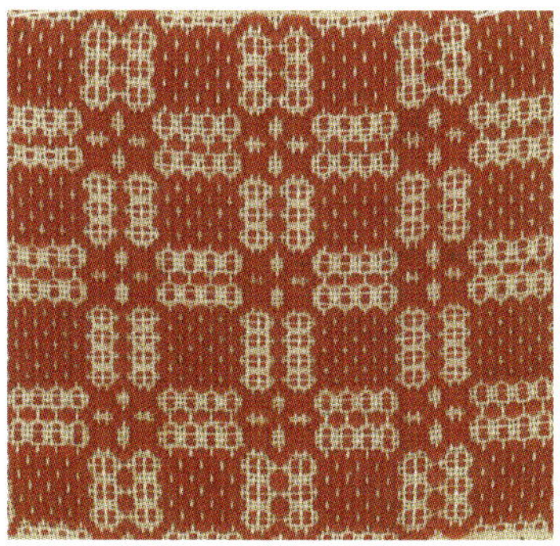

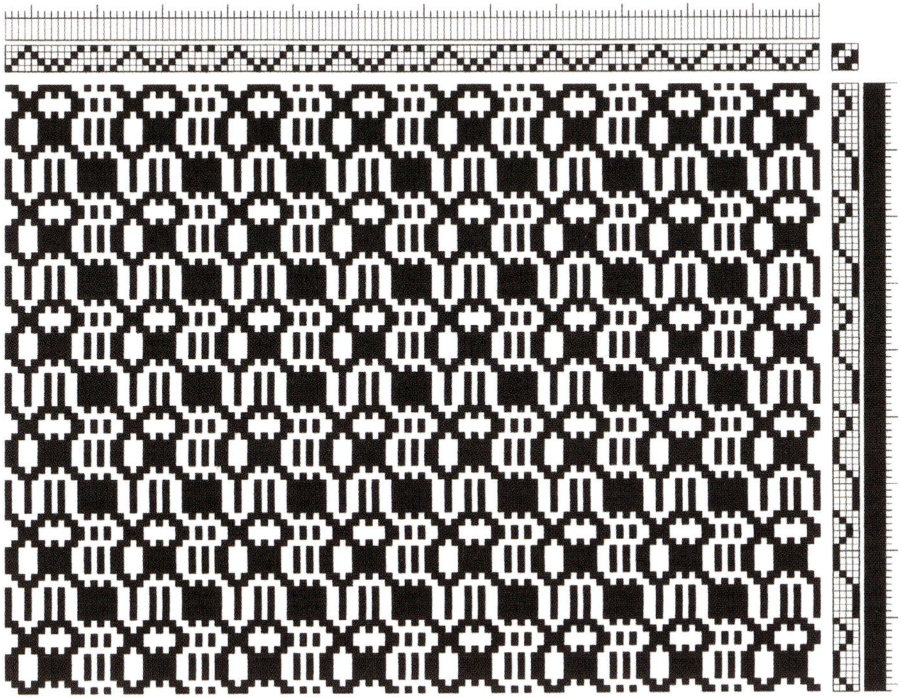

Figure 162. *Hooks and Eyes* **(Design 71).** Reduced to 84%.

Figure 163. *Pinwheels* **(Design 72).** Reduced to 84%.

4. Recently Discovered Patterns

Miss Hayes' passion for weaving and pattern design is evident. In the last days of her life, she was designing new patterns while being treated for cancer at the Miriam Hospital in Providence, Rhode Island. Her Workbook contains thirteen drafts that never made it to sample cards. One has the title *Miriam Hospital* and is, in fact, a draft from that name. It is also the name of the place she spent her last ten days.

In her Workbook, following *Pinwheels* (Design 72), there are four final pages with thirteen threadings and drawdowns (see Figures 164 to 167). We have numbered these thirteen patterns 73 through 85, and have given them names, if Miss Hayes added any notations. They are probably all name drafts. The first page includes her name draft code. She did not provide skeleton drawdowns, treadling variations, or other weaving notations, so she probably never got these designs to the loom. Even those drafts that she crossed out, we decided to keep.

Vilma Yatter 1 (Design 79) is asymmetrical and in Design 80 the motif is mirrored, creating a symmetrical image. Using Miss Hayes' code, Sally DuBois worked out threadings and drawdowns for both versions of *Dexter Training Ground* (Design 73 and Design 74) and verified that they are name drafts. Sally did the same for *Gastric Ulcer* (Design 77), for which Miss Hayes had faintly penciled in the letters over the threading on her work sheet, and for *Miriam Hospital* (Design 78). Sally then worked on the very last threading in this group. Using the code and the dots, but not the Xs, in the threading she worked out a name draft: Merry Christmas. Sally chose to name it *December Decoded* (Design 85), as Miss Hayes might have done, not using the words from the threading. This cheerful and charming draft was probably the last one Bertha Gray Hayes worked out, during her last days in Miriam Hospital. These thirteen designs have been woven by Tony Kormos. We were very excited to find these hitherto unknown patterns and eager to have them published.

Design 73. *Dexter Training Ground 1*
Design 74. *Dexter Training Ground 2*
Design 75. *Juliet 1*
Design 76. *Juliet 2*
Design 77. *Gastric Ulcer*
Design 78. *Miriam Hospital*
Design 79. *Vilma Yatter 1*
Design 80. *Vilma Yatter 2*
Design 81. *Unnamed 1*
Design 82. *Unnamed 2*
Design 83. *Unnamed 3*
Design 84. *Unnamed 4*
Design 85. *December Decoded*

As we continued our research in Miss Hayes' notebooks and materials, we subsequently found an additional seven drafts. They are designated as Designs 86 to 92. Even though their chronology is unclear, they were surely developed before Miss Hayes was hospitalized.

Design 86. *Jitterbug - enlarged*
Design 87. *Old Fashioned Garden*
Design 88. *Summer and Winter Weave*
Design 89. *Meigs Mountain in Crackle Weave*
Design 90. *Meigs Mountain - bookmark*
Design 91. *Rosette*
Design 92. *Afterthought*

On the back of the cardboard to which her sampler of *Jitterbug* was stapled, she added a threading she called *Jitterbug - enlarged*, which we have numbered Design 86. She doubled the size of the original pattern from sixty-two to 120 ends. Also from the Workbook, glued at the bottom of her work page for *Meigs Mountain* (Design 6), she added a threading of ninety-two ends in crackle weave, based on the skeleton drawdown. She called it *Meigs Mountain in Crackle Weave* (Figure 188). We have numbered it Design 89. Notice that each of the four threading blocks is penciled in a different color. These ninety-two ends are one repeat as compared with twenty ends in a repeat of *Meigs Mountain* in overshot.

Included in the Red and White Album of skeleton drawdowns is a drawdown for *Meigs Mountain*, and the one following she called *Meigs Mountain - bookmark*. By reversing the overshot threading, Miss Hayes had created a new pattern, which we call Design 90. (Compare Figures 25, 188, and 190.)

Summer and Winter Weave and *Meigs Mountain in Crackle Weave* are the only two Bertha Gray Hayes patterns we have that are not overshot. Because threading blocks of summer and winter and crackle are made up of four warp ends rather than two, as with overshot, these two patterns are quite large. We felt these drafts should be included in her book, along with computer-generated drawdowns, but no samples have been woven.

The Butternut Workbook contains nineteen drafts with drawdowns, only two of which she labeled "original." The other seventeen drafts with drawdowns in the Butternut Workbook are taken from various sources, either from Atwater or from classes she took at the National Conferences. Among these, *Ladies Delight* (Figure 181) is a fine example of her beautiful penmanship and meticulous record keeping. The colored threads, the counting out of warp ends for her 240 and 600 looms, and her terminology are shown here. She referred to the four shafts as "Back," "NB" (near back), "NF" (near front), and "Front," and to the heddles as "needles." She worked out many of her threadings for 239 or 599 warp ends, and then chose to use the prewound spools of 240 or 600 ends, placing two ends in the last "needle." She included four treadlings for *Ladies Delight* on another page: one she named "Waffles," another "Corduroy Roads," which is a straight twill treadling.

She wrote that "Old Fashioned Garden is Reverse of Rose Path (an accident) Original" and added seven treadling variations for this pattern. A two-block, four-shaft "Design for Summer and Winter Weave Original" was "Designed while with Mrs. Johnson, Rockport, Mass, July 1931."[38] We have numbered them Design 87 and Design 88.

In the WGRI collection of Bertha Gray Hayes' materials are thirty-six empty large brown envelopes of the sort that might have been used at the Providence Gas Company. These are numbered one through thirty-five and thirty-eight, with a name of one of her patterns written in the corner of each envelope. The numbers do not match those on her sample cards. Of the names given on these envelopes are three pattern names not included on her sample cards. One of these was *Flower of Cromaine - enlarged*. We know she developed and wove this pattern, because Mrs. Gallinger and Mrs. Atwater wrote letters thanking her for it, as well as *Flower of Cromaine* (Design 1), saying how they would use each. (See the letters, Figures 5, 6, and 7). We do not have a draft for *Flower of Cromaine - enlarged*.

Two other drafts, also hitherto unknown, are *Rosette* and *Afterthought*, which we have numbered Design 91 and Design 92. These handwritten drafts, like several others, were glued to the outside of envelopes and are reproduced in Figure 191. We chose to end our collection with *Afterthought*, as it truly was an afterthought for Miss Hayes. The first fifty-four ends are the same threading as *Plaza* (Design 42); however, she doubled *Plaza*'s secondary motif by adding twelve ends to make a larger, different pattern.

These are all the patterns in the WGRI Bertha Gray Hayes Archives. The great pleasure Miss Hayes found in her weaving and in her friends led her to develop a web of personal connections among weavers across the country. Perhaps, in their collections, more of her designs and weavings survive and will come to light.

Thirteen Handwritten Drafts from the Workbook, Designs 73 to 85

Figure 164. *Dexter Training Ground 1* **(Design 73),** *Dexter Training Ground 2* **(Design 74), and name draft code.**

Figure 165. *Juliet 1* **(Design 75),** *Juliet 2* **(Design 76), and** *Gastric Ulcer* **(Design 77).**

Figure 166. *Miriam Hospital* **(Design 78),** *Vilma Yatter 1* **(Design 79),** *Vilma Yatter 2* **(Design 80),** *Unnamed 1* **(Design 81), and** *Unnamed 2* **(Design 82).**

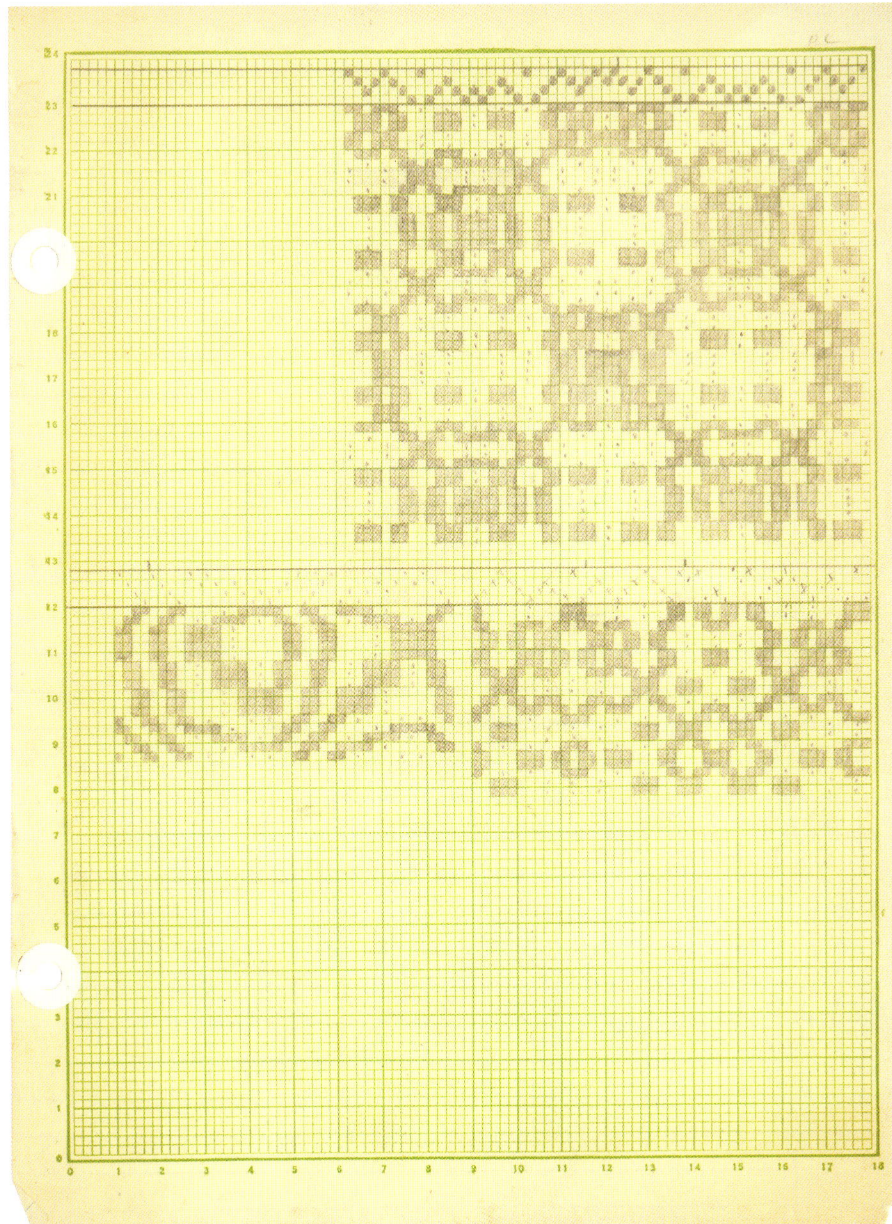

Figure 167. *Unnamed 3* **(Design 83),** *Unnamed 4* **(Design 84), and** *December Decoded* **(Design 85).**

Woven Samples and Computer-generated Drawdowns, Designs 73 to 85

Figure 168. *Dexter Training Ground 1* **(Design 73).**

With the reader in mind, the drawdowns were created at a consistent 24 epi and are therefore at a slightly larger scale than the woven samples (30 epi.) The tie-up is rising shed.

Figure 169. *Dexter Training Ground 2* **(Design 74).**

Figure 170. *Juliet 1* **(Design 75).**

Figure 171. *Juliet 2* (Design 76).

Figure 172. *Gastric Ulcer* (Design 77).

Figure 173. *Miriam Hospital* (Design 78).

Figure 174. *Vilma Yatter 1* **(Design 79).**

Figure 175. *Vilma Yatter 2* **(Design 80).**

Figure 176. *Unnamed 1* **(Design 81).**

Figure 177. *Unnamed 2* (Design 82).

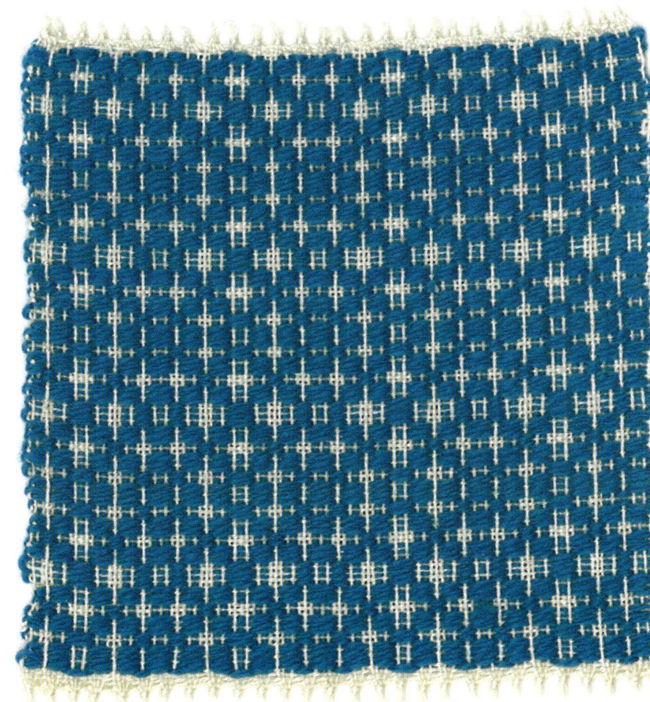

Figure 178. *Unnamed 3* **(Design 83).**

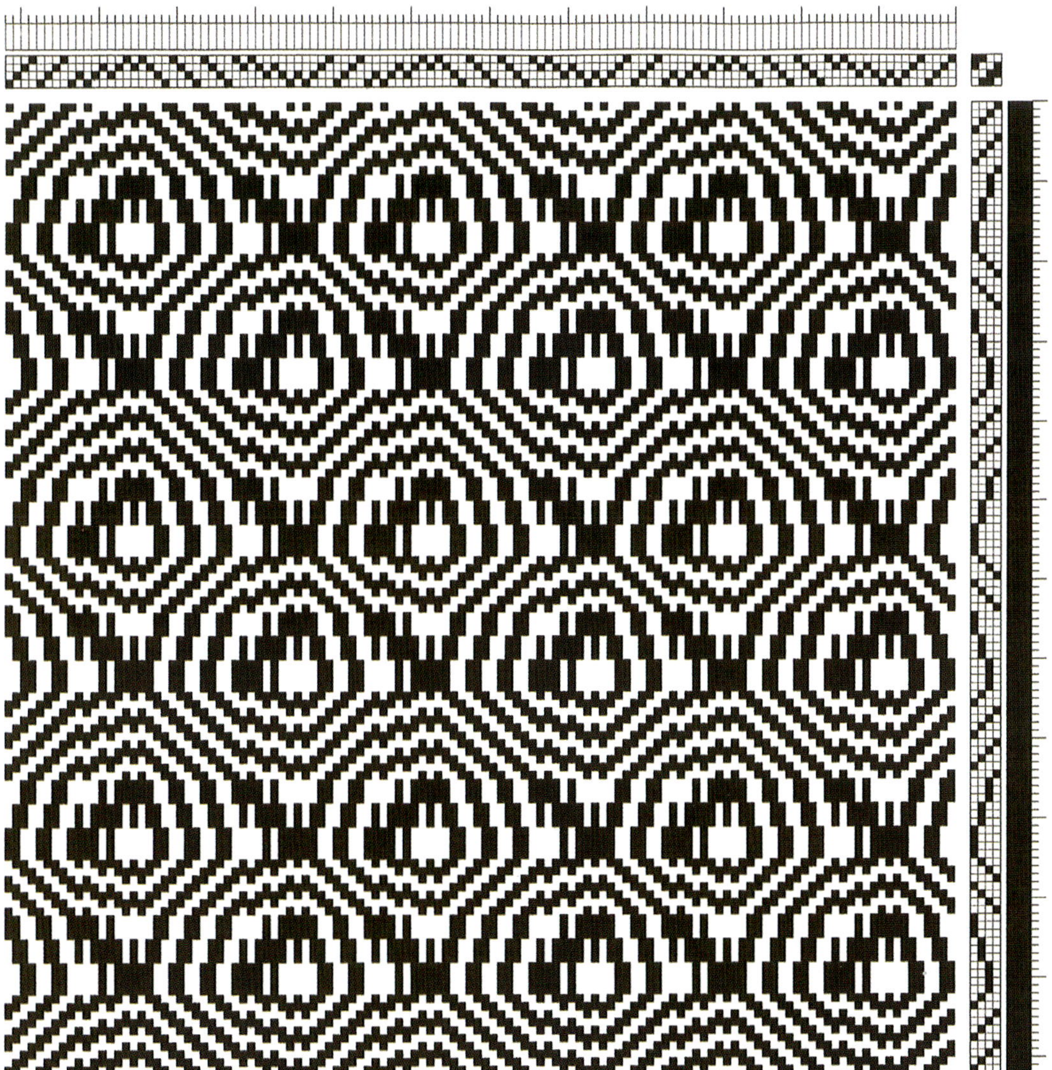

Figure 179. *Unnamed 4* (Design 84).

Figure 180. *December Decoded* **(Design 85).**

Additional Handwritten Drafts, Woven Samples, and Computer-generated Drawdowns, Designs 86 to 92

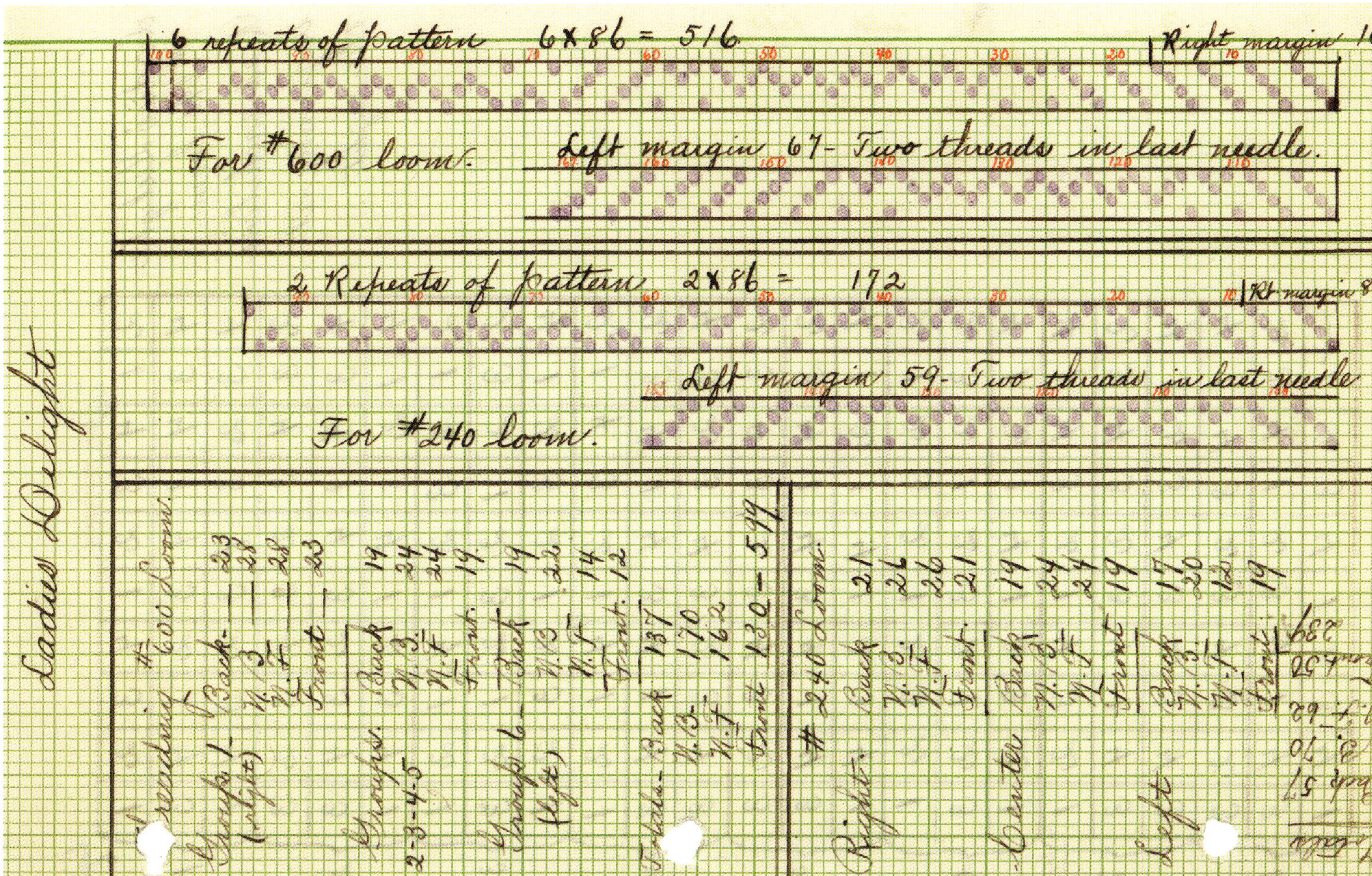

Figure 181. *Ladies Delight*, **from Butternut Workbook.**

With the reader in mind, drawdowns were created at a consistent 24 epi and are therefore at a slightly larger scale than the woven samples. Exceptions are Design 88 and Design 89, which were created at 40 epi. The tie-up is rising shed.

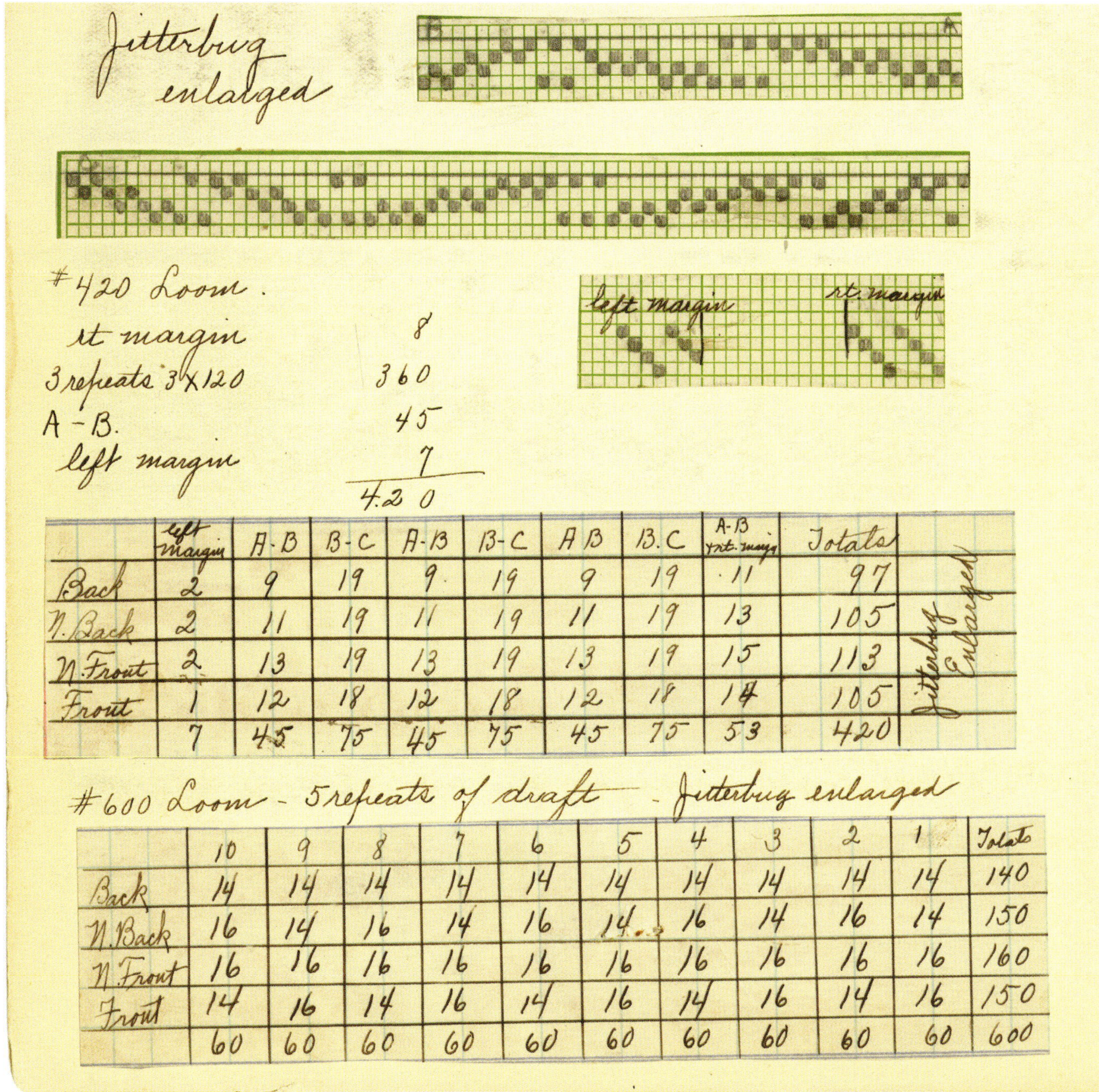

Jitterbug enlarged

left margin   rt. margin

#420 Loom.

rt margin	8
3 repeats 3 X 120	360
A - B.	45
left margin	7
	420

	left margin	A-B	B-C	A-B	B-C	A B	B.C	A-B rt. margin	Totals
Back	2	9	19	9	19	9	19	11	97
N. Back	2	11	19	11	19	11	19	13	105
N. Front	2	13	19	13	19	13	19	15	113
Front	1	12	18	12	18	12	18	14	105
	7	45	75	45	75	45	75	53	420

Jitterbug Enlarged

#600 Loom - 5 repeats of draft - Jitterbug enlarged

	10	9	8	7	6	5	4	3	2	1	Totals
Back	14	14	14	14	14	14	14	14	14	14	140
N. Back	16	14	16	14	16	14	16	14	16	14	150
N. Front	16	16	16	16	16	16	16	16	16	16	160
Front	14	16	14	16	14	16	14	16	14	16	150
	60	60	60	60	60	60	60	60	60	60	600

Figure 182. *Jitterbug - enlarged* **(Design 86), from Workbook.**

Figure 183. *Jitterbug - enlarged* **(Design 86).**

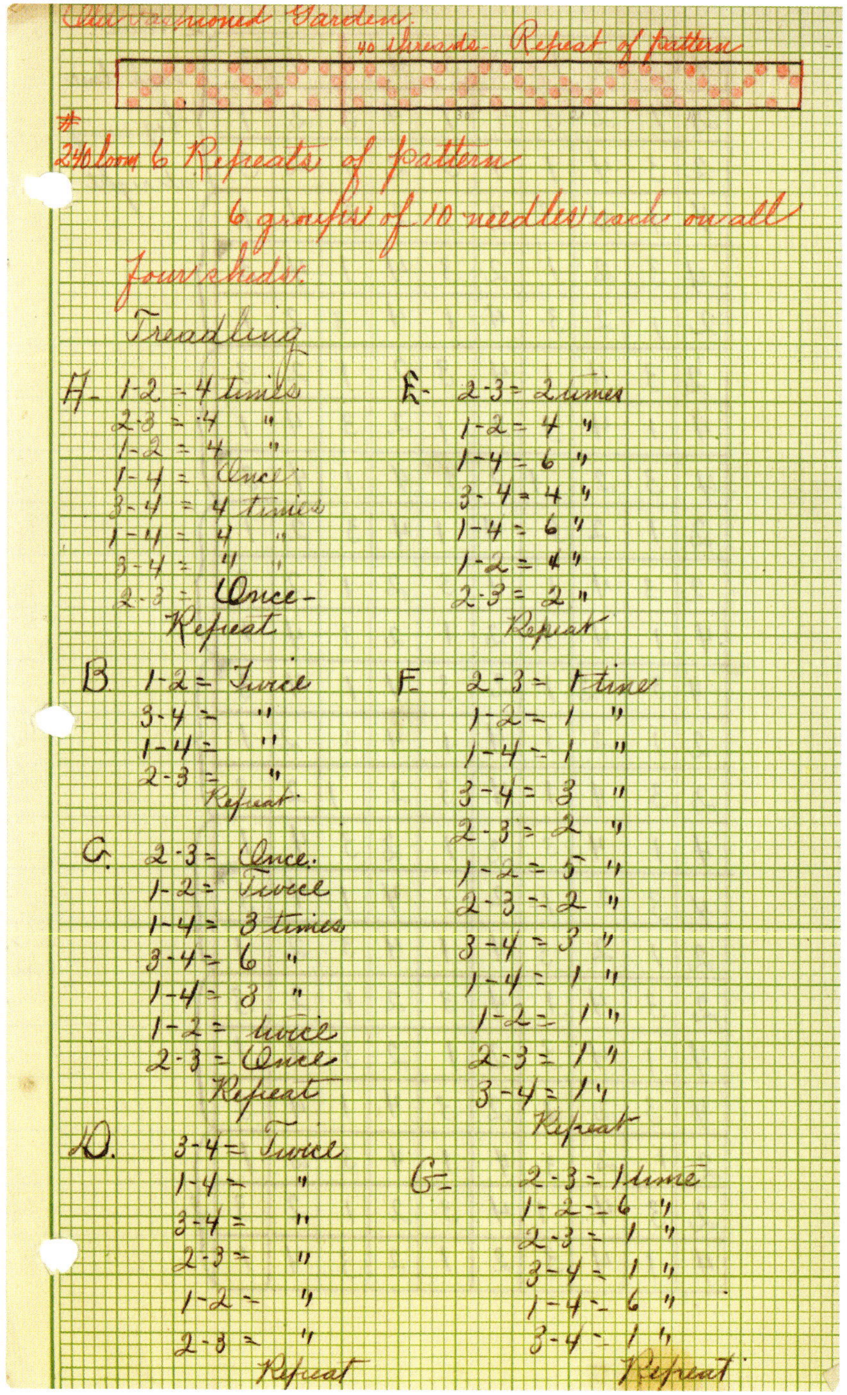
Old Fashioned Garden.
40 threads - Repeat of pattern
#
240 loom 6 Repeats of pattern
6 groups of 10 needles each on all four sheds.

Treadling

A- 1-2 = 4 times
2-3 = 4 "
1-2 = 4 "
1-4 = Once
3-4 = 4 times
1-4 = 4 "
3-4 = 4 "
2-3 = Once-
Repeat

B 1-2 = Twice
3-4 = "
1-4 = "
2-3 = "
Repeat

C. 2-3 = Once.
1-2 = Twice
1-4 = 3 times
3-4 = 6 "
1-4 = 3 "
1-2 = twice
2-3 = Once
Repeat

D. 3-4 = Twice
1-4 = "
3-4 = "
2-3 = "
1-2 = "
2-3 = "
Repeat

E- 2-3 = 2 times
1-2 = 4 "
1-4 = 6 "
3-4 = 4 "
1-4 = 6 "
1-2 = 4 "
2-3 = 2 "
Repeat

F. 2-3 = 1 time
1-2 = 1 "
1-4 = 1 "
3-4 = 3 "
2-3 = 2 "
1-2 = 5 "
2-3 = 2 "
3-4 = 3 "
1-4 = 1 "
1-2 = 1 "
2-3 = 1 "
3-4 = 1 "
Repeat

G- 2-3 = 1 time
1-2 = 6 "
2-3 = 1 "
3-4 = 1 "
1-4 = 6 "
3-4 = 1 "
Repeat

Figure 184. *Old Fashioned Garden* **(Design 87), from Butternut Workbook.**

Figure 185. *Old Fashioned Garden* **(Design 87).**

Figure 186. *Summer and Winter Weave* **(Design 88), from Butternut Workbook.** Reduced to 84%.

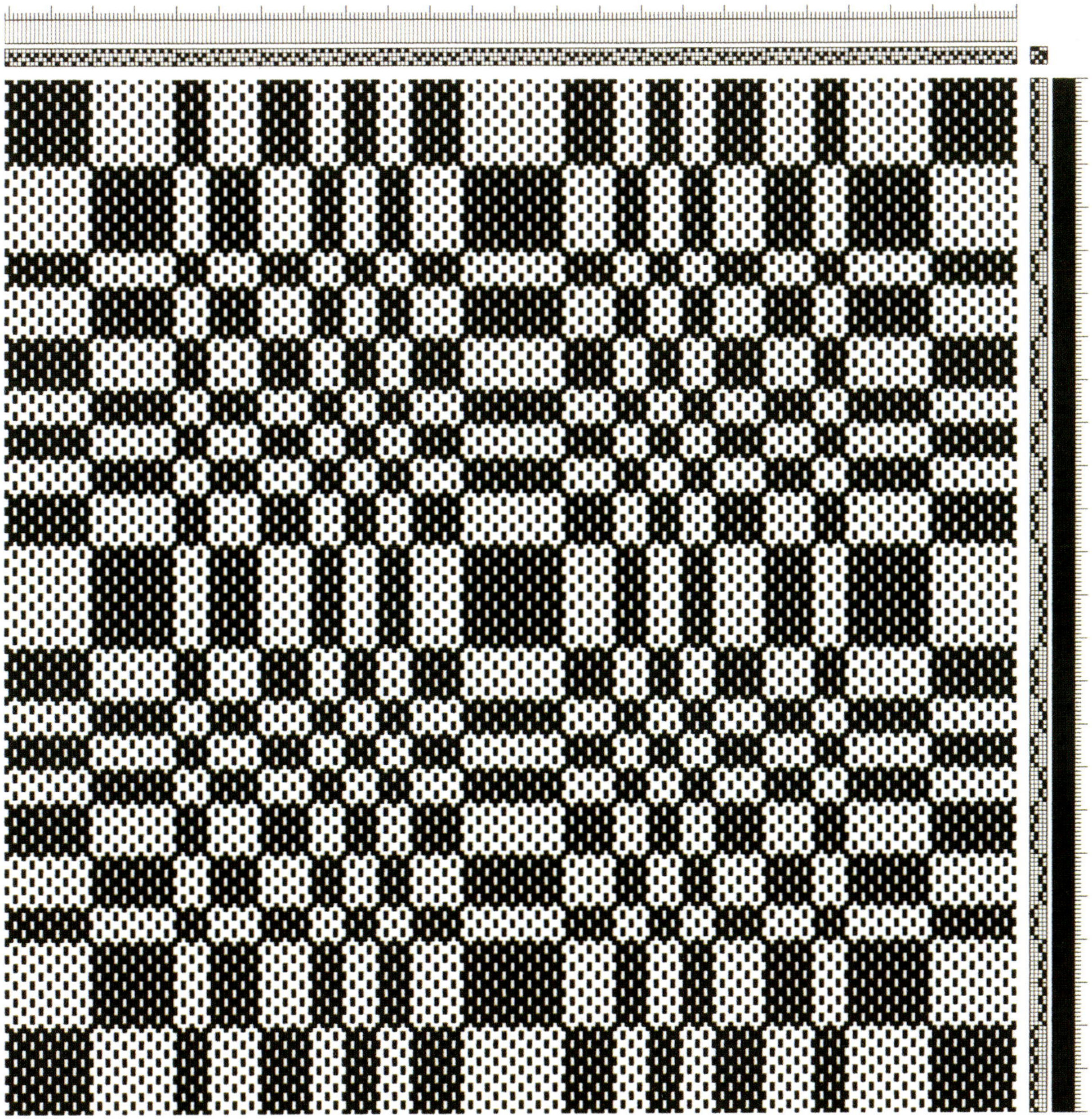

Figure 187. *Summer and Winter Weave* **(Design 88).**

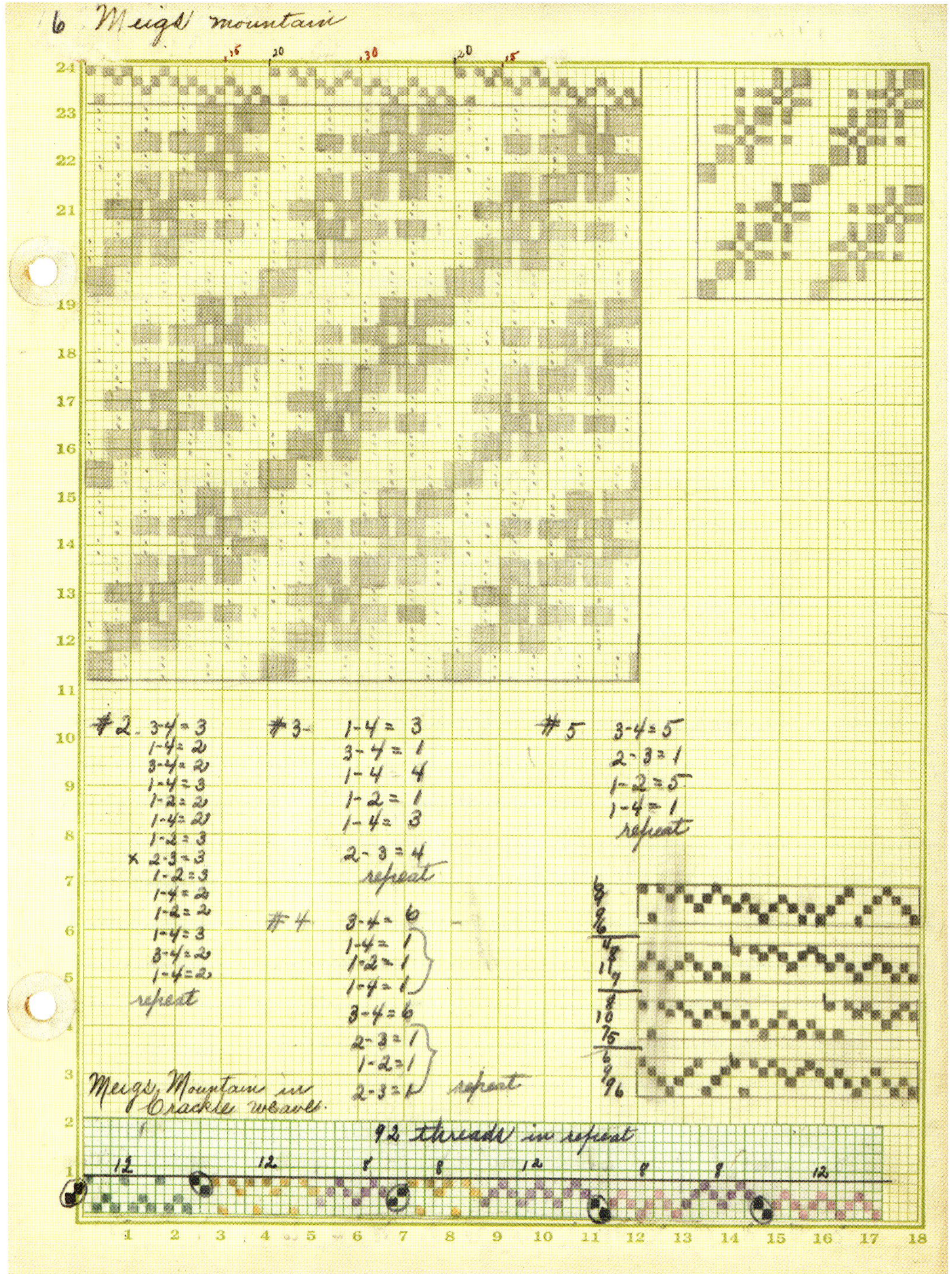

Figure 188. *Meigs Mountain in Crackle Weave* **(Design 89), from Workbook.**

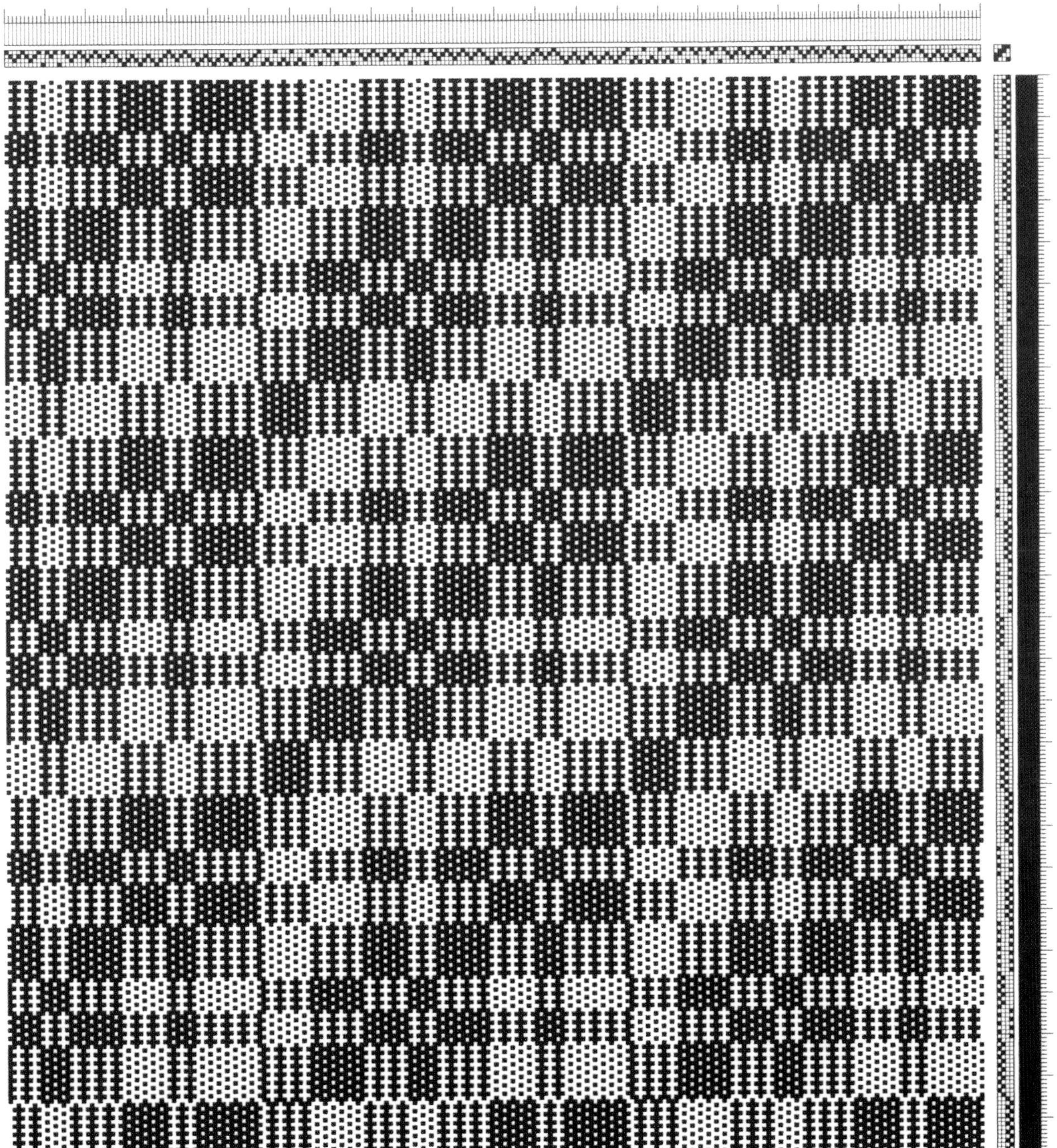

Figure 189. *Meigs Mountain in Crackle Weave* **(Design 89).**

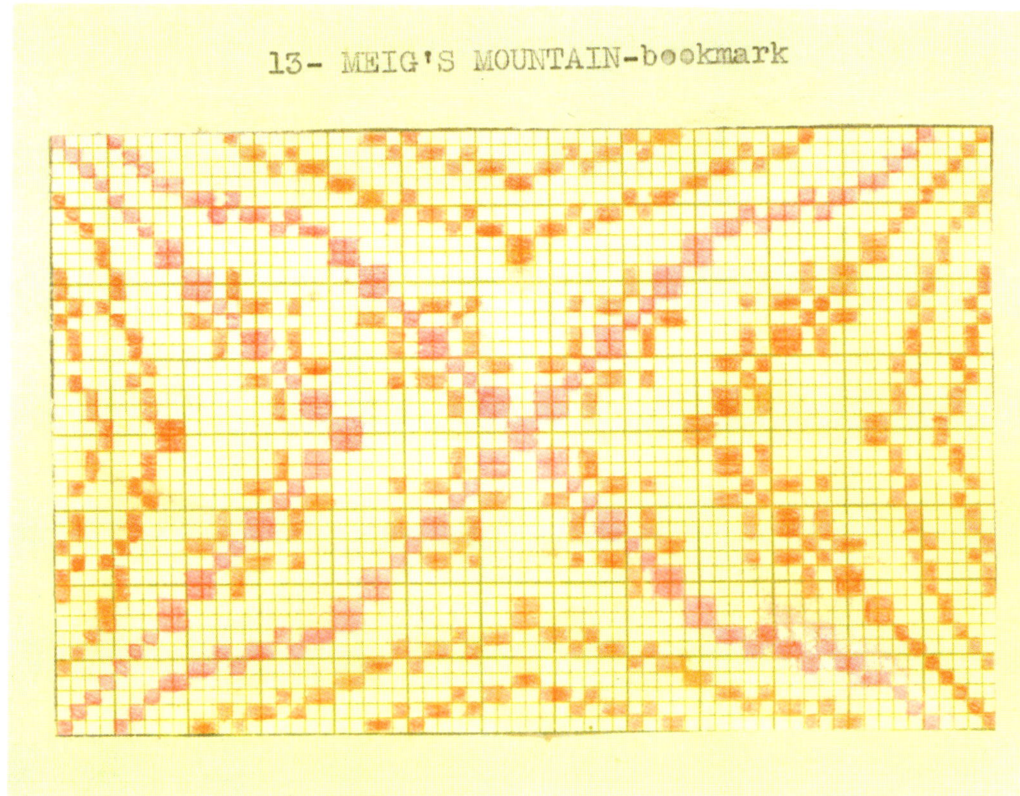

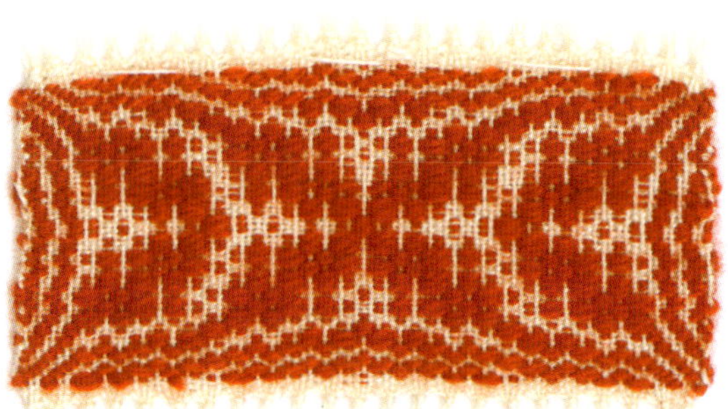

Figure 190. *Meigs Mountain - bookmark* (Design 90), from Red and White Album.

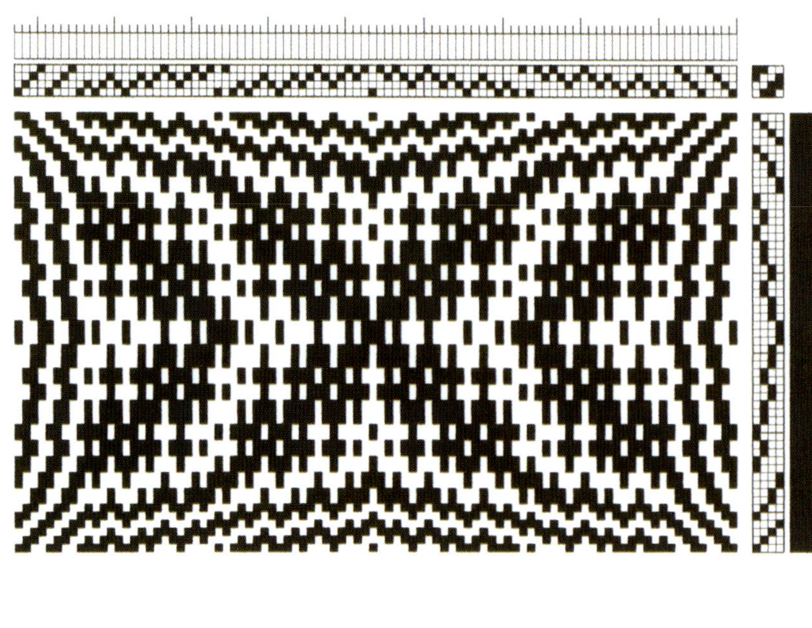

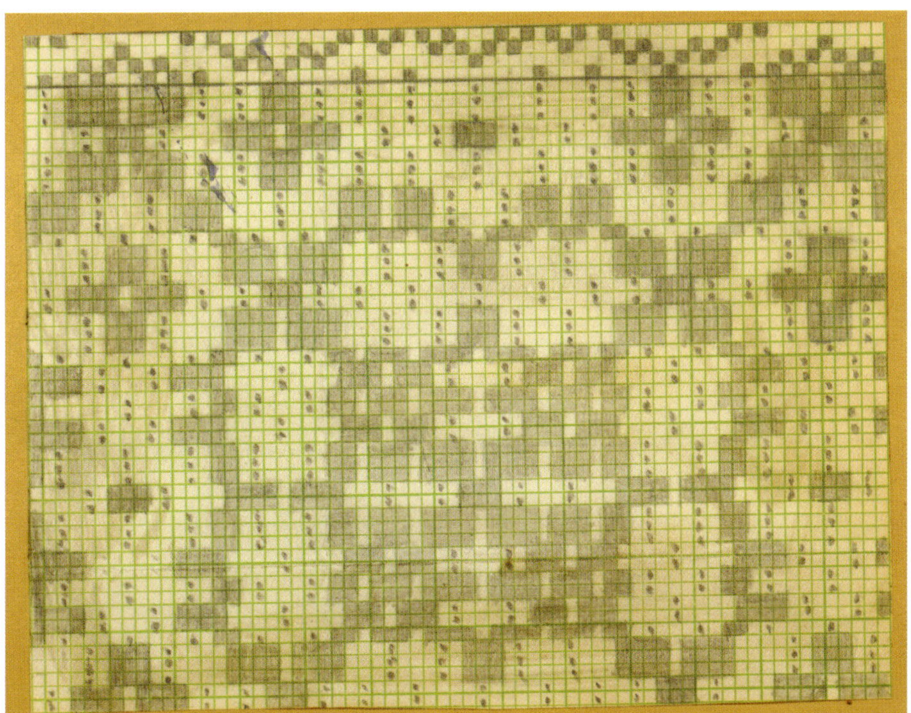

Figure 191. ***Rosette*** **(Design 91) and** ***Afterthought*** **(Design 92), from brown envelopes.**

Figure 192. *Rosette* **(Design 91).**

Figure 193. *Afterthought* (Design 92).

5. Other Weavings by Miss Hayes

In her Workbook, accompanying the pattern drafts, are eight neatly hemstitched weavings. Most of them measure seven inches by ten inches, have 240 warp ends of 20/2 cotton, and are sett at 30 epi. (See Figures 194 to 201.) The most remarkable of these weavings is her runner woven in the *Meigs Mountain* pattern (Figure 195). She wove eight bands of treadling variations to the center, and then mirrored her treadling by weaving the blocks in reverse order. Where a diagonal line of pattern blocks can be seen, it reverses from one end of the runner to the other, making it truly symmetrical. Another weaving is a well-worn guest towel in the *Remembrance* pattern. She wove each end with six bands of treadling variations (Figure 196).

The Figures in our book end with a stunning example, *Theme Song*, typical of Miss Hayes' work in its asymmetry, use of color, and visualization of a rousing theme. It uses the Morse code of dot, dot, dot, dash, and a V for victory and exemplifies the patriotic spirit of a country at war.

Design 1. *Flower of Cromaine*
Design 6. *Meigs Mountain*
Design 7. *Remembrance*
Design 10. *Hoosier Tallyho*
Design 31. *Jitterbug*
Design 32. *Lambeth Walk*
Design 47. *Stagger*
Design 51. *Theme Song*

Figure 194. *Flower of Cromaine* **(Design 1).**

Figure 195. *Meigs Mountain* **(Design 6), detail of table runner.**

Figure 196. *Remembrance* **(Design 7), detail of guest towel.**

Figure 197. *Hoosier Tallyho* **(Design 10)**.

Figure 198. *Jitterbug* **(Design 31).**

Figure 199. *Lambeth Walk* **(Design 32).**

Figure 200. *Stagger* **(Design 47).**

Figure 201. *Theme Song* **(Design 51).**

6. The Story Continues

The idea for this book began with a shoebox full of seventy-two sample cards. As our involvement with Miss Hayes grew, we discovered unpublished patterns, and became aware of a very interesting person. We have come to know her as courageous, hardworking, creative, artistic, willing to share her newfound knowledge, whimsical, warm and friendly. Her courage brought her from her hometown of Middleborough, Massachusetts, to Providence, Rhode Island, to work a six-day-a-week job. Handweaving was an outlet, in the early mornings and late evenings, to explore her creative talent and design her many patterns.

She went on to share her new knowledge with other weavers in New England and across the country. Her designs often were centered around name drafting and filled with playful references to the world in which she lived. And in that world, she found many friends and admirers. Mrs. MacAllister writes:

> Bertha was in a class by herself, so devoted to those she loved, so true, so unselfish. I believe Creative Crafts did much to bring her out and give her courage to go on with her rare talent of designing and drafting.[39]

Miss Hayes will continue to provide inspiration for the handweavers of today and tomorrow. The WGRI has much in the Bertha Gray Hayes Archives that should be shared with others: patterns for their charm and originality, Workbook pages for their meticulous notations, and her anecdotal notes for a look at a weaver/designer at work. By including computer-generated drawdowns, the WGRI hopes this book will serve as a tool, as well as an inspiration, for many projects.

The WGRI curated an exhibit of Miss Hayes' materials and thirty-six pieces woven by guild members inspired by Miss Hayes' designs. Weavers continue to add to our exhibit, which has traveled to three venues. As we prepare for future exhibits, present day weavers, with more sophisticated handlooms, cannot help but marvel at how much she wove, and enjoyed doing so, on her preferred loom, the No. 240 Structo.

Miss Hayes was a self-taught weaver who used a traditional weave structure to create her own individual patterns. She preferred fine threads for her miniature designs. As a way of creating her "Personalized Designs," she adapted a technique learned from Mrs. Genevieve Shields.[40] Using this method we now call name drafting, she made each pattern unique, often commemorating events, places, and people. An important characteristic of her overshot work is asymmetry, a feature not found in most weaving of her time. She liked to take her traditional work a step further by using unusual color sequences and a variety of treadlings.

Miss Hayes sought out contacts with other weavers by attending the first nine National Conferences of American Handweavers. She published articles on her work and corresponded with other weavers. She delighted in sharing her work, both as gifts and to sell. Well-known weavers of her day valued her work, describing her patterns in journals, newsletters, and a publication devoted to her original designs.

As our knowledge of Bertha Gray Hayes grew, we knew that we had to share her life and her work with other weavers. In this book, her history and her original designs, including those recently discovered, are finally available to the public.

Glossary

As drawn in – Term used for the sequence of treadling blocks that is the same as the threading block sequence. Pattern blocks are squared and appear on the diagonal. Also called "tromp as writ."

Atwater, Mary Meigs – "The dean of American handweaving" first taught women in Basin, Montana to weave, then went on to teach weaving to soldiers as occupational therapy, founded the Shuttle-Craft Guild, developed a correspondence course for weaving, published a monthly newsletter for twenty-two years, wrote several books, taught at guilds and conferences in the United States and Canada, and traveled extensively researching ethnic weaving. There was not a weave structure she didn't find interesting and worthy of study. For a look into the life of this remarkable woman, read her autobiography: *The Life of a Weaver*.

Block – Rectangular pattern element shown against a contrasting background. A block is created by a repeated threading unit and a repeated treadling sequence.

Card weaving – An ancient method of weaving in which cards or tablets produce a warp-faced fabric of great strength. Warp threads pass through holes in the cards, which, when rotated, form a shed and twist to produce unique patterns. Also called tablet weaving.

Crackle – Twill-based pattern weave composed of four-thread units (three-shaft point twill units). There are four possible pattern blocks on four shafts, and the supplementary-weft pattern floats are tied down every fourth warp thread on a plain weave ground. Pattern blocks do not weave alone, but weave with either of the adjacent pattern blocks, giving an overlapping effect.

Davison, Marguerite Porter – Weaver active in the Pennsylvania Craft Movement in the first half of the twentieth century, gathering weaving patterns from many sources. *A Handweaver's Pattern Book* ("the green book"), first published in 1944, is a must-have for beginning weavers. It contains hundreds of four-shaft patterns in many different techniques, each with many treadlings. She wrote other books in addition to being an active teacher and weaver.

Dent – Vertical opening in a weaving reed. The reed is named by the number of dents per inch, e.g., a fifteen-dent reed.

Draft – Diagrammatic representation of warp ends in the shafts and of the treadling sequence to produce the desired cloth.

Drawdown – Diagram of the interlacement of warp and weft threads in a textile, derived from the threading, tie-up, and treadling.

Draw in – To thread the heddles.

Dukagang – Swedish embroidery weave technique having a supplementary weft inlaid on a plain weave ground. The supplementary weft floats over three and under one warp for the distance of the motif. The same warp end is always used to tie down the pattern weft, resulting in vertical ribs and giving a columnar effect in the motif. It is easiest to weave this fabric wrong side up. Miss Hayes used a rosepath threading for dukagang weaving.

End – Individual warp thread.

epi – Abbreviation for ends per inch or the number of warp threads per inch.

Float – Length of pattern weft lying on the surface of the fabric, passing over two or more warp threads to form the pattern.

Flossa rug – Knotted pile weave commonly woven in Sweden.

Gallinger, Osma (later known as Osma Gallinger Tod) – Weaver, teacher, and author who founded the National Conferences of American Handweavers. She was director of Creative Crafts, published a monthly newsletter, *Shuttle Service*, and a series of leaflets, as well as various craft books, including one on handweaving, and one on rug weaving co-authored with her daughter, Josephine Del Deo.

Harness – See "Shaft."

Heddle – Wire or string loop, with an eye through which a warp end is threaded, allowing the warp to be raised or lowered to permit passage of the weft thread. Heddles are mounted in a frame called a shaft.

Indian braid – Interwoven strands made by hand-manipulating multiple threads as practiced by North and South American indigenous peoples.

Leno – Hand-manipulated lace weave formed by crossing adjacent warp ends, or warp pairs, to form a new shed in the design area. Alternate rows are woven in plain weave to secure the design. A type of gauze.

Monk's belt – Two-block supplementary-weft pattern weave, usually on four shafts. A simplified overshot. The two blocks do not share shafts. For example, if block A is on shafts 1 and 2, then block B will be on shafts 3 and 4.

Overshot – Twill-based supplementary-weft pattern weave, usually on four shafts. The overshot weave structure is identified by its three distinct areas: the balanced plain weave area, the pattern area of weft floats, and the half-tone area with pattern and ground weave showing equally.

Plain weave – Also known as tabby, the simplest weave structure. Each weft thread goes over one warp thread, and then under the next, alternating that sequence in the next row. This may be woven on two shafts.

Reed – Part of the loom having a consistent number of dents or spaces per inch, thereby determining the ends per inch in the cloth. Also used to beat in the weft.

Rosepath – Threading based on the twill structure. The usual four-shaft version is threaded 1-4-3-2-1-2-3-4, and can be woven with or without a tabby. An alternate threading is 1-2-1-4-3-2-3-4. Rosepath is commonly used in decorative Scandinavian textiles.

Sample – Example of a weaving, not a finished piece.

Sampler – Similar to a sample, but with two or more treadlings on the same threading to show other examples of the weave.

Sett – Number of warp ends per inch, determined by the reed.

Shaft – Frame in the loom to hold heddles, through which warp ends are threaded. Four shafts are needed to weave overshot. Also known as "harness."

Shed – Opening of the warp that permits passage of the shuttle carrying the weft.

Skeleton drawdown – Abbreviated drawdown, showing how the threading and treadling units relate, rather than how individual threads interlace. Also called profile draft or block draft.

Sley – To draw the warp ends through the reed.

Summer and winter – Supplementary-weft pattern weave requiring two shafts for tie-down threads, and one shaft for each pattern block. The weft floats over three warp ends and under one in the pattern areas, and under three warps and over one in the background areas, on a plain weave ground. Pattern blocks may be woven alone or in combination with any of the other blocks, giving great design potential for weaving with looms having more than four shafts.

Tabby – Plain weave, especially when used for weave structures having a pattern on plain weave ground. Pattern and tabby weft shots often alternate.

Tidball, Harriet – Weaver and teacher. She taught weaving at the "Division of Rehabilitation of the Blind" in Montana and at Montana State University, as well as at conferences and guilds. Following Atwater, she became director of the Shuttle Craft Guild and editor of their monthly periodical from 1946 to 1957. She wrote *The Weaver's Book*. She traveled to Central and South America and Great Britain to research ethnic textiles and textile design.

Treadle – Lever or pedal used to raise or lower one or more shafts, thereby creating a shed.

Tromp as writ - See "As drawn in."

Warp – Threads stretched lengthwise on the loom.

Weft – Threads traveling crosswise, perpendicular to the warp, passing through the shed.

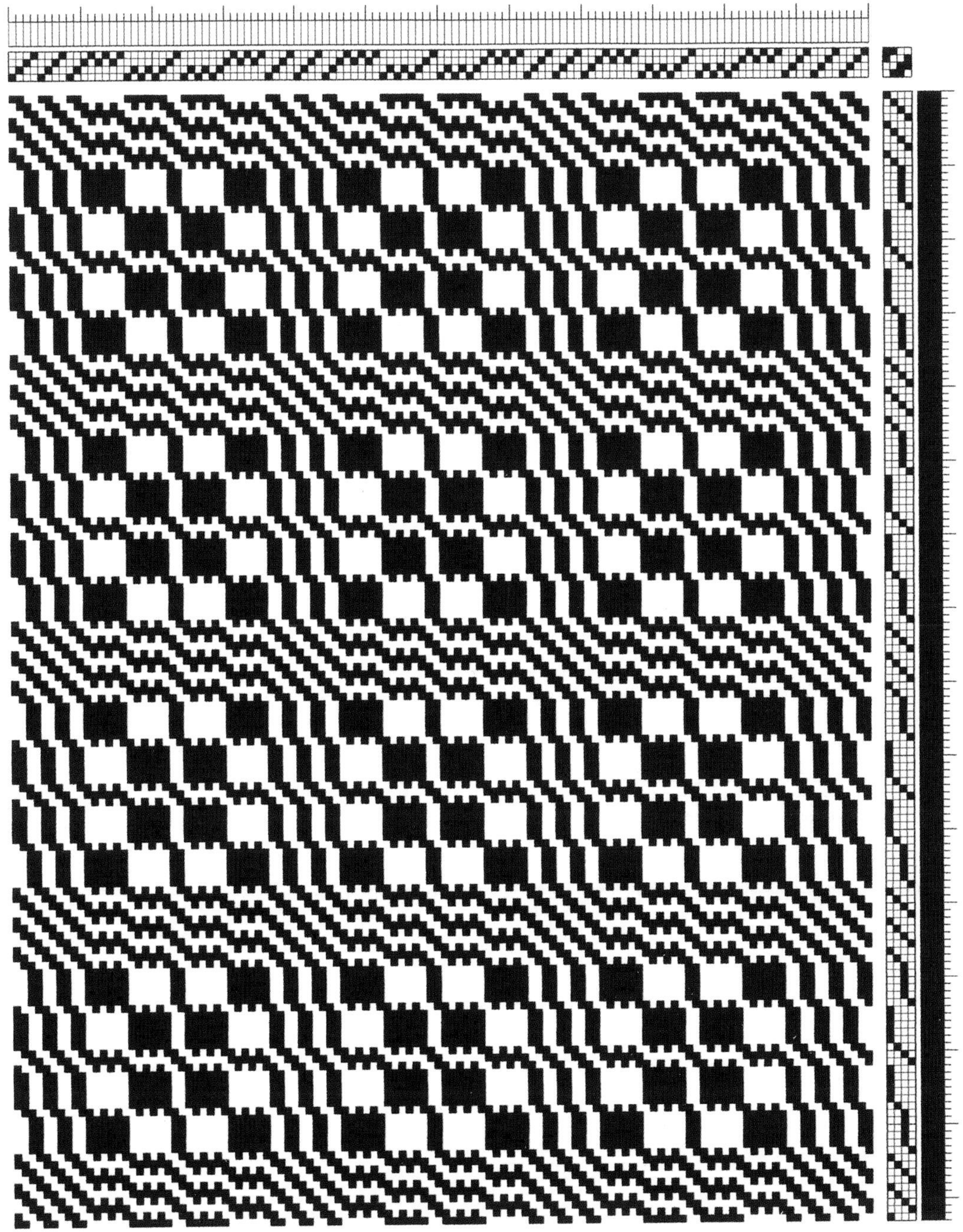

Endnotes

Preface

1. Harriet Tidball, *The Shuttle Craft Guild Handweaver's Bulletin*, XXXIII, no. 8,9,10. 1956: 3-21

Introduction

2. Mary M. Atwater, *Shuttle-Craft Bulletin*, September 1940: 1-3
3. Marguerite P. Davison, *A Handweaver's Pattern Book*, (Swarthmore, Pennsylvania: privately printed, 1950)
4. Town Clerk's Records, Middleborough, Massachusetts
5. Rhode Island Department of Health, Providence, Rhode Island
6. Providence City Directory, Providence, Rhode Island
7. Providence Gas Company employees, Pearl Spencer and Madeleine Ray Durfee, personal communication to Sally DuBois, 1983
8. Jane McKivergan McNaughton and Mary Ruth McKivergan, personal communication to Norma Smayda, November 2008
9. Conference Journal
10. Weavers' Guild of Rhode Island Bulletin, 1947

Chapter 1 Bertha Gray Hayes' Development as a Weaver

11. Pink Scrapbook
12. Ibid.
13. Josephine Del Deo, personal communication to Norma Smayda, May 4, 2008
14. Website of the Cromaine District Library, Hartland, Michigan, 2007
15. Osma Couch Gallinger, *The Complete Book of Bertha Hayes' Patterns: 75 Drafts and Design Effects Created by Bertha Gray Hayes* (East Berlin, Pennsylvania: Creative Crafts, 1957)
16. Conference Journal
17. Ibid.
18. Ibid.
19. Ibid.
20. Ibid.
21. Atwater, Ibid.
22. Davison, Ibid.
23. Davison, *A Handweaver's Source Book: A Selection of 224 Patterns from the Laura M. Allen collection* (Chester, Pennsylvania: John Spencer, 1953)
24. Gallinger, Ibid.
25. Ibid.
26. Ibid.

Chapter 2. Bertha Gray Hayes' Weaving

27. Bertha G. Hayes, "Bags for the Woman Who Reads," *The Weaver*, VII, no. 1, (Jan-Feb 1942): 29-30
28. Mary B. Hill, "The History of the Structo Artcraft Loom," *The Spinning Wheel Sleuth, Handlooms: Supplement #2*, April 1999
29. Theresa Trebon, "Structo Looms," *The Weaver's Friend: A Publication for Rag Rug Weavers*, Fall/Winter 1994
30. Hill, Ibid.
31. Hayes, "Bags for the Woman Who Reads," Ibid.
32. Gallinger, Ibid.
33. Workbook
34. Bertha Gray Hayes, "Christmas Card Weaving," *The Weaver*, VI, no. 4, (Oct-Nov 1941): 4-7
35. Gallinger, Ibid.
36. Bertha G. Hayes, "Bag in Featherstitch Technique," *The Weaver*, VI, no. 1, (Jan-Feb 1941): 12-14
37. Hayes, "Bags for the Woman Who Reads," Ibid.

Chapter 4. Recently Discovered Patterns

38. Butternut Workbook

Chapter 6. The Story Continues

39. Osma Couch Gallinger, *The Shuttle Service*, XIV, no. 2 (February 1948)
40. Gallinger, *The Complete Book of Bertha Hayes' Patterns:* Ibid.

Bibliography and Suggested Reading

Atwater, Mary Meigs. *The Life of a Weaver.* Loveland, Colorado: Interweave Press, 1992.

______. *Shuttle-Craft Guild Bulletin,* September 1940, 1-3.

______. *Manual of Instructions for Structo Artcraft Looms.* Freeport, Illinois: Structo Manufacturing, 1930.

Gallinger, Osma Couch (later Osma Gallinger Tod). *The Complete Book of Bertha Hayes' Patterns: 75 Drafts and Design Effects Created by Bertha G. Hayes.* East Berlin, Pennsylvania: Creative Crafts, 1957. (This was reprinted by The Mannings in 1982.)

______. *The Shuttle Service* XIV, no. 2 (February 1948).

______. *The Weaver IV*, no. 1 (Jan 1939): 23-24.

______. *The Weaver V*, no. 1 (Jan-Feb 1940): 17, 30.

Davison, Marguerite P. *A Handweaver's Pattern Book.* Swarthmore, Pennsylvania: privately printed, 1950.

______. *A Handweaver's Source Book: A Selection of 224 Patterns from the Laura M. Allen Collection.* Chester, Pennsylvania: John Spencer, 1953.

Hayes, Bertha G. "Bag in Featherstitch Technique." *The Weaver* VI, no. 1 (Jan - Feb 1941): 12-14.

______. "Christmas Card Weaving." *The Weaver* VI, no. 4 (Oct-Nov 1941): 4-7.

______. "Bags for the Woman Who Reads." *The Weaver* VII, no. 1 (Jan-Feb 1942): 29-30.

Hill, Mary B. "The History of the Structo Artcraft Loom." *The Spinning Wheel Sleuth, Hand Looms: Supplement #2.* (April 1999).

Tidball, Harriet. "The Bertha Gray Hayes Miniature Patterns (First twenty patterns, alphabetically arranged, to be continued.)" *The Shuttle Craft Guild Handweaver's Bulletin* XXXIII, no. 8 (August 1956): 3-21.

______. "The Bertha Gray Hayes Miniature Patterns (Concluded. Alphabetically arranged, through number 70.)" *The Shuttle Craft Guild Handweaver's Bulletin* XXXIII, no. 9 (September 1956): 2-18.

______. "New Publication of the Bertha Gray Hayes Drafts." *The Shuttle Craft Guild Handweaver's Bulletin* XXXIII, no. 10 (October 1956): 18.

______. *The Weaver's Book.* New York City: Macmillan, 1961.

Trebon, Theresa. "Structo Looms." *The Weaver's Friend: A Publication for Rag Rug Weavers.* (Fall/Winter 1994).

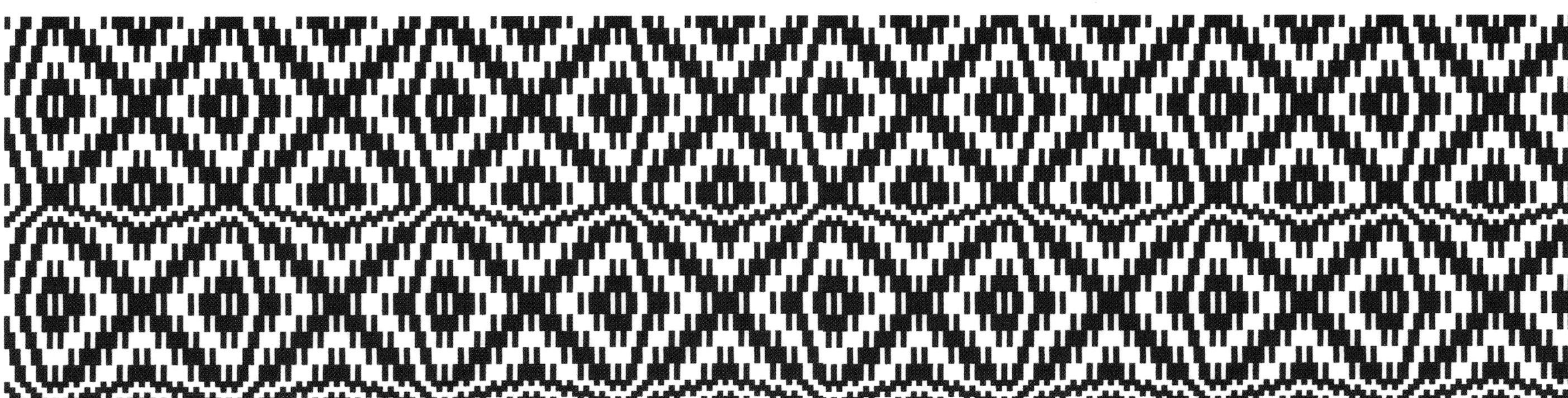

Index

Afterthought 10, 164, 165, 191
Archives, Bertha Gray Hayes 9, 165
as drawn in 11, 25
asymmetry 12, 19, 25, 33, 194, 202
Atwater, Mary Meigs 9, 12, 14, 16-21, 23, 30, 33, 34, 165
Auld Lang Syne 25

Bagatelle 35
bags, woven 13, 14, 19, 33
Baird, John 34
Balaliaka 25
Bardwell, Edna 25
Batchelder, Mrs. 13
Bernat floor loom 23
block 12, 23, 32, 165, 194
Blossom 25, 27, 34
Boan, Isabel 9
Bomber Flight 25, 27, 34, 35
bookmark 10, 31, 164, 165
braids, Indian 10, 30
Butterfly 25
Butternut 10
Butternut Workbook 10, 11, 165, 181, 184, 186

Cameo 28
card weaving 17
Cheerio 16, 21, 32, 34
Chintz 21, 34
Chrostowski, Claire 9, 12
cigarette pack case 18
Complete Book of Bertha Hayes' Patterns, The 19
Conference Journal 10, 12, 16, 18
Crackle 10, 33, 164, 165, 188
Creative Crafts 9, 10, 16, 19, 21
Cretonne 34
Cromaine Crafts 16, 21
Crouse, John Robert 16, 21

Davison, Marguerite P. 9, 12, 19
Daybreak 13, 21, 25, 34
December Decoded 164, 167
Del Deo, Josephine Couch 16, 21, 32, 34
Dexter Training Ground 25
Dexter Training Ground 1 and 2 24, 25, 164, 166
Dick Blick 23
Domino 25, 30, 34
draft 9, 10, 12, 16, 18, 19, 21, 23, 25, 30-33, 35, 164, 165
drawdown 9, 12, 23, 25, 30, 31, 110, 164, 165, 168, 182
DuBois, Sara (Sally) 9, 10, 164
dukagang 25, 31

envelopes, large brown 10, 30, 165, 191
epi 23, 31, 34, 110, 168, 182, 194
erector sets 23
Estes, Josephine 23
Estrellita 31, 35
Fantasia 31
Fascination 25
featherstitch technique 33
Filigree 25, 27
float 12, 32
Flossa rug 30
Flower of Cromaine 16, 21, 26, 165, 194
Flower of Cromaine - enlarged 165

Gallinger (Tod), Osma Couch 9, 10, 12, 16, 18-21, 32, 165
Gallinger Gem, The 21
Gallinger Gem - miniature, The 25, 26
Gastric Ulcer 164, 166
Gilbert Company, A. C. 23
Gone with the Wind 25, 35
greeting cards 25, 31

half-tone 12
Handweaver's Pattern Book, A 19
Handweaver's Source Book, A 19
Hartland Area Project 16
Hayes, Ansel (son) 13
Hayes, Ansel Gray 13
Hayes, Bertha Gray 9-14, 16, 18-21, 23-25, 30-35, 164, 165, 194
Hayes, Maria Elizabeth Dunlap 13
Hazelwood 21
hexagonal warp beam 23
Hooks and Eyes 25
Hoosier Tallyho 21, 194, 197
Jitterbug 19, 25, 33, 164, 194, 198
Jitterbug – enlarged 10, 164, 182
Johnson, Mrs. 165
Juliet 1 and 2 164, 166

King-Seeley Thermos Company 23
Kormos, Antonia (Tony) 9, 10, 35, 164

Labyrinth 30
Ladies Delight 165, 181
Lambeth Walk 34, 194, 199
leno 30
logo 10, 34
Lothrop, Hazel 21

MacAllister, Mrs. 13, 202
McKivergan, Thomas, Jane and Mary 13, 21, 34
Meigs Mountain 21, 34, 165, 188, 194, 195
Meigs Mountain in Crackle Weave 10, 33, 164, 165, 188
Meigs Mountain – bookmark 10, 31, 164, 165, 190
Middleborough, Massachusetts 13, 32, 202
Miriam Hospital 164
Miriam Hospital 164, 167
modernistic type 12, 19
monk's belt 14
Morse code 25, 194
Mosaic 25

name draft 12, 13, 21, 23, 25, 30-33, 164, 166
National Conference of American Handweavers 9, 10, 12, 13, 16, 19, 20, 21, 23, 25, 30, 33, 165
Needlepoint 16, 35

Old Fashioned Garden 10, 164, 165, 184
Olive, The 25
overshot 9, 10, 12, 14, 19, 23, 25, 30, 32-34, 165

Parachute 25
Parquetry 34
pattern block 12, 23, 32, 194
Peace-1945 25, 34
Peggy's Choice 30
Personalized Design 31, 32
Petite 9
Pink Scrapbook 9, 11, 12, 14, 15
Pinwheels 25
plain weave 12, 25, 31, 32, 34
Plaza 165
Primrose 28
Providence Gas Company 10, 13, 30, 33, 165
Providence, Rhode Island 13, 19, 164, 202

ration books 32
Red and White Album 10, 11, 30, 32, 165, 190
reed 23
Remembrance 21, 194, 196
Ring Around a Rosey 25, 32
Rosette 10, 30, 164, 165, 191

sample 10, 12, 14, 16, 19, 21, 25, 30, 33-35, 164
sample cards 9, 10, 12, 18, 19, 30, 34, 35, 164, 165
sampler 19, 23, 32, 195, 196, 198-201
Saunderstown Weaving School 9
Serenity of Salem 21, 25, 34
sett 23, 34, 194
sewing basket 13, 32
shaft 9, 12, 23, 25, 32, 34, 35, 165
Sherburne, Susan 25
Shields, Mrs. Genevieve 12, 202
Shilhan, Thelma 9
Shuttle Service Leaflets 9, 16
Shuttle-Craft Course in Weaving 9, 12, 14, 15
Shuttle-Craft Guild Bulletin 19
skeleton drawdowns 9, 10, 23, 25, 30-32, 165
Smayda, Norma 9, 10
Spencer, Pearl 13
Stagger 16, 21, 194, 200
stamp, metal 9, 10, 12, 34
Stars of Victory 21, 34
stocking tops 33
Stormy Weather 25
Strong, Daisy 18
Structo loom 9, 19, 23, 24, 31
Structo Manufacturing Company 23
Summer and Winter Weave 10, 164, 165, 186
Superhighway 19, 25, 29, 30
Sweet and Lovely 34
symmetry 31-33, 35, 164, 194

tablet weaving 17
Tangerine 25
Tanner, Mrs. Bertha 12
Theme Song 25, 194, 201
thimble holder 13, 18, 25, 32
Thomas, Nina Lillian 25
Thompson Manufacturing Company 23
Tidball, Harriet 9, 10, 12, 19, 20
tie-up 10, 35, 110, 168, 182
Treasure Island 35
Tremaine, H. A. 16, 21
Turntable 25

Unnamed 1, 2, 3 and 4 164, 167

Victory 25
Vilma Yatter 1 and 2 164, 167

Waldenweave 21, 31, 35
Waldenweave – enlarged 34, 35
Waldenwoods 16, 19, 21
warp 12, 21, 23, 25, 31-35, 165
warp spools, pre-wound 23, 24
Weaver, The 19, 31, 33
Weavers' Guild of Rhode Island (WGRI) 9, 10, 12, 13, 165
weft 12, 31-34
Wibraska 29, 30
Wishing Well 30, 31
Workbook 9, 10, 23, 25, 30, 33, 35, 164, 165, 182, 188, 194
World War II 12, 25, 33
Wreath Rose 12

Yankee, The 21, 30, 32, 33

Zigzag 35